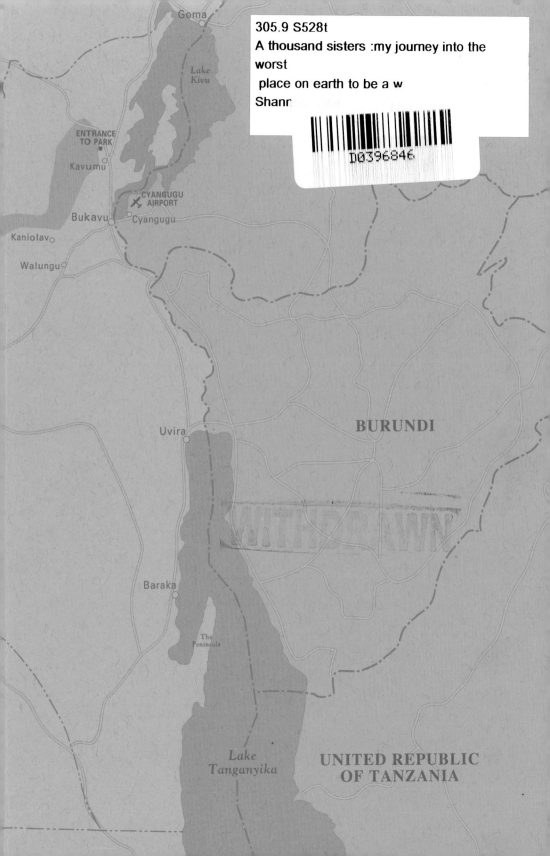

Goma

Lake
Kivu

ENTRANCE
TO PARK

Kavumu

CYANGUGU
AIRPORT

Bukavu   Cyangugu

Kaniolav

Walungu

Uvira   BURUNDI

Baraka

The
Peninsula

Lake
Tanganyika   UNITED REPUBLIC
OF TANZANIA

A Thousand Sisters

MY JOURNEY INTO THE WORST PLACE ON EARTH TO BE A WOMAN

LISA J. SHANNON

Foreword by Zainab Salbi

founder of Women for Women International

SEAL PRESS

"Lisa Shannon's beautifully written memoir is for anyone who thinks one person can't make a difference in the world. A page turning read, *A Thousand Sisters* could inspire the biggest skeptic. Hard to put down."

—EMILY DESCHANEL, ACTRESS AND ACTIVIST

"*A Thousand Sisters* asks the question, 'Can one person get off her couch and touch the lives of those in need on the other side of the world?' This memoir answers, with poignancy and passion, 'Yes, she can!'"

–JERRY FOWLER, PRESIDENT, SAVE DARFUR COALITION

A THOUSAND SISTERS
My Journey Into the Worst Place on Earth to be a Woman

Page 225. Komunyakaa, Yusef. © 1998
"You and I Are Disappearing," from *Dien Cai Dau*.
Reprinted with permission by Wesleyan University Press.

Published by
Seal Press
A Member of the Perseus Books Group
1700 Fourth Street
Berkeley, California

Library of Congress Cataloging-in-Publication Data

Shannon, Lisa, 1975-
  A thousand sisters : my journey of hope into the worst place on earth
to be a woman / by Lisa Shannon.
    p. cm.
ISBN-13: 978-1-58005-296-2
ISBN-10: 1-58005-296-7
 1. Shannon, Lisa, 1975- 2. Women and war—Congo (Democratic Republic)
3. Women refugees—Congo (Democratic Republic) 4. War victims—Congo
(Democratic Republic) 5. Civil war—Congo (Democratic Republic) 6.
Humanitarian assistance, American—Congo (Democratic Republic) I.
Title.

  HQ1805.5.S53 2010
  305.9'0695082096751—dc22

                          2009025391

9 8 7 6 5 4 3 2

Cover and interior design by Domini Dragoone
Printed in the United States by Edwards Brothers
Distributed by Publishers Group West

FOR CONGO'S COUNTLESS QUIET HEROES
AND
STEWART SHANNON,
MY FATHER AND NOW SILENT GUIDE

When we stood close

Together and your eyes

Looked into my

Eyes, I felt that

Invisible

Threads passed from

Your eyes into

My eyes and

Bound our hearts

Together.

When you left me, and journeyed across

The sea, it was as

If fine threads still united us,

And they were tearing at the wound.

By Edvard Munch

Contents

A THOUSAND SISTERS

BY ZAINAB SALBI

*T*HE CONFLICT IN the Democratic Republic of Congo has taken more lives than any other war since World War II, resulting in the death of more than 5.4 million people and the ongoing rape of hundreds of thousands of women. Despite these gruesome statistics, the conflict rages on amidst muted international response and blanket impunity for rape and war crimes in which all sides are implicated. It has been more than 10 years now, but every day, scores of Congolese people are still falling victim to some of the worst acts of violence known to humanity (if you can believe there can be a *worst act of violence*)—from the killing and mutilation, to the raping of women, men and children, violence continues to happen and the number of victims continues to grow. The world has yet to rise up with the political will to stop this war and the atrocities committed against not only the Congolese people but all of humanity as well.

It is hard not to be angry when you have witnessed the rape of your mother in front of your eyes, the killing of your child, the burning of your home, or the pillaging of all that you have worked so hard to build. The question for survivors is never their anger at injustice, but rather how to express that anger in a healthy way that can lead to building rather than destruction, to reconciliation rather than hate, to a profound perspective that marries both the beauty and the ugliness of life. A survivor's need for action is understood and in many ways expected, even though at times that action can be destructive both for the self and the other.

That's the predicament of the survivor. Then there are the questions with which the rest of the world must wrestle: What if one has the privilege of not directly experiencing or even witnessing firsthand injustice in front of one's eyes? What if one never has to know what it feels like to be lynched, whipped, raped, chained, mutilated, enslaved; or know the pain of witnessing a loved one be killed without being able to do anything about it? What if one doesn't know what it feels like to lose a home because a bomb fell on it, or because it was invaded by soldiers or rebels in the middle of the night while you were sleeping in your own bed; or be forced to walk days and weeks in the middle of the forest without any food just to save your life and that of your loved one? What then? Is that carte blanche to ignore, to pretend, to do *nothing?*

For much of the world it is. Much of the world is content to stand by and do nothing while the war rages on in Congo, while people die by the millions, and while women are raped by the hundreds of thousands. But, thankfully, it is not so for everyone. There are activists worldwide who do what they can on behalf of others who are oppressed, though they may not share that plight.

These are the people who realize that their own privilege—the privilege of not witnessing atrocities, the privilege of being heard, or having the resources to survive—is a responsibility to humanity, a responsibility to be shared with others, and a responsibility to this world. That story, the story of a few individuals acting upon injustice even though they have not witnessed it firsthand has always existed, and that is the story that adds to the hope survivors share when they triumph over the evil they have witnessed.

With every story of injustice, there were always those who refused to stand silent, who made a conscious choice to act, regardless of the consequences, the price, and the impact on one's life. It was a few individuals who had never been part of the slave trade who decided to act in the late eighteenth century in London, England, leading eventually to the global abolitionist movement. It was three white civil rights workers who were slain making a stand for equality in Mississippi in 1964. Like the abolitionists before them, they were making a political statement that slavery and segregation were not "black problems," they were everyone's problem and responsibility to solve. Similarly, individual white South African activists made the point that Apartheid was a moral responsibility for all to end.

We see that in every story of injustice there is a movement for the good, one in which there are always survivors who decided to dedicate their lives to ending it, as well as those who have not been victims but know of their moral responsibility to stand up and fight. Lisa Shannon is one of those individuals who has decided to take a stand against an evil that does not oppress her directly but offends her with its very existence. She runs for Congo women.

Lisa Shannon is a woman no different than those who stood up against slavery and apartheid before her, who decided to act, watch, hear, and even go into the heart of horrors as she did to witness the atrocities and listen to those who have seen evil. For survivors, their perseverance is a triumph over evil, the sheer force of *will* to survive and to stand tall. For Lisa, hers is a heroine's journey of a woman who did not shy away from the ongoing horrors in the world. She is a woman who was not afraid to confront conflict in the Congo, who did not worry about how much it would cost her personally to engage. Hers is a story of compassion, clarity, determination, strength, creativity, and love. It is a story about the power of believing in the possibility of making a difference, in the possibility of good to triumph over evil, and in the power of love to triumph over hate.

I have witnessed the joy Lisa created in the hearts of women who have survived the horror of the war in Congo. I have seen their embrace, heard their laughter, and shared their joy when they learned that this one woman cares so much. Lisa loved them so much that she traveled halfway around the world to talk with them directly, touch them, assure them that there is still hope in this world, and that it is still possible for life to go back to normal. And, by organizing the Run for Congo events, she showed them that women all over the world care enough to run, and run in order to draw attention to their suffering and to create change.

Through the most honest and sincere portrayal of emotions, balanced with an astute understanding of the politics associated with the conflict, *A Thousand Sisters* gives a human face to war by showing that the beauty and resilience of Congolese women shines through even the darkest of times—through their sheer determination to stay alive, or love the child they bore out of mass rape; to process the pain they endured and the horrors they survived; to laugh despite all odds, dance despite all pain, believe in humanity despite all of the inhumanity they have witnessed; and to keep life going in the midst of death. That is what women always do in war, and they do that in the Democratic Republic of Congo. Lisa has borne witness to that; she has captured their strength expertly in this book.

A Thousand Sisters shows the power of communication, of reaching out, of building bridges of hope. It is the story of individual women from around the world who decided to take full ownership of their voice and their resources and become one thousand philanthropists, one thousand advocates on behalf of one thousand women whose resources have been stolen and whose voices have been ignored. The horror in Congo has been going on for so long, it feels as if the world has put the sounds of the women's cries of injustice on mute. Lisa and a few American women have decided to turn up the volume, to shine the spotlight: they have listened and acted.

Public diplomacy, friendship, and peace come in many different forms, and Lisa's journey of sponsoring Congolese women proves that it also comes from individuals who have made the conscious decision to act, to represent the beauty of who they are as individuals. Her story shows the power of connecting through our humanity, connecting through our common love for simple things—our trees and gardens, the sound of running water, and all that we have in common, regardless of where we are and where we come from.

I would like to offer a special thanks to Oprah Winfrey, whose vision and passion led her to cover the story of the women in Congo before anybody else brought awareness to the issue. If Oprah had not given me the opportunity to share the story of Congolese women, I would not have had the privilege of meeting Lisa and the thousands of other women who decided to act.

I will close with this final thought: a Bosnian journalist once told me that war shows you the worst side of humanity and in that same moment it shows the most beautiful side of humanity. Lisa's story is a testament to the beauty of humanity that exists in the darkest and most depraved times of war. It is a beauty that has sparked the united action of women who gather in support of their Congolese sisters across the globe, who gather to speak out, and who gather to create change.

Rumi, a 13th century Sufi poet, wrote :

Out beyond the world of right doing and wrong doing
There is a field.
I will meet you there.
When the soul meets in that grass,
the world is too full to talk about.
Ideas, language, even the phrase each other *no longer makes any sense.*

I hope Rumi forgives me if I suggest that in between the worlds of war and peace, there is a field, and women are meeting in that field. Lisa is there; Honarata is there; Fatima is there; Violette is there; Barbara is there; so many other sisters are there. If you are not there already, come join us, for the "world is too full to talk about. Ideas, language, even the phrase *each other* no longer makes any sense." We are just sisters gathering in a field, and we shall run— run and dance—dance until the end.

AUTHOR'S NOTE

*T*HIS IS A TRUE STORY. In a place as extreme as Congo, there is no need to make anything up. Everything in this book happened; the vast majority of it happened on videotape. Most of the dialogue has been transcribed directly from video, as it was translated to me in the moment. Some interviews are compressed, having taken place over multiple meetings. Some portions are not presented in the exact order of actual events. There are no composite characters. Congo, nonetheless, is an active war zone and I have a duty to protect those I met and interviewed. Most names have been changed, primarily for safety reasons, and in some special cases (as clearly noted in the text) details of context were omitted due to serious safety concerns.

Congo in a Nutshell

AT THE END of the Rwandan genocide in 1994, more than two million Hutu refugees fled over the border into Zaire. Among them, approximately 100,000 Hutu *genocidaires,* known as the Interahamwe, found safe harbor, melting into refugee camps facilitated by the United Nations.

In the absence of an international effort to identify Interahamwe, in 1996 Rwanda and Uganda sponsored rebel leader Laurent Kabila to invade Zaire. The Hutu refugee camps were destroyed. The remaining Interahamwe retreated to Congo's forests, where they re-branded themselves as the Democratic Liberation Forces of Rwanda (the FDLR).

Backed by Rwandan troops, Kabila ousted Zaire's long-time kleptocratic dictator Mobutu. Kabila was installed as the new President of the country and renamed it The Democratic Republic of the Congo.

The alliance between Rwanda and Kabila was short-lived. In 1998, again citing security threats posed by the Interahamwe (FDLR), Rwanda and Uganda invaded once again, now backing the militia Rally for Congolese Democracy (RCD), which took control of North and South Kivu provinces. Ragtag splinter groups and homegrown militias jumped into the fight, including the Mai Mai, a local defense force known for its use of witchcraft. Kabila formed his own alliances with neighboring countries like Zimbabwe, Angola, and

Namibia, dragging half a dozen countries into the conflict that grew to be termed Africa's World War.

In January 2001, Kabila was assassinated. His son, Joseph Kabila, took over as President of DR Congo. The conflict technically ended in 2003 and many countries or their proxy militias returned home. In the summer of 2006, with heavy international support, Congo held its first elections since independence, and Joseph Kabila became the first democratically elected President since 1960.

Despite this, chaos continues to reign in eastern Congo.

Congo hosts the largest United Nations peacekeeping force in the world, with 20,000 troops and a robust mandate to protect civilians. But given the enormity of the country and its chaos, the UN force, also called MONUC, is "pathetically spare," while the Congolese army, a force of 125,000 troops, is comprised primarily of former militias integrated into this notoriously corrupt, ill-disciplined army.

The FDLR remain, still known by the locals as Interahamwe, "Those Who Kill Together." Though they have shrunk to an estimated 6,000 to 8,000 combatants, they control 60 percent of South Kivu.

National Congress for the Defense of People (a.k.a., CNDP), a Congolese-Tusti defense force led by General Laurent Nkunda (widely reported to be backed by Rwanda), has caused major unrest and massive displacement in North Kivu through 2008. Nkunda was arrested in 2009.

The United Nations has accused all nations involved in the conflict of using the war as a cover for looting Congo's vast mineral wealth. Rwanda, Uganda, and Burundi, as well as Congolese government officials, have made hundreds of millions of dollars off of the Congo plunder.

The result? As of January 2008, more than 5.4 million people had died due to the conflict, making it the deadliest war since World War II. Forty-five thousand continue to die every month. Sexual violence is rampant. Congo has been widely termed "the worst place on earth to be a woman."

Journalist Lisa Ling has termed Eastern Congo, "The worst place on earth. And the most ignored."

CHAPTER ONE

Congo Rushes

THE CALLS COME during the remote, panic-inducing hours of morning. I scramble for my cell phone; a number beginning 011-243-99 appears on my caller ID. Congo calling. Sometimes it's the United Nations, a Sergeant Something-I-Can't-Make-Out, with a heavy South Asian lilt, who requests my immediate reply but is never again reachable. The president of a militia calls for a job reference after being fired for "political affiliations incompatible with humanitarian work." Or it's the distant voice of my Congolese driver, Serge, who says, "Some f——ing job." He is using his precious phone minutes to prank call me. We both giggle until he hangs up.

The Democratic Republic of the Congo—otherwise known as the worst place on earth. Home to Africa's First World War, the deadliest war on the planet since World War II. I've spent months trying to shake that place, but it keeps knocking at my door, like a bill collector or an old lover anxious to wrap up unfinished business.

This morning is different, though.

"Do you remember there?"

Yes, Eric. I remember there.

It's news from the village of Kaniola. One Sunday, many months ago, I walked through its far-flung settlements, which are scattered along the ridgeline, butted up against vast stretches of forest. Since the 1994 Rwandan genocide, the forests, thirty miles inland from the Rwandan border, have been ruled by Hutu militias known as Interahamwe, a Rwandan word meaning "those who kill together." The group is also known as the *Forces Democratiques de Liberation du Rwanda,* or FDLR.

I thought about Kaniola just the other day while strolling past the Old Portland houses and walnut trees that line my street, sipping my takeout tea. I'm not religious, so Biblical passages almost never cross my mind, but that psalm flashed in my head: *Yea, though I walk through the valley of the shadow of death* . . . I realized that if there is anywhere on earth that qualifies as the valley of the shadow of death, it's Kaniola. In the five and a half weeks I spent in Congo, the most horrific stories I heard came from that valley. I walked through it and I felt no fear. *I've done that, literally.*

I chuckled to myself.

This morning, sitting in front of my laptop with another cup of tea, staring at my email in-box, it is not amusing in the least.

My friend Eric, a Congolese conservationist with whom I maintain regular contact, writes, "I am forwarding you an article about seventeen persons who were killed by knives in Kaniola. Do you remember there?"

Of course I remember.

The international news report outlines the attack. "It was a reprisal. They targeted houses. They silently entered the house. They started by strangling some victims before stabbing them to stop them raising the alarm. . . . The assailants left a letter saying they would return in force."

Twenty injured. Eighteen kidnapped. Seventeen killed.

On my second read of the article, I stop cold at a line I initially missed: "The victims included the father of a girl kidnapped by the FDLR and recently freed by the army."

From the hundreds of people I interviewed in Congo's war-ravaged

South Kivu province, I heard plenty of stories of abductions and countless reports of the army *running away* from the Interahamwe. But I heard only one account of the army protecting civilians, a shocking story because these kinds of heroics are so rare. In Kaniola, I met three girls who'd been abducted by the Interahamwe and rescued by the Congolese Army.

Is this article about that same family? *It must be.*

It will be days before I hear from one of the United Nations majors who escorted me that day, who confirms my guess. "If you remember the last walk, it was that same area."

I went to Kaniola on a tip, a shred of paper, on a day I had nothing better to do. I spent less than a day there—just a Sunday morning—walking through the village, hoping to talk with the rescued girls. We visited the girls' home and spoke for more than an hour with the cool-tempered teenagers, their brother, and their desperate father. Afterward, their dad turned to us and asked pointedly, "Now that we've talked with you, what are you going to *do?*"

I drag out the plastic storage bin packed with videotapes from my trip, long since left in a corner of an empty room, its contents unviewed. I'm up late, combing the unfiltered, raw footage, which are called "rushes" in the film industry. Finally I find the Kaniola tapes.

It's peaceful enough there. Certainly, there is no gore. (I never once saw a dead person in Congo.) Still, I notice my hands shaking as I watch. I have to stop, pace the hall, and return to inch through the footage, frame by frame, until I land on the clearest image of each person I so much as scanned with the camera that day. I capture them in still frames. I export them, save them, print them out in pixilated eight-by-tens, and file them in a white plastic three-ring binder.

I missed so much when I was there. I had heard that when you cross the border into Congo, the look in people's eyes changes. I noticed it the first day, then never again. Now, as I scan the video footage, it seems so obvious. I study their eyes. Countless people have referred to that look as one of numbness or shell shock. Journalist Lisa Ling once called it "a look of utter death."

As days fly by and I continue to dig deep into the footage, I stumble across a shot of myself on my second day in Africa, standing on the Rwandan side of the border with a rickety wooden bridge in front of me. I'm about to cross over. I'm already disheveled from the thirty-five-minute flight from Kigali, Rwanda.

That's odd. In the footage, I am blinking rapidly. My eyelids are fluttering. I didn't feel afraid at the time, but as I watch myself, I'm clearly scared.

Why did I invite that place in? Why did I pursue it, track it down?

It wasn't because I wanted a feel-good pet project. I needed a solution.

CHAPTER TWO

The Greenest Grass

*I*IT ALL STARTS with *Oprah,* as these things so often do.

It is August 2004 and I am sitting in my therapist's office. She zeroes right in. "You've been watching *Oprah* a lot lately."

I am not one to advertise my daytime TV habits, but my four o'clock appointment with Ms. Winfrey has recently become the sturdy anchor in my day. "How did you know that?"

"Depressed people who are at home during the daytime always watch the show."

Wait, depressed? I don't have a clue where she's getting that. To me, depressed is someone in a dingy bedroom in mid-afternoon, blinds closed, watching the digital clock click from 2:12 PM to 2:13 PM to 2:14 PM, or rattling around the house in day-thirteen socks. That is not me. Some stress issues? Sure, and there is my dad's end-stage cancer. But I feel fine.

I have a great life. At twenty-nine, I am on a solid trajectory, working my plan. I have a little Victorian house with a flower garden in a hip, walkable Portland neighborhood; a creative business with cash-flow charts that tell me freedom is just around the corner; and a good man to snuggle with at night.

My quirky English business partner, Ted, is also my significant other. We aren't married, but there's no need. We have a bond just as strong, with all the legal protections to match. We are a corporation.

Ted is wonderful, truly. Everything I've always had on my list. Kind. Creative. Fun. Cool. Though he's fifteen years my senior, at forty-four, he prefers to think of himself as twenty-two. Playful and charming to the bone, he can squeeze a smile out of even the most sour grocery-checkout lady or snarky video store clerk. He's not one to talk much (did I mention he's English?), but we have between us the quiet harmony of best friends.

We shoot lifestyle stock-photography, the kind of images you see on display in health food stores, dental brochures, and advertisements for online dating services. The beauty of the stock shot is that it can be used to sell anything. One aspiration fits all. A winning photograph will convey two things: perfection and genuine emotion. Correction: The *illusion* of genuine emotion, which, it turns out, can be manufactured with a few rounds of "One, two, three, yay!"

Ted shoots; I art direct and produce. I haul perfect size-2 models out to a cloudless beach or field of the greenest manicured grass and tell them to lift their arms to the sky like wings so we can capture pictures that will rise to the top of online image searches tagged with the keyword "freedom."

We call it "image pollution," just to be clear we're in on the joke. At parties, Ted likes to say facetiously that we've sold our souls. For us, stock photography is strictly a means to an end. As though such things can be coaxed from the universe—or from hundred-dollar-an-hour models, for that matter—Ted often rocks back and forth as he shoots, chanting, "Happiness. More happiness."

CHAPTER THREE

Sometimes Death is More Like a Labor

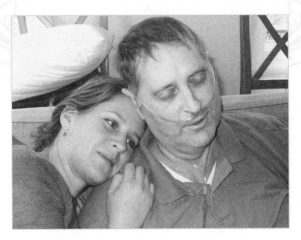

THE LABORED BREATHING starts late at night. They call it "the death rattle." Though it is my job to stay near my dad in case he needs anything, I sleep through it as though it isn't happening. My blankets and foam pad are piled on the dining room floor amid the chaos of oxygen tubes and pills, the hospital bed shoved in one corner, and the antique dish-cabinet in the other. I drift in and out of sleep, ignoring all the cues that this is his final night.

In the morning, my mom calls hospice. The nurse arrives and announces that he is now in the active dying process.

There is a grasping half-light in Dad's eyes and his desperate breathing continues, increasing in intensity. The nurse warns us that this slow release of life could go on for days—that "sometimes death is more like a labor."

Hours pass. His blood steadily retreats up his arms and feet, leaving his skin bluish green and translucent. His pajamas are soaked with sweat. Someone grabs scissors and cuts them off, leaving his six-foot-four frame naked, swaddled in pink sheets.

Everyone leaves the room, so I sit down next to him and hold his hand.

A Vedic prayer I learned in college comes to mind. I haven't said it aloud for years. *What the hell. We're alone.* I lean in close and sing the prayer.

He cranes his head toward me to listen. The nurse comes back, sees Dad fading, and corrals everyone into the room. "This is it!"

I sense panic and crying behind me, but I don't look up. I continue the prayer until someone puts a hand on my arm and I hear, like sounds from a distant radio, "He's gone."

I step away, disconnected, like someone who slipped out to the restroom and missed a crucial point in a movie. I want to lean over to the nearest person and whisper, "What did I miss?" Instead, they cry, while I study his body. Sprawled on the hospital bed, my father looks like a giant, pale green frog.

The nurse shuts off the oxygen pump.

After they roll Dad away in the burgundy velvet body bag, all that is left on his hospital bed is his outline on the pink sheets. I sit in the room for a long time, and again the next day, until the bed is broken down and taken away. The dining room table returns to host distant relatives who will eat from Chinese takeout boxes on the spot where he died.

SEVERAL CRISP FALL DAYS LATER, the sun in my eyes obscures the people who are scattered down the hillside of a modern, 1960s-era graveyard, its flat headstones and manicured grass overlooking Portland's Sunset Highway. I stare at the one-foot-square, simple wooden box of ashes with my mind locked on the impossibility of the math. How can my father, who was six-four and weighed 250 pounds, fit in that little container—even reduced to ashes? What percentage of his body is this?

I try to calculate. We are burying just a portion of his ashes. The rest will be displayed in bits and pieces. Some are split between three pink and green cloisonné mini-urns on my mother's mantel. Some are in a "Granddaddy" Build-a-Bear made for my niece. Some will be scattered at the family cemetery, in a wheat field where my father spent his summers as a child. I abandon the math. This all seems a bit silly. And he was not a silly man.

Dad was a government servant. His preference was for all things simple: pleated polyester pants, microwave dinners. His favorite things were blood-and-guts action movies and hours of philosophical conversation over morning coffee. He was a therapist who treated Vietnam vets' war trauma, though he did not fight in the war himself. Growing up, I heard bits and pieces about his work and some horror stories from Vietnam. But Dad's "guys," as he called his clients, seemed more like mythical characters to me until we had a living wake—a memorial service held before someone dies—a couple of weeks ago, and I noticed a crusty guy wearing a trucker cap in the back row, unobtrusively showing his support.

On the other hand, Mom is a nervous lady, given to melodrama. She's a former Southern beauty queen, and with her heavyset frame and salt-and-pepper hair, she can look ultrasophisticated when she chooses to streamline. But on most days she prefers black socks under tan sandals, paired with wrinkled, cropped khakis and oddly layered T-shirts that, more often than not, she slept in the night before. By midday she's tugging at the ends of her shirt, combing her hair, and declaring, "I feel so frumpy!"

Now that Mom has lost her lifetime love, I stand back and allow her center stage in her rather public grieving process. At today's wake, I wander around stiffly, avoiding the sympathetic hugs and talk of how I'll be able to feel his presence "if only I open my heart."

My mom and sister mourn, as they will for months. Sitting on the edge of my parents' bed, they cry it out. They purge the closets of his extra-extra-large, tall-size flannel and Oxford-cloth shirts (striped and plaid) and his white V-necks. They keep their eyes on the sky, watching for eagles to circle above the house, insistent that his "spirit animal" carries messages from beyond.

I don't cry. He doesn't appear in my dreams. I avoid my parents' house. It's not that anything has changed that much. But I'd imagined that after Dad died I would be upset. In fact, I don't feel much of anything, and as I think about it, I haven't felt much of anything for quite some time. I call it "creepy normal." On my trips to the grocery store, when visiting with friends, and during my afternoons with *Oprah*, it's like I'm still sitting in the converted dining room—in the green wingback chair—with his body, silent and still, like I'm waiting to wrap up an unfinished conversation.

There's something that bothers me, something Dad told me a few weeks before he died. He had structured his life around family, friends, and service work. He connected very deeply with people. Yet he viewed himself as a loser. Why? Because he didn't think he'd made enough money. Like so many other men, he judged himself through the lens of status. In his mind, a couple of rental investment properties didn't cut it.

I, on the other hand, have never had trouble making money. But now that Dad is gone, I find it hard to remember what the goal is supposed to be. *This?* Ted and I designed our home as a background for photo shoots: white-on-white-on-white décor, accented with bold doses of nothing. It's the kind of purity you can purchase on a long afternoon at IKEA—perfectly generic.

We periodically swear off business talk during our nightly dinners out, declaring some nonwork "personal time," but we never seem to find another topic worth pursuing. Our conversation always careers towards production plans. My malaise never comes up. When I watch Ted across the table, I notice how he refuses to look me in the eyes. I wonder if it's possible to be this close to someone, locked in a twenty-four-hour-a-day, aura-meshing marathon, and still feel lonely.

Can't we push the reset button?

AFTER DAD DIES, I don't go back to work. I cannot step on another plane bound for sunny Southern California. I can no longer retreat behind the camera wearing this season's Banana Republic collection in all black, size 14, hoping it hides my forty-five-pound weight gain, which I'm afraid screams: *I don't know who I am anymore. I am disappearing.* I can't lead models in one more round of "One, two, three. Yay!" I will not sit through one more lecture from a stock-photo library rep who mocks lovely little-girl models as "weird looking" or "horsey faced."

Instead, as Ted will point out later in division-of-labor arguments, I sit on the couch and do precisely nothing for months. Four months, to be exact.

This leads us to try Paris. The plan is to visit the city—it will be my first time there—to celebrate my thirtieth birthday. I want to mark the territory of the next decade with something new and different. Because I have a sneaking feeling that now may be the time to get away . . . from all this.

Ted and I visit his family in England, where I catch a horrible cold. By the time we reach Berlin for a quick visit with friends, I have both the flu and strep throat. As though I can will myself to feel better, I go out one night, but the smoky Berlin bars throw me into a nonstop coughing fit. The next day, while Ted explores the city's museums, I stay in bed watching shadows shift around our hosts' dark guest apartment. I trace lines in the wide-board floors, scan the bookshelf and attempt to make sense of the German titles, and drift in and out of sleep, trying not to swallow. By the time Ted returns, we hit "eject." We're supposed to fly to Paris in the morning, but we fly home instead.

I wind up back on the couch in Portland, watching *Oprah*.

On January 24, 2005, Oprah features a twenty-minute segment on women in the Congo.

"During World War II, a lot of people pretended not to know what was going on. Well, there's another holocaust going on. This time, in the Democratic Republic of the Congo. And if you are like most people, you probably had no idea."

What?

In the report, journalist Lisa Ling describes a conflict born out of the 1994 Rwandan genocide. After the mass killings, the Hutu militias responsible were pushed west over the border into Congo, where they retreated into the forests and began to terrorize the local population. The militias that were formed to fight them soon began fighting each other. Eventually, half a dozen countries were involved in the conflict, which became known as Africa's First World War.

Oprah adds, "And the violence continues *today,* as we speak." *Women* have suffered the worst of it; rape and sexual slavery are widespread, and once they've become victims, women are usually rejected by their husbands.

"Four million people have died. *Four million people.* And no one is talking about it," Lisa Ling reports. "I think it's the worst place on earth . . . and the most ignored."

Wait. Wait. Wait. Let's be clear. The militias responsible for the Rwandan genocide are still out there? Killing people?

Oprah says, "They are hoping somebody in the world will hear their screams for help."

Could I be one of those people?

Zainab Salbi, founder of the Washington, D.C.–based nonprofit Women for Women International, appears on the show. The articulate, thirtysomething Iraqi American woman suggests sponsoring a Congolese woman for $27 a month. Oprah concludes, in an unusually pointed tone, "Now that you know, you can't pretend you didn't hear it."

I'll do that. I'll sponsor a woman.

The show ends. Ted shouts from the next room, "Would you like some tea?"

The phone rings. I chat with my mom for a couple of minutes. I check email then initiate the daily discussion, calling to Ted in the next room. "Where should we have dinner?"

Walking down the hall, heading for my tea, I remember the show. I know how this will go. My mind will drift to cash-flow charts scrawled on yellow legal pads. I'll log onto modeling agency sites to see what new face might spark a shoot idea. I'll move on. Weeks, months, maybe years will stack up, and I'll think back to those faces, those numb eyes I saw on *Oprah,* and wonder, *What if I had tried to help?*

I have to do it now, before it becomes one more thing I meant to do. I stop, turn around, go back to the computer, and sign up to sponsor two women. I am one of six thousand viewers to sign up as a sponsor because of Oprah's show.

THE WOMEN'S FACES don't retreat, though. And I continue to feel like something is missing in my life. I'm hungry for something all my own, beyond Ted and Lisa, Inc. I want to do something, but I can't think of what. There is this faint sense, somewhere in the background, of a person I haven't seen in a long time: the person I always imagined I would become.

I remember the day when I was eleven and my older sister, Marie, and I met my mom for lunch downtown, where she worked as a legal secretary. Afterward, Marie and I walked to the bus stop. I took the last available seat on the bench, next to an African American lady. Marie stood beside me as we waited. A few minutes later, a disheveled homeless man, probably drunk, approached. He asked, "Can you spare any change?"

One of us responded. "Don't have any, sorry."

He turned to the lady next to me, who gave him the same polite answer.

As he turned to walk away, he sputtered none too quietly, "F——ing n——."

It was one of those moments when time slows, like during a traffic accident. My heart beat heavily. An impulse overtook me. *I can't just let that go.* I jumped to my feet and blurted out, "You are a *racist!*"

My skin burned. Everyone milling around the bus stop stood still. My sister was shocked. The lady was shocked. I was shocked. Yet I continued. "I don't want to hear your garbage!" I said. "You have no right to judge people by the color of their skin. You need to watch your mouth!"

The man looked at me for a moment, then turned around and shuffled away, murmuring, "Damned kids . . ."

Then there was that time after a gym-class volleyball game, during my freshman year of high school, when I noticed a group of boys swarming around the net. It was another problem with Trevor Samson, the school geek. This time he was in a verbal sparring match with a popular kid, one of those who commuted to school from their prestigious, sprawling West Hills homes in spanking new Jeep Cherokees. I didn't care that Trevor and I had a lot in common—we'd been in middle school together, and we came from the same part of town. We weren't friends. I didn't like him. He was a nerd's nerd: obnoxious. Vulnerable. Pathetic.

The confrontation heated up quickly as I edged in closer to see what was going on. No teachers were in sight. More than thirty boys, mostly of the West Hills breed, had gathered around and were egging on the aggressor. They wanted to see a fight. As people started pushing and violent threats were hurled, Trevor was saying all the wrong things—the kind of defensive garbage that only fuels the confrontation. Boys shouted from the crowd, "Kick his ass!"

Without considering the social risk, I pushed my way past the pack and stepped between Trevor and Mr. Popular. I stuck my finger in Chip-or-Chad-or-Seth's face and declared, "Stop!"

A kid with the chiseled features and glowing tan that seem to come with a moneyed background shouted from the herd, "Shut up, you f—ing hippie bitch!"

I stood my ground, squarely in front of Trevor, shielding him with the hard fact there is no social status to be gained from hitting a girl. The crowd disbanded.

Later that year, I saw an ambulance in front of the school. Down the main corridor, covered in bandages, came Trevor; he was being wheeled out by paramedics. Someone had cornered him in the locker room and beaten his head against the cement floor until he collapsed, bloody. The teacher who found him called 911.

A lot of us, when we were kids, couldn't stand to see a starving stray cat. *It's not right,* we'd think. *Something has to be done.* Then, somewhere between ages fifteen and twenty-five, the feeling fades. We shut up. We get "real." We learn to mind our own business.

I've been no exception.

STILL, ABOUT A WEEK LATER on my last-day-of-my-twenties party, I abandon social graces and herd the conversation back to Congo at every turn. "No, you don't understand. Four million people have died. Don't you think we should do something? Let's have a fundraising party or bake sale or walk. . . ."

I am met with awkward silences, blank stares, and polite changes of subject.

Despite attempts to map new terrain for myself, I wake up on the morning of my thirtieth birthday without a clue about where I am headed. Ted says he has a surprise for me. Whatever it is, I welcome the change.

On my last birthday, we were in San Diego prepping a photo shoot. We spent hours in sprawling malls, driving from one chain store to another. We roamed the aisles at Target, Ross, and the Saks Fifth Avenue outlet, hunting for size 2 summer dresses and swimsuits. By the time evening came around, we abandoned plans to eat at the nicer strip mall restaurant, opting for rice and beans at the Baja Fresh across the parking lot to avoid the long lines outside the marginally fancier place. Back at the hotel, Ted presented me with my birthday treat—a card picked up while we were prop shopping. I stayed up late, wrapping empty boxes in flower-print and striped gift paper and tying them with inviting bows for the next day's shoot, a fake child's birthday celebration.

So wherever I am headed to inaugurate my thirties, it's already something better. When we get in the car, I have no idea: The beach? The mountains? The desert? The train? A drive? The airport? I'm not used to this lack of control, "Can you at least tell me when I'll know?"

"Soon," Ted teases.

When we pull up at the airport, I am just as lost, even after we check in for our flight to San Francisco.

As we sit in the airport terminal, I spot a newsstand with the February issue of *O, The Oprah Magazine,* which has an article on women in Congo.

Minutes later, in the crowded waiting area, I read the article, then its online expanded version, "Postcards from the Edge." One woman describes a militia dragging her away to the forest to rape or kill her. She pleads for her life. One of the militia responds, "Even if I kill you, what would it matter? You are not human. You are like an animal. Even if I killed you, you would not be missed."

I decide to run.

CHAPTER FOUR

Lone Run

I AM NOT A feel-the-burn kind of girl. I am a casual runner. Make that very casual.

Years ago, my then roommate and I decided to train for our first marathon. We trained consistently for about a month, then scheduled our first fourteen-mile training run. We procrastinated until late afternoon, forgot our water, and set out in ninety-five-degree heat on an endlessly flat, sun-exposed cement path. (I still call it "The Corridor of Hell.") Our chatter about frozen dessert could only keep us distracted for so long, and around mile ten, it trailed off into the sound of panting and footsteps. My running buddy asked, "How are you doing over there?"

"Exhausted," I admitted.

"Want to stop?" he asked.

"Got your cell phone?"

"No," he said, then he pointed to a convenience store. "But I bet they have a pay phone there."

We called a cab to drive us back to the car. I collapsed in the back of the taxi, delighted to declare that giving up was one of the nicest things I'd ever done for myself. That marked the end of my marathon ambitions.

Now, back from our San Francisco trip and over my midwinter bug, I find a five-mile run long, but doable. Though I've tried to enroll friends to join me in creating a run or walk for Congo's women, not one of them has agreed. They don't know anything about the conflict and aren't interested in learning. So I'm doing this alone. Because everyone and their cousin's boyfriend do 5Ks and marathons to raise funds for every cause imaginable, I need to take it a step further. I realize I need an effort that can't be faked: something extreme. Something that will get my friends and family to see how seriously, how personally, I take the situation in Congo.

So I decide to run 30.16 miles, the entire length of Wildwood Trail, a muddy, rugged forest trail which zigzags up and down Portland's West Hills. My goal is to raise thirty-one sponsorships for Congolese women through Women for Women International, one sponsorship for every mile I run.

I'm not sure I can do it. That's why at first I keep it a secret.

Everyday I hit the trail alone. Each week I go on the longest run of my life. I hire an ultrarunning coach and follow her training schedule to the letter. Ted drops me at the trailhead in the morning. While he works for hours, grocery shops, and does laundry, I pound miles of trail, getting smacked in the face with branches and spider webs. If I'm lucky, I brush them off my face or hair. Less lucky for me and the spider, I sometimes get a surprise high-protein snack.

I REALLY NEED TO PEE. Never mind public toilets; I am ten miles from the nearest porta-potty. Without any other option, I climb off the trail to the most secluded, dense underbrush I can find and I squat. When I continue on my way, I run like a snail. I crawl, shuffle, wince, and spend miles trying to forget what I'm doing. I try all kinds of mental tricks, from counting my steps to reciting the Vedic prayer I sang to my dad when he died and composing letters to my future Congolese sisters. Anything to distract myself from the searing pain that shoots from my sciatic nerve. Anything to get through the remote stretches of the park where I don't see another jogger for hours. When I reach the more populated section, everyone is faster than I am. As college girls in bushy-bushy ponytails bounce straight past me, I reassure myself: They are probably on mile two; I'm on mile eighteen.

Another jogger rounds a corner and says, "Nice job!" as he passes. I mumble on an exhale, "Thanks," and then get misty-eyed! No one ever warns you that on these long stretches, with the body's resources beyond tapped, you get wiggy.

On the final stretch, I feel like I'm running while I have the flu. I was overly optimistic about my pace again. Ted has been sitting dutifully in the car, waiting almost an hour for me to round the last curve of the trail and emerge, sweaty and exhausted. When I see him waiting with a cold bottle of water and a sandwich, I think, *That's love.* My gait disintegrates to a crumpled, stiff shuffle back to the car.

After a hard run like this, I collapse for the rest of the day, avoiding social functions if I can. If I can't, I simply accept that forming complete sentences is not within my realm of possibility.

Over months of training, my toenails fall off; some fall off twice. Bloody blisters, severe leg pain, and sores caused by chafing are daily companions. Thanks to the sun hitting my sweaty upper lip for miles, overpowering my sunscreen, my summer look has a special new accent: the mustache tan. Sooo sexy.

It's raining? I run anyway. I'm in pain? I run anyway. I'm tired? I'm busy? Ted and I have a fight? I run anyway. When it all seems too much, I try to picture the women living in eastern Congo. Their faces are always a blank, but I try to imagine what they are doing. They can't pick up a cell phone and call a cab to take them out of the war zone. So I keep going.

Though I signed up as a sponsor in January, it is April before I receive a packet from Women for Women with a postage stamp-size image of my first Congolese sister, Therese. The photo is dark, distant, and blurry. Her head is smaller than my pinky fingernail, and I can barely make out her face. She stands against a white wall, shoulders raised in discomfort, but her eyes are clear. Holding the photo feels like magic. Congo feels a little closer. Therese was born in 1970, she's married, and she has no formal education. From now on, I picture her on my long runs and fantasize about what I might say one day if I met her in person.

Four months into my training and two months before the run, it's time for another reality check. I need to raise ten thousand dollars. I've never done any fundraising or public speaking. My only ideas are to send out a bulk email and to invite ten friends over for a screening of Oprah's Congo segment. One of my best friends, Lana—a savvy Portland casting director known for her fundraising prowess—advises otherwise. "Don't invite ten friends over to your place. Ask those ten friends to each invite ten friends to their houses."

I don't have ten friends to ask, but six friends finally agree to it. I squirm at the prospect of asking people for money, so I keep it simple and take a no-pressure approach. I give a little talk, show the *Oprah* video clip, and ask people to sponsor a woman in Congo, pledge a flat donation, or just read more about the conflict.

Another friend asks me, "What's the hardest part? I bet it's not the running." She is right: It's feeling alone. When I talk about Congo, it's not just that people don't know about the war, it's that they assume there must be a reason no one is talking or doing anything about it. When I invite a thoughtful, politically aware friend out for coffee and try to convince her to host a house party, she questions the logic of my effort. "Why help women there, where it's a total mess? Why not help other needy women someplace where it is stable?"

I'm glad I'm wearing sunglasses because I'm so frustrated I choke up. I know my emotional argument won't get me very far, but it's all I've got. "Because they don't feel like human beings."

This friend hosts a house party after all, where we raise eight sponsorships!

I try to read more, but news on Congo is shockingly spare.

There is one book I devour: Adam Hochschild's *King Leopold's Ghost*, a haunting account of Congo's colonial history. In the late nineteenth century, with the help of the adventure-crazed Welsh explorer Henry Morton Stanley, Belgium's King Leopold staked out the Congo Free State as his own private colony. Under the auspices of science, religious conversion, and protection from Arab slave traders and from their own ignorance, he enslaved the Congolese people en masse to extract Congo's treasure trove of natural resources, from rubber to ivory. Leopold used his plunder to build pleasure palaces on the French Riviera and bankroll the Paris shopping sprees of his teenage mistress, who once boasted of spending three million francs at one dress shop. During King Leopold's thirty-year rule, the population of Congo was cut in half, with a staggering net loss of ten million people. Novelist Joseph Conrad labeled it "the vilest scramble for loot that ever disfigured the history of human conscience."

Yet in a strange and inspiring turn, the first major international human rights movement was launched against Leopold's oppressive regime by a modest English shipping clerk with no greater credential or connection to Congo than having read the subtext of the shipping records. Endless shipments of rubber and other natural resources were being imported from Congo, while only guns and soldiers were being exported back. That could only mean one thing, he guessed: slavery. Armed with the evidence, E. D. Morel recruited citizens and dignitaries from around the world and led the charge to end Leopold's brutal treatment of native people. His campaign led to the handover of the Congo Free State from King Leopold to the government of Belgium in 1908. It remained a colony until 1960, when it was granted independence.

E. D. Morel's story is a shot of pure inspiration, especially because I've been combing the Internet, searching for any other grassroots folks working for Congo. While the movement to end the violence in Darfur has gained momentum by mobilizing religious groups, students, moms, movie stars, journalists, and big news organizations, as far as I can see, the field for helping the people of Congo is painfully empty.

AT THE END of my first twenty-two-mile training run, Ted greets me with the camera for a spontaneous photo shoot. Imagine how beautiful I look after twenty-two miles, red-faced, my body caked with salt. But we need a picture for *The Oregonian*. They have responded to my mom's pitch to do a feature article on my run. It is the only story they will publish on the Congo in 2005. After it runs, checks from people I've never met begin to appear in the mailbox, in amounts from US$5 to US$500.

Eventually I receive my first letter from Therese. It is written in Swahili and accompanied by a version that has been translated into English by Women for Women International's Congo staff.

> *Dear Sister,*
>
> *Hello! I'm happy to write to you today. I'm happy with the $10 you are sending me. I'm using $5 of it in selling charcoals and $3 a chicken to raise as well as $ for medical care. I'm making a profit of $2 through my activity.*
>
> *My husband was taken to the bush by the Interahamwe soldiers. I don't have much to say.*
>
> *Your friend,*
>
> *Therese*

The worn paper filled with Swahili cursive makes everything I'm running for suddenly feel concrete.

ON THE BIG DAY, I'm determined to run the whole trail, against the adamant advice of my trainer. ("You must walk the hills. You will walk the hills.") At mile twenty-five, I hit Pittock Hill, by far the most brutal stretch. It's a mile and a half of punishing incline. I inch my way up in a shuffle-run. I call on every mental trick I can muster to get one foot in front of the other. But I run, I don't walk. Finally, I can see my sister and niece Aria waiting for me at the top with water and pretzels.

As the trail flattens out, I know I can do it. I'm home free. Better. Though I practically crawl through my last few miles, I'm on fire! A hiker walks past me. A grandma and her fat dog are gaining on me fast. But I refuse to walk. I run every step of those 30.16 miles. As I descend the final hill, a crowd of thirty or so people waits in the cool, early autumn drizzle—family, friends, girl scouts having a bake sale, but mostly people I've never met—all cheering.

I cross the finish line beaming.

Then I announce the final fundraising totals. We've raised more than US$28,000. Eighty Congolese women and their kids will now have different lives. And this is just the beginning.

CHAPTER FIVE

Ms. Congo

*I*IT'S STILL DARK when we step out of the cab at Manhattan's Riverside Park. Rain and blustery winds soak my lightweight jogging shorts as I lug an oversize suitcase out of the trunk. I am here with my one never-say-die volunteer: my mom.

The cab pulls away, leaving my mom and me to set up the First Annual New York Run for Congo Women in a downpour with gale force winds.

I can't say we weren't warned. Last night, we got a call from the park service asking if we plan to cancel due to the severe weather. No way, I told them.

Word has spread. After my solo run, I started getting random emails from people who want to get involved. I ran the numbers and landed on a new goal: a million dollars, which will pay for three thousand sponsorships. That's just a hundred runners (or walkers, swimmers, cyclists, bakers, or whatever) raising money for thirty sponsorships each. Or three hundred people raising money for ten sponsorships each. Or a thousand people, three sponsorships each.

My mom has appointed herself my full-time assistant. Sounds like a dream come true, but the mother-daughter dynamics are a challenge. Especially since *I've* been trying to keep *her* organized since I was five. Mom has developed a little habit. During the question-and-answer period of my public appearances, she takes the microphone and talks about the depth of Congo's suffering, and she always ends in tears. It's an issue, but she works hard and long. Despite her unmeasured approach and regular fits of panic (the organizational tasks are tough on her nerves), we're pulling it off.

Over the year since my Wildwood Trail run, Run for Congo Women events have sprung up in ten states and four countries. Some are simple solo runs, some are community or group runs. Tracey, in suburban Texas, has trained all summer in 110-degree heat. Robin, a mom in North Carolina, runs with her son. Carrie, in Ireland, takes out a permit at a manor house and more than forty people join her on a run around the grounds. My friends in London are reaching out to their church to sponsor their walk. More than a hundred people showed up for the Second Annual Portland Run for Congo Women.

With all the interest, I decided to take the run on the road. I took out permits in New York, San Francisco, Chicago, and Washington, D.C., hoping to spark a movement.

We have more than forty registrations for the First Annual New York Run for Congo Women. With this morning's rainy weather, I'm not optimistic about the turnout. We've already gotten several emails asking if we're still on.

Yes, we're still on. When it rains in Congo, women still hide in the bushes from the militia. They sleep in the rain. Kids get sick and die. We're running today. No excuses, no deterrents.

My mom takes temporary refuge in a coffee shop a couple of blocks away from the start line, while I hold down the fort in my skimpy running clothes and Mom's oversize, ankle-length trench coat. It whips and snaps against my blotchy, red, goose-bumped legs.

Alone, sick of my own spin, I abandon the internal pep talk. I squint to keep the wind and rain from thrashing at my eyes. The driving rain stings, drops pelt me like needles. It's so cold that I have to concentrate just to hold still and control the reflexive shaking. The banner blows off. I climb up the retaining wall and bury myself in the tree branches to re-tie it with my icy fingers. I find no comfort or inspiration from the statue of Eleanor Roosevelt looming over me as the dimness of nighttime lifts bit by bit. The rain continues unabated. I decide that this moment is officially harder than mile twenty-nine. There will be no break from the cold for hours.

At eight o'clock, our start time, it's just me and my mom. A cab pulls up and all the country directors from Women for Women emerge. I just met Christine, the organization's country director for Congo, in Chicago a few weeks ago. She is a vibrant, open, regal Congolese woman. We are both thirty-one years old and five foot ten, so she instantly branded me her "twin sister."

One runner with cropped blond hair shows up in a pink jogging suit. She introduces herself as Lisa Jackson. We wait another twenty minutes in the rain, just in case. Finally, we run the five-mile there-and-back course in the atrocious weather. We finish and escape to a local diner, where Lisa hands me a promotional postcard for her documentary-in-progress, *The Greatest Silence: Rape in the Congo.*

ASIDE FROM LISA JACKSON, I've come across only a few other grassroots Congo activists: The Washington, D.C.-based Friends of Congo, who join me in organizing the first D.C. Run for Congo Women; a six-person-strong Chicago-based coalition, headed by a Presbyterian couple; and a woman in California who collects tea bags and combs to send to rape victims at the Panzi Hospital in Bukavu. Collectively, we seem to be the movement for Congo.

But I receive an email from another potential activist who lives in a town nearby. She is a Women for Women sponsor who also saw the Congo report on *Oprah*. Its subject line: I WANT TO DO MORE. Anxious to foster leadership in what I hope is growing into a movement, I hop in the car and make the three-hour drive to help Kelly engage her church in a Hike for Congo Women project. An ultraorganized, sweet-spoken former model and a devout Christian, she is yoga-chic, with the requisite alterna-girl nose ring and flowing hair. Kelly spends her working life as a Pilates instructor and her free time blogging; she describes herself as a "peacemaker, justice seeker, healer, and dreamer." Despite the suburban love nest she shares with her husband, at 35 she has the kind of idealism and passion that would make her right at home in a women's studies class on almost any college campus.

I'm thrilled to have a Congo partner in crime. We take off to a grassroots advocacy conference in D.C., where we chase policy wonks down hotel corridors, quizzing them about how to launch a movement. At the Darfur discussion panels, I'm the woman in the back of the room asking, "Why is there no advocacy focus on Congo?" After the conference, I continue the outreach effort and pick up the nickname "Ms. Congo" in the process.

Kelly and I return to Washington to meet with every Africa or relief or genocide prevention organization that will talk to us. We are also spinning plans for a trip to Congo. I leave Ted at home to fend for himself on these trips, and he doesn't object; we can use the space.

Kelly and I schlep our way up Pennsylvania Avenue, exhausted after wrapping up our seventh meeting of the day. The Capitol stands in front of us in its undeniable grandeur, but the beauty is lost on me in my end-of-day brain-fry. I'm sticky in my black wool business clothes and weighed down from the oppressive humidity. I want to shake off the day. Instead, we talk in loops, regurgitating and processing everything we heard in our meetings. Almost everyone we've met has their hands full with Darfur or HIV or debt relief. Some are very supportive, promising to do what they can. Others are quick to lecture us. "You need to get it: You can't save Congo."

I'm so tired I can't even track what I've just said. I've all but checked out from the conversation when I hear Kelly refer to my efforts as "just pity."

Just pity? As a child of New Agers (bless my mother), I'm all for self-reflection. But given Kelly's quiet manner, I'm surprised at her quick jump from analyzing her own motivations to judging mine. It hits me like a slap.

So this is what it's like under the microscope: Now that I've stepped out, the pressure is on. I'm expected to work from the exactly perfect, most enlightened and politically correct place in my soul. Flawed methods and motivations will be observed and noted. This is a problem; I have not spent semester after semester studying how to be an activist. I have no idea what I'm doing. Like a lot of people, I'm afraid I won't make a difference, but mostly I'm afraid of doing it wrong. In public.

Should I curl up in the fetal position and process? Do I need to stop and go see a therapist or spiritual guide to deal with my ego? Wait to be perfect before I start? What about effort polluted by ego and naiveté, buoyed by grandiose dreams? What if I can't save Congo, but I try anyway? Would it be better to do nothing?

Did the abolitionists really think they could end slavery?

Did the anti-apartheid movement really think it could ban apartheid?

Does Save Darfur really think they can save Darfur?

Who do they think they are?

Defensive, I spit back, "I'm doing this because I care."

WHILE I AM IN WASHINGTON, my mom calls to tell me that a batch of letters has just arrived from our Congo sisters. The letters are full of news about their children, their favorite classes in the program, their business activities, prayers and blessings, and their hopes for the first democratic elections in their country since 1960, which are scheduled to take place this summer. My mom faxes the letters to the nearest Kinko's. One stands out.

> *Dear Sister,*
>
> *We are doing well here in Bukavu. I was very happy to get your letter and to realize that there is someone caring for me so that I can go on living. As I am handicapped of one of my legs, God arranged it in such a way that you can do what I could not do for my family. May God Bless you for that.*
>
> *In 2005, robbers dropped in at night in our home and killed my husband and cut off my leg. They also killed one of my children and*

burnt my house. Here in Bukavu, I am an internally displaced person.
I come from an area located sixty kilometers drive from Bukavu.

I am a mother of four.

War is a very bad thing. But I'm thankful God has enabled you
to comfort us.

Thanks.

Generose

I march her letter over to Oregon Senator Ron Wyden's office, where he's holding his weekly meet and greet for constituents. I'm the only person who shows up, so we talk for a half hour about Congo. He reads Generose's letter.

"They cut off her leg!" he says, shocked. "There are so many horrific situations like this, but what makes Congo stand out is the brutality. When were you there?"

Embarrassed to admit it, I answer, "I've never been to Congo."

I'm so tickled that a letter written by a woman in the Congo has landed in the hands of a U.S. Senator. I stop by Union Station and pick up postcards of Washington monuments framed with cherry blossoms and I write to Generose. I make rudimentary diagrams that outline the way the U.S. government is structured, so that Generose will understand how high up her letter has gotten. I suppose I want to offer her one of the few shreds of silver lining available after a loss, the modest comfort that a loved one's death has not occurred in a vacuum, but that something meaningful might spring from it.

A batch of new sponsorship packets arrives around the same time. The photos of new sisters always seem to have the self-conscious look of those who are unaccustomed to being photographed, but these four portraits say something else entirely. Though their paperwork looks no different than that of other Congolese women, their furrowed brows and downcast eyes convey distress. They look transparent, beaten down. Something especially bad must be happening in or around the Women for Women center they all attend called Walungu.

Back at Women for Women's D.C. headquarters, Sumana, the group's media person, tells me she wants to pitch my story to national magazines. Later that day we hop across the street to rummage the magazine racks at Borders, hoping to spark some ideas. As I thumb through women's magazines, Sumana leans over to me and whispers, "I know that woman. She's with [a major national magazine]." Without blinking, she pounces on her long-lost colleague. They swap updates about the last few years, since their joint stint in the White House press corps. Then Sumana launches into her Women for Women pitch, motioning for me to join them. "You have to hear Lisa's story. Well, Lisa, you'll tell it best . . ."

Pitch myself? Ugh. I stumble—practically choke—while the reporter listens politely. When I finish, she turns back to Sumana. "We get hundreds of pitches for stories on someone who crawled across the country on hand and knee for some good cause." She sizes me up. "Have you been to Congo?"

"No. Not yet."

She turns back to Sumana and says, "We might consider a story on letters between women, but just make sure it's not who you'd expect. You know, not someone who looks like they eat granola."

Whoa there, lady. I don't eat granola. It has way too much sugar.

Sumana jumps in, trying to salvage the contact. "I know a sponsor who would be perfect . . ."

I retreat to the magazine rack, trying to hide out behind *Elle* or *Glamour* or *Cosmo*, wondering what part of this perfectly pressed, all-black suit from Saks Fifth Avenue identified me as granola. All I can figure is that my silver 1920s art nouveau choker, a collector's item, apparently screams "hippie" in this Ann Taylor town. In any case, I don't need to be told my story isn't suited for a national magazine. I never dreamed it might be until Sumana mentioned it.

Fortunately, *Runner's World* and *O, The Oprah Magazine*—and later, *Fitness* magazine—disagree. Nine months after the meeting with Sumana, they all publish stories about me and the run, and the timing couldn't be better. Congo legislation is stalled in committee in the House following a unanimous pass in the Senate. It's cosponsored by Senators Barack Obama and Sam Brownback. (You can't get more opposite sides of the aisle than that!) But rumor has it the committee chair is holding it up so as to not aid Obama's rising star. I head over to D.C.'s Union Station, a couple of blocks from Capitol Hill, and stock up on as many copies of *O* and *Runner's World* as I can stuff into my bag, then I join the small constituency from Chicago, about six people total, for their self-proclaimed "Congo Lobby Days." We lug the magazines up and down the halls of Congress, asking for support of the bill.

When we talk with a couple of Republican staffers, I give them the magazines in an effort to prove there is a national, grassroots groundswell of support for Congo. They scan the articles. "A million dollars," says one. "How much have you raised so far?"

"Fifty thousand," I say, then quickly change the subject.

Who knows if it helps, but a handful of Republican staffers promise to call to check the bill's status, which will put pressure on the committee chair to pass it through for a floor vote. In a week, I will get an email from a legislative aide. The last statement in the Congressional Record, just prior to the unanimous passing of the bill, will be praise for Run for Congo Women and the way it has blossomed into a global effort to support the women of the DRC.

IF I SCORED POINTS IN D.C., I certainly haven't scored any at home. I had imagined that my drop-everything-to-stop-a-war behavior would recharge a relationship that has had no space for the past five years. But my all-consuming volunteer work schedule and my Congo-first, business-second attitude have gotten old for Ted. I see his point—I have put our financial goals on hold. But I think I've earned some flexibility after putting in years of sixteen-hour workdays and months-long stretches without a day off.

In any case, people have started to notice. Long after the event, my mom confesses that at the Portland run volunteers pulled her aside to report Ted's visible disenchantment with me. It was in the air that day. After the run, he went out for beers with a buddy while a neighbor drove me home. In my post-30-mile stupor, I threw up out the window (much to the disgust of her teenage kids sitting next to me!) and spent the rest of the afternoon sprawled on the bathroom floor alone.

At this point, there's no getting around it. Ted's icy silence speaks volumes. I'm in breach of contract. I'm not free to do my own thing until delivery of a French country home, a Ducati Supersport, and a new Rolex. Anything less is just selfish.

The slow burn of betrayal is mutual. I'm desperate for us to try to work it out. But as our relationship descends into a series of seething, resentful fights, I find myself on the defensive, snapping, "I'm a human being, not a lifestyle."

On the June day that we were supposed to get married, I can't help but feel ripped off. In an alternate universe, I would be in the Val d'Orcia, dancing under a string of lights in the courtyard of a medieval Tuscan inn, overlooking ancient olive groves.

Ted asked me to marry him on New Year's Day. We don't believe in long engagements, so we set a June date, but in late March the Italian country inn cancelled our booking (something about an auto accident), and it was too late to find another venue. We said we'd do it next year. Maybe.

Now Ted is gone. He's taking an extended "break" in Berlin, while I've been bestowed the freedom to date whomever I choose. It is not a freedom I've asked for or want.

I'm sure he won't call today. Best not to wait around. Time to go for a run.

The phone rings; it's my friend Lana. "Have you checked your email yet today?"

"Why?"

"Just do."

I open my inbox to find a message presumably emailed to our entire guest list. *Evite Reminder: Ted and Lisa's Wedding.*

Just so all of my friends and family really, really remember exactly what is *not* happening today. Mercifully, none of the recipients ever say a word.

Why mope? I leave for my run.

I get out of the car at the trailhead and stretch next to the two-lane road sandwiched between the river and the airport. It's mostly used by truckers as a back route to industrial parks and freeways. I like it because the path is paved and flat. It's my "I don't feel like running" course.

I notice a man on a bicycle in the distance. I've learned how to distinguish recreational bike riders from the transient car thieves that comb isolated parking lots off this road. This guy is of the car thief variety so I stay near my car, waiting for him to pass. I don't want to lose my stereo.

He doesn't pass. He rides straight up to me and stops. He's normal looking enough, but tattered and greasy around the edges in a way that reads transient. He blocks my way to the path and thrusts out his hand for me to shake.

"I'm James."

"Hello, James," I say, keeping my hands to myself.

"What's wrong? You won't shake my hand?" he says in an unsettling, sharp voice. "What's your name? Why won't you shake my hand?"

Alarm bells start to blare in my head. Isolated road, no clear path forward or back. Truckers whizzing by, oblivious.

I hold up my hands and gesture towards the path as if to say, "Back off."

This does not fly.

"What? You're too good to shake my hand?" He thrusts out his hand again in confrontation. "Just shake my hand and I'll leave you alone. Hi. I'm James."

I shake his hand.

"I'm Lisa. Nice to meet you."

He doesn't let go of my hand and barks, "What's my name?"

"James."

"What's my name again?"

"James."

"See? Was that so hard?"

He lets go of my hand, turns his bike around and begins to walk away.

I take a few steps toward the trail. He stops, turns back and spits, "I hate people like you."

A dead calm comes over me. This is not the nonsensical raving of a madman, but cool, palpable rage. Staring at me, he says, "I hate women."

I remain detached, as if watching a child throw a temper tantrum. In an effort to soothe him, I start to say, "I'm sorry you are in so much pain." But all I can get out is "I'm sorry" before he interrupts, shouting, "*Sorry?* No. *No.* You better get out of here!"

I'm calculating. He's blocking my path to the car. If I start to run up the trail even a hundred yards, I will not be visible to traffic. I will be completely isolated. He could easily follow me on his bike and attack. With no way forward and no way back, I stand still.

"I said you better get out of here—I'll hurt you," he threatens.

I stare at him with icy reserve. He is testing me, playing at controlling me, and he's clearly aggravated that I refuse to obey. If I turn my back to run, it will be an invitation to chase.

I back away, moving steadily toward the trail with my eyes on him, as he shouts louder and louder. "You better run! Don't walk. Run! You better run! *Now!*"

Then he spews like a drill sergeant. "Run now! Run now! Run now!"

I peel around toward the road and walk directly onto the two-lane highway, holding up my hands like a prisoner surrendering. A yellow semitruck slows and stops in front of me. I'm safe, blocking traffic, watching James slink away on his bike and disappear down the road.

Driving home, I think about all the brides who shape-shift into Bridezilla on their big day. It rains, or the orange-peach on the cake clashes with the pink-peach on the flower girls' sashes, and they declare, "Crisis!" I want to tell them it could be worse, much worse. I wonder if today qualifies as the Worst Wedding Day Ever. Wedding called off. Sitting here in Portland instead of Italy. Groom left for Berlin. Bride accosted by a sociopath.

I'll joke with friends about it in the weeks that follow, until one of them will point out, "That's not the worst wedding day ever. The worst is to have the day go perfectly, but you've married the wrong guy." Well put, though we are both wrong. It won't be until I get to Congo that I will hear about the worst wedding day ever.

Today, walking into the kitchen door of our little Victorian bungalow, I'm not amused. I try to call my mom, Lana, even Ted in Berlin. No one is home. I sit on the prop couch in my empty house. It doesn't feel like home. It feels more like a disease.

Meanwhile, Congo has become magnetic. I don't care what I might lose. Numbness has made room for craving. I want to tear my life to shreds and see what's left.

CHAPTER SIX

I'd Like to Buy the World a Coke

BRITISH AIRWAYS FLIGHT 0065, London to Nairobi. I wake up on one of the empty four-seat "couches" in coach (lucky for me, it's not a big week for African pleasure holidays), untangle myself from the synthetic blankets, and check out the seatback flight map. We're in African airspace. I study the territory: Mogadishu, Darfur Mountains, Kigali, Lake Kivu.

We land in Nairobi at night, when it's too dark to get a sense of the place. At sunrise, on the ride back to the airport to catch my plane to Rwanda, I notice that beyond the stretch of modern office buildings, hotels, and high-end car dealerships lining the main road, there's a scattering of windswept trees. I decide I love Africa. The feeling builds as the plane takes off and cruises above long stretches of Kenyan and Tanzanian savannah, rolling red hills, and the stunning Lake Victoria, which stretches out like an ocean. When we're flying over it, there's only water visible in all directions. I'm shamelessly excited. I scan to see if the other passengers share my enthusiasm. It's all I can do to not squeal with delight to everyone in the plane, "We're in Africa!"

Instead, I peel myself away from the window and read the Lonely Planet guide to Rwanda, tagging pages that describe the genocide memorials I hope to visit, refreshing my memory and filling in the gaps by reading the history section. Rwanda is a fitting place to begin my journey because the war in Congo began with the 1994 genocide there.

For hundreds of years, Rwanda has been comprised of three ethnic groups: Hutu, Tutsi, and Twa. Historically, these ethnic lines were loose, and intermarriage was common. But Belgian colonists wanted ethnicity in writing. They measured people's noses, counted their livestock, and issued ethnic identification cards accordingly, grooming Tutsis to be the ruling class, despite their minority status. There were several outbursts of major ethnic violence over the course of the twentieth century, but tension reached an all-time high in 1994. When the plane carrying Rwanda's Hutu president was shot down that April, Hutu extremists vowed to kill all the "cockroaches," as they called Tutsis, igniting a four-month bloodbath. Hutu extremists, known as Interahamwe, slaughtered 800,000 Tutsis and moderate Hutus. The international community did not intervene.

It was ultimately a Tutsi-led rebel army that secured the country in July 1994 and ended the genocide. When the Tutsis took over the government of Rwanda, two million refugees flooded over the border into what was then known as Zaire (and is today known as the Demoratic Republic of the Congo). Among them were countless thousands of Interahamwe—Hutu *genocidaires*—who found safe harbor by melting into refugee camps that were facilitated by the United Nations High Commission on Refugees (UNHCR). While regret-steeped aid dollars from around the world poured in to rebuild Rwanda, no effort was made to identify—and bring to justice—the thousands of Interahamwe hiding in Congo's refugee camps.

They soon became the catalyst for Africa's World War.

As the plane descends, we see the landscape: lush, rolling hills dotted with a patchwork of postage stamp-size farms, clay huts, tin roofs, and banana plantations.

Rwanda is beautiful. The city of Kigali rolls out across steep hills. Its roads are lined with flowering trees and filled with orderly traffic. Everything seems in good repair. The 1994 genocide seems incomprehensible.

Though I don't stay at the InterContinental, a.k.a. Hotel Rwanda, my hotel is a lovely four-star place with gift shops and terraced gardens; it's filled with African dignitaries and European businesspeople.

I want to visit the genocide memorial schools, where bodies and bones are still on display, or the churches, where all the personal effects of those killed have been left exactly as they were at the time of the massacre.

After settling in, I hire a taxi to go to the Kigali Genocide Memorial Center, abandoning hopes of visiting the churches after the driver quotes a $200 fare for a two-hour drive. We pull up to a large cement building that's surrounded by linear pathways and gardens. The memorial center was built on top of a mass grave that holds more than 250,000 genocide victims. Massive cement slabs run across the front; a metal opening allows visitors to peek inside at coffins decorated with crosses piled on top of each other. A couple of floral arrangements wrapped with bows and cellophane crackle in the breeze as the faint voices of children chatting with their neighbors drift in from the hills.

Inside, I walk past walls filled with snapshots of victims. With each photo of a child, a few details of his or her life are listed:

> *Francine Murengezi Ingabire*
> *Age: 12*
> *Favorite sport: Swimming*
> *Favorite food: Eggs and chips*
> *Favorite drink: Milk and Fanta Tropical*
> *Best friend: Her elder sister Claudette*
> *Cause of death: Hacked by machete*

I wonder if Congo will ever have a memorial like this.

On the drive home, I chat up my taxi driver, who speaks some English. I tell him my destination. He volunteers, "I studied in Goma and Bukavu in the 1970s, but I've not returned since." He pauses for a moment. "Laurent Nkunda is over there straightening it all out for us. He's taking care of that situation."

I know about Laurent Nkunda. His attacks have been in the headlines. But my taxi driver's comment is hardly a shock. Nkunda is widely known to be backed by Rwanda. He's the leader of the rebel group the National Congress for the Defense of People (CNDP), claiming to protect his fellow Congolese Tutsis from Interahamwe aggression. But his militia is known for the same atrocities as any other, and the presence of Nkunda's CNDP has resulted in the displacement of more than 750,000 people.

My driver chews on his thought for a moment, then adds, "In Congo, they hate Rwandans. If we go there, they kill us."

We are quiet for a while.

He says, "You should let me drive you to Bukavu. Forget your flight."

I picture myself crouched in the back of this taxi as we crawl across the border into Congo, trying to be inconspicuous in a car with Rwandan plates that's boldly labeled KIGALI CITY CAB.

"I will take you! It is no problem!"

"You are kind. But no thanks."

At dinner on the hotel terrace, I watch the other guests. Much to my relief, I notice a woman traveler sitting by herself. *Women travel by themselves in Africa all the time. I'll be fine.* Several minutes pass, then a male colleague joins her.

In my brief stay in the hotel and around Kigali, I don't see another lone woman traveler.

All the same, by morning I am starting to feel confident while listening to the birds, enjoying the relaxing breeze, and having a lovely breakfast amid flower gardens. Watching businesspeople in their tropics-friendly, oh-so-colonial business wear, I think, *Rwanda, easy. Africa, no problem. Orchid Safari Club is probably a lot like this four-star hotel, with terraced views and lovely buffets. Bukavu might be an awful lot like Kigali—clean, organized, with calm, happy people. Maybe everyone is being dramatic when they talk about Congo. Maybe it will be no big deal.*

I stop at the front desk to check out. A fellow guest, an older gentleman who seems to be a seasoned African traveler, nods hello. "How's your stay going so far?"

"Brief. I'm flying to Congo in a couple of hours."

He remarks flatly, "Well, that will be a different experience, won't it."

WHEN I LEAVE THE HOTEL, the doorman calls a taxi for me. I wait by the curb next to a white South African with red, leathery skin who is wearing a khaki safari vest—a cue that he is an old-school African journalist. I'm not surprised when he introduces himself as a television producer. He's shooting a documentary about Francophile Africa for South African television. My taxi driver, a former employee at the French Embassy, is among his subjects. I agree to allow his Rwandan crew to ride along with me to the airport. While we wait, he asks, "Where are you headed?"

"Congo."

I stare ahead, waiting for the requisite sizing up. But standing side by side on the curb, we both maintain a forward gaze. He's quiet, then offers, "That place . . . Be careful. You can't trust anyone. Last spring, I was in Goma for three days."

I continue to stare forward.

He asks, "How long are you staying?"

"Five and a half weeks."

On the short drive, my destination catches the camera crew's attention. "The Congo, huh?"

"What's your take on the conflict?" I ask.

"The Congo people brought it on themselves. They harbored *genocidaires*, you know. They welcomed killers into their country. So, now they have problems. Whose fault is that?"

Congo's bad karma aside, it is hard to argue the facts. I don't. The cameraman chimes in. "We have a saying here in Rwanda about the Congo: The end of logic. That is where Congo begins."

THE TINY AIRCRAFT ascends and spends thirty-five minutes bouncing around the clouds before descending to a tiny landing strip carved out of a hilltop on the Rwandan side of the Congo border. It is a picturesque, remote African airport with a simple fence, one red-and-white cement building, and a few rusty hangars in the distance.

My first look across the border to Congo is a stunning view of Lake Kivu and the rolling blue hills beyond. I collect my bags and leave the airport.

I have made arrangements with my "Congolese twin," Christine, to pick me up, but when I come out no one is waiting. I sit down on my bags, watching as other passengers are picked up or wander down the hill. An airport guard lounges nearby. A woman swings her keys, following behind schoolchildren in red dresses and backpacks who walk holding hands.

Kelly is arriving in Bukavu today too. To be honest, it's a relief to know there will be a friendly face from home waiting on the other side of Lake Kivu. She flew into Goma, via Kinshasa, with a church delegation led by a California-based Congolese expat, and we have plans to meet up as soon as I arrive.

Finally, a Range Rover with a Women for Women logo pulls up. Christine hops out for an embrace of welcome. *Karibu!* Welcome!"

She seems to have changed since we met in the States; perhaps it's because I'm seeing her now in her native environment. Her stature is striking. She carries herself with the dignity of African royalty. The ongoing half-joke at Women for Women is that Christine could someday become the first woman president of DR Congo, and it doesn't seem so much a stretch. Her wedding is only a month away and she is in the thick of planning a celebration for five hundred guests.

We drive down the tree-lined, paved road that runs above Lake Kivu. Christine explains, "There was a problem with Orchid Safari Club. They are fully booked with a group for the next few nights, so I've made arrangements for you to stay elsewhere."

I have been emphatically warned by Ricki, a staff member at Women for Women headquarters. "Orchid is the *only* place to stay," she told me. "Nowhere else is secure."

It was a major point of discussion, actually, when Kelly announced she wanted to do a homestay for a few days. When I ran the idea past a few veteran Congo travelers, they all said the same thing. No way. Not safe.

"What is Kelly doing in Congo, anyway?" they all asked.

In her own words, I told them, she wants to "cry with the women. To grieve with them."

My policy-wonk friends scoffed, but hey, more power to her. There will be plenty of time to sing "Kumbaya" with the people. And I'm happy to be with a friend and split expenses. I do, however, have a tangible goal. Congo needs a movement. We only raised US$60,000 in the second year of Run for Congo Women—nowhere close to the million dollars I hope will spark a movement. But if we can put a human face on the horror, and document all facets of the conflict in a film, we would have ammunition for advocacy meetings. We could raise that million dollars through screenings and house parties, and generate a buzz that could ignite the grassroots movement for Congo. A good omen landed in my email in-box just before my departure: A producer from a major news network is interested in an American angle on the conflict. They might want my story and footage!

Goals aside, the security threats are real. Before I left, Ricki also impressed on me how quickly things can go wrong when she filled me in on her visit to Congo.

"We were there in April 2006," she told me. "Zainab was shooting follow-up footage for *Oprah*, and I was supposed to show our program to a judge for the Conrad Hilton Award, a major humanitarian prize. The first day, Zainab went to the Bukavu ghetto to follow up and we set out to a rural area to meet women.

"We didn't make it.

"We got in the car with the driver and Christine, who has four different cell phones, one just for security updates. She got a call. We couldn't go down this street, a main road in Bukavu. Students were protesting. It was Easter break and the police shot someone. Protesters marched with his body over to the governor's house and left it on the front steps.

"We immediately did a U-turn. Thirty seconds later, I saw two huge UN tanks in front of us, coming down the road, heading towards the protesters. One of the tanks passed, turned their gun at me—like two feet from my head. But I was thinking, okay, they are experts, they aren't going to shoot me.

"The first tank passed and the second tank was coming our way. The only thing between us was a guy on a motorcycle. The tank swerved into our lane and we heard the motorcycle getting crushed. The rider started screaming.

"The tank stopped there. The guy's legs were pinned underneath, and the UN tank didn't roll off. One of the UN guys was just looking around, calm, surveying the scene for a good few minutes, not emotional at all. He was looking each way while the guy was screaming. A woman was right next to our car yelling at the UN to get off the guy! There were maybe fifty people around. Everyone was yelling. Finally, the tank rolled off the guy and just rolled on down the street, leaving him there. Congolese people picked him up and dragged him out of the street. Then everyone turned toward our car, and they saw me sitting in the front seat. They saw my big sunglasses. Christine told me they thought my sunglasses were a video camera of some kind, they thought I was filming. They started to crowd around the car, screaming. Our driver just pulled out and escaped up a dirt road. All the while, the Conrad Hilton judge was in the back seat.

"We decided to do interviews at the office instead of in the field.

"At the office the next day, we heard that the security situation was getting worse. Zainab said I should go back to the hotel and pack our bags, and we could be on a plane in a few hours. 'Just lie down in the back of the car on the ride back to Orchid,' she told me. So the Women for Women car pulled up in the middle of the street and I was walking from the office gate to the car, when all of a sudden I heard 'pow-pow-pow-pow.' About a hundred scared-shitless Congolese were running towards me. Christine yelled, 'Don't run! Don't run!' But I ran straight back to the gate, and all these people were crowding around, trying to get back into the compound while the security guys were trying to close the gates.

"I stuck my arm in through the crowd and they pulled me in. Zainab was just standing there asking, 'What's going on?'

"I decided I wasn't going anywhere. So I started to film the rest of Zainab's interview, then we heard shots again, right outside the gate. I dropped the camera and ran around the compound in circles, because there was nowhere to go. Zainab just laughed and said, 'It's worse in Iraq.'

"I was like, 'Stop laughing. It's not funny.'

"She says, 'I laugh in these situations.'

"We left that afternoon."

RICKI'S WARNINGS ARE flashing in my head like a stoplight, so the news about Orchid being overbooked does not land well. In the States, I am not known for my restraint when unhappy. Now I feel as if I have one foot on the brake and one the accelerator. Every minute of my countdown to Congo, every warning, presses down harder on both.

But I've also been forewarned: People in Congo don't get mad. It would be viewed as a temper tantrum—it's something you don't do, like crying in a board meeting. As one Congo travel veteran warned emphatically, "If you lose it, just pack up; leave. You might as well never come back. You will have permanently lost the respect of the Congolese."

So I smile at Christine and laugh. "Flexible is the name of the game in Congo," I say. "It's no problem."

We pull off to the side of the road and I get my first glance of the border crossing, just a simple bridge, shorter than a city block. I recognize it from Lisa Ling's report. I pull out my broadcast-quality HDV camera.

I position myself with the bridge in the background. Christine holds the camera for me, trying to be low-key. It's illegal to film borders. I try to control my face twitching and I dive right in with the commentary. "I'm standing on the border of Congo . . ."

As we approach the bridge, leaving Rwanda behind, I'm amazed that this old, rotting wooden bridge from Belgian Congo is all that separates the country from Rwanda. On the other side of the bridge, a man lifts the old metal gate and lets us through.

Whew. That was easy.

We drive up a hill about two city blocks before we hit the real border crossing, on the Congo side. Men in shabby tracksuits, sporting Kalashnikovs, lurk by the side of the road. I get out and enter a small cement-block room, where Congolese border officials size me up, stamp my paperwork, and usher me out again. Back in the SUV, three men approach and survey the car's contents, standing uncomfortably close to my window, glaring. One of them presses my hosts for God knows what. His eyes confirm the folklore—they tell me I'm in Congo, with their hard, glazed-over look that makes me wonder what he's seen, what he's done, and if there is a soul left inside.

Christine meets him with a laugh. *Is she teasing him?* I can't tell, but I'm taking mental notes. *Laugh. Laugh. When in danger, laugh. Everyone is your best friend.*

They want to search the car. My driver shoves cash toward the man and says something. Christine translates, "The driver told that guy to buy himself a Coke."

As we pull away, I hum to myself that Coke ad from the eighties, the one they played during Saturday morning cartoons.

I'd like to buy the world a Coke,
And furnish it with love . . .
Something, something, turtle doves . . .
It's the real thing.

CHAPTER SEVEN

The Real Thing

WELCOME TO BUKAVU, a far cry from Rwanda. I stare out my Range Rover window, which is rolled all the way up tight, and comb the scene on Bukavu's main drag. The landscape is identical to what I saw in Rwanda. Hills jut along the lake, forming pockets and outcrops draped with greenery. Each hill, dotted with compounds, is a mirror image of the next one.

In Bukavu, however, the signs are everywhere that all is not well. It feels raw and dusty. Corroded shopfronts and old lakeside villas stand like outlines in chalk, sketches of a dignified past, imprints of a grandeur that has been stripped and rotted under the chokehold of chaos. I can picture the villas filled with pleasure seekers—people on holiday alongside Mobutu in the lush gardens, savoring tropical fruit and tea with sugar and milk. Today, the old villas are either roofless, crumbling shells or they're shrouded by high cement walls capped with razor wire and jagged shards of glass, men in hand-me-down security uniforms stationed at their rusty gates.

Open-air jeeps marked "UN" crawl up and down the streets; they are mounted with giant machine guns and cramped with Pakistani army guys whose hands never wander far from the trigger. Traders line the streets with wooden crates; they're selling phone cards, cassava flour, soaps, or clothes that look they were rescued from Goodwill bins. The washed-out roads are more like dry riverbeds. I was warned I will need an SUV to drive anywhere outside of Bukavu, but by the look of things, I'll need an SUV to get anywhere inside Bukavu too. The air is different here. Rwanda breathes; purged of demons, cleansed with soft rains and the government's progressive agenda, it hums with prospects. Not so in Congo. The air here is thick with paranoia, like rancid garbage dumped by strangers and left to fester in the yard.

Women, like pack mules, carry loads of cassava flour, firewood, stone, and other commodities up steep hills. Sometimes their cargo is twice their size. With the impassible roads and gutted local economy, there are few vehicles left and all the livestock and bicycles have been looted. The transport of last resort is the backs of women. They transfer petty goods to keep the essentials of life and the local economy crawling forward. Those loads must weigh, what, 150 pounds? Hunched over, women lug the loads with straps slung around their foreheads, digging into their skin. They are sweating, steady, focused. It's a struggle journalist Ted Koppel once compared to the Greek myth of Sisyphus, who was destined to keep rolling a boulder up a mountain, only to have it roll back down, again and again, for all eternity.

Surprisingly, the Congolese seem to be quite fashion-conscious. Their clothes are neat and pressed, with their hair in colorful braids or wigs; they wear traditional African wraps and dresses or sport American cast-offs: T-shirts, fashion jeans, and sporty tennis shoes. Many look worthy of a Diesel ad campaign. One local hipster seems perfectly packaged to open an indie rock concert as he saunters around in a tiger-print cowboy hat and a faux-fur-lined jacket, peering out from behind trendy sunglasses.

But all that primping can't hide the unmistakable mark of war in these people's eyes. I notice the eyes again when we arrive at the Women for Women compound, a two-story whitewashed building surrounded by round, open-air classrooms built of wood and straw. Morning classes disbanded some time ago, but three women linger in the courtyard garden of cosmos and marigolds.

Two of them inch towards me, curious. With the impenetrable language barrier between us and no one around to translate, we smile and attempt a few false starts at conversation that can't get beyond "Hello."

"My name is Lisa," I say, pointing to myself. "Lisa. Lisa. I am a sponsor."

They say something back in Swahili, but it is completely lost on me. We smile with resignation. I watch an older lady standing at a cautious distance. She doesn't smile, barely looks at me. I see the glazed-over look, the same one I saw in the guy at the border. I move closer to her. We say nothing.

Inside, staff members abandon their lunch to enthusiastically embrace me. "So you are Lisa Shannon!" They ask about all manner of personal details: my home, my cats, the would-be wedding. They have translated hundreds of my letters, seen my photos countless times. A tall, full-figured lady says, "You tell your sister I say hello! We are both big ladies; I am her Congolese twin!"

I'm grateful for the warm reception, though headquarters in Washington made something clear. When staff members from headquarters visit offices in other countries, they stay no more than three days. No way will the staff host my five-and-a-half-week visit. The Congo office is slammed, short staffed. Christine was gracious enough to pick me up from the airport, give me access to their office for Internet use, and assign a staff member to arrange all my meetings with my sisters, which will not start for another week. Other than that, I'm on my own.

That's fine by me. I crack my Moleskine notebook open to my list of contacts, which is neatly printed in the back, a patchwork of nongovernmental organizations (NGOs) operating here. Christine lends me a cell phone. I settle into the second-floor office with metal picture-frame windows that overlook Lake Kivu and spend the afternoon steadily working my way down my list: The International Rescue Committee, International Medical Corp, CARE, UNICEF, The Red Cross, Panzi Hospital, a child soldier center, and conservation groups. I contact all of them by email and phone, and I even leave the compound to make a couple of quick visits to the International Rescue Committee and International Medical Corp, escorted by Women for Women's staff driver, moving from compound to nearby compound, as if they are secure islands.

Of the NGO's young, disaster-hopping expats, only half return my initial call or email. The remainder say hello, talk enthusiastically of the programs they would like to show me, then never return a call or email again. It will take weeks for me to get it. My credentials, or lack thereof, don't warrant their time. The Congolese on my list, however, all immediately arrange visits so that I can learn about their programs.

Christine interrupts my outreach efforts to introduce Hortense, a wild-haired single mom. Her big eyes, thin lips, and petite frame—though it is swallowed by her oversized office outfit—remind me of a woman in a Renaissance painting; she has a passionate, unmeasured manner. Christine glows as she describes Hortense. "She knows all of the women, every participant's story. She will arrange and accompany you on all of your meetings with sisters. She is very good, this one. I really must give her a promotion."

The Orchid Safari Club has my reservation after all. In addition to being safe, the club's supposed to be the best people-watching spot in Bukavu. All of Eastern Congo's power players drift through: government officials, mining executives, aid workers, Ukrainian bush pilots, journalists, military commanders. On the way in, I notice a sign posted on the door: Dear guests, We thank you to not come into the restaurant with firearms. The manager

Inside, framed botanical orchid prints hang off-kilter and mold creeps along their edges. A water buffalo head mounted above a stone fireplace overlooks the dining room, which is dressed with white tablecloths and semiformal place settings. French doors fold back, opening from the restaurant onto the terrace, where lounge chairs with views of the flowering gardens and Lake Kivu are scattered. Tribal African songs drift in from the hills, mingling with Orchid's ambient classical music.

A man in his mid-seventies lunches alone at one of the tables, looking over some paperwork. He's the owner and, I imagine, the Last Belgian in Congo. He spends his days wandering around the terrace and restaurant, greeting guests and directing the Congolese staff. We exchange casual smiles. He says something in French that I don't understand. Because of the language barrier, I am never able speak with him.

But the rumors fly. I will collect bits and pieces about him—perhaps fact, perhaps urban legend. They say he was born to Belgian colonists on a plantation and has never married, but owned this place with his brother who died a few years ago. Rebels invaded the hotel once, and he hid with the staff above the guestroom ceilings. On another occasion, legend has it, he was shot in the foot and had to retreat to Belgium for nine months of medical care. They say the Rwanda-backed RCD militia once camped out at the hotel for a long stretch and still owe him US$60,000.

The Last Belgian seems to me a breathing museum piece, the last of his species, like Congo's answer to a Tennessee William's character or the tropical male equivalent of Scarlett O'Hara, haunting the halls of Tara. He seems to be playing the tragic leading role in the final stage production of a faded colonial dream, making his final stand in his small Orchid kingdom, ordering around Congolese staff members dressed in red oxfords, black pants, and bow ties. They radiate the stiff friendliness of obligation, though in private conversation with patrons they are rumored to admit they despise their employer. I would not guess it, even though their graciousness feels manufactured, as in, "Madame would like some tea?"

As for safety at Orchid, that apparently lies in the eye of the beholder. This evening, military commanders are in the house. Never mind the sign on the doorway; they've brought their girls and guns. I watch a commander, his uniform buttons straining with postmeal bloat, while three girls sit by him quietly, smiling and laughing on cue. This is the kind of place that allows the illusion of elegance or influence or power if the lights are low, visitors' eyes are squinted or don't scan the corners of the room, conversation is kept vague, and nobody asks too many questions.

The Orchid staffers show me to my room and give me a key, which, out of defiance or nostalgia, is still labeled ZAIRE. I dump my bag in the room, a nouveau Elizabethan safari cottage with a bold, flower-print bedspread in 1970s orange, green, and tan, along with Tudor-style wood accents, a dim light, and a slow fan. The bed's mosquito netting has tiny rips and tears. In the bathroom, the rim of the yellowed plastic tub is lined with peeling, mildewed caulking.

Christine picks me up and we stop at her home on the way to dinner. Though she is the country director of an international NGO, Christine lives in her childhood home while awaiting her wedding next month. I sit in the dim living room—though it's late January, there are Christmas decorations still in the corner—with her younger brothers and sisters and a six-year-old orphan with that unmistakably vacant, glazed Congo stare.

Christine has just convinced her family to take the boy in. He has suffered severe neglect and illness and has only been here a few days. The adults are in the next room while the other children are fixated on a Congolese TV show shot on low-end video, something about men breaking into a woman's home. I call the orphaned child over to me and he sits obediently, stone-faced, at my side. He doesn't move. He won't interact. I can't elicit a smile. He is a little island.

I don't notice that look again in Congo. Yet back in the United States, when I review my video footage, it will be there, in the eyes of nearly every person I interview.

CHRISTINE AND I APPROACH the guesthouse where Kelly is staying with her group tonight, located on Bukavu's main road, near the boarder. She invited us for dinner so we can hammer out the details for the remainder of our trip. After a draining day, I'm exhausted and desperate for the anchor of a travel buddy.

Kelly greets Christine and me at the guesthouse door, which has been left open and unlocked beyond an unguarded metal gate. The group's bags sit exposed in a bunkroom, with the door flung wide. I reach back and touch my camera bag, as though I could forget the twenty-five pound monster that will stay glued on my back for the duration of my trip. Kelly fills me in on their journey so far. "Kinshasa was rough," she says. "Very aggressive. Tons of people. But here, everyone is so mellow. It's pleasant, safe to walk around. . . ."

Are we in different countries?

The place is spare and lit with fluorescent lights. I'm introduced to the church delegation as we take our places at the table for a traditional Congolese meal of whole, deep-fried fish, which my vegetarian credentials excuse me from eating. Something feels off. Conversation is strained and tense with the pale, sweaty missionaries. An American doctor quizzes me about Run for Congo Women and my contacts in D.C., while fussing with precise spellings as she takes notes. Patrick, the group leader, jumps in and asks occasional questions. But each time I start to answer, he turns away to talk to someone else.

Kelly casually drops into conversation that she's hired her own car and driver and plans to do the homestay for the duration of her time in Bukavu, which is several weeks shorter than my planned stay. I stare at the fish skeletons on their plates, at the way the other guests pick at the bones.

Patrick looks at me and asks, "What are your plans?"

My plans. Not *our* plans.

Now I get it. I'm not in Congo with Kelly. Though she's happy to occasionally piggyback on my outings that appeal to her, Kelly has no intention of making this a joint trip.

I watch them pick at the deep-fried fish heads, the breaded eyeballs, as reality settles in: *I'm in Congo alone.*

Though everyone who knows me would call me an "independent woman," I wouldn't choose a situation like this. I let go of trying to earn my bad-ass credentials years ago. At twenty-five, I drove ten hours across Oregon to go on a lone camping trip in a remote canyon on the Idaho border. When I got there, I pitched my tent, made myself a beautiful meal over an open fire, and watched the sun set over the canyon walls before I thought how much better it would all be if I were not alone. The thought gnawed at me through the evening until I decided, *This sucks.* Then, while I'm in my spot more than an hour from the nearest paved road, a van drove by. As I lay awake in my sleeping bag, I couldn't stop thinking about the isolation of this place. If something went wrong, no one would question my absence for days. That night, I thought to myself, *Point proven.* At midnight, I packed up and drove home. Within a year, I was with Ted.

It's not that I can't be independent; it just isn't my preference to be alone. If I had the choice of going to dinner by myself or with a friend, I would choose the company. If we needed to prop shop at Target, I was always happier to go with Ted. The preference became a habit, full days of work-lunch-work-dinner-bed-work that rolled into years of zero space. Soon enough, friends were more likely to remark on our model partnership than my independence. Occasionally, with a quick slip of the tongue or one too many glasses of wine, we were introduced as Tisa and Led.

I walk back across the Orchid grounds armed with only a flashlight. The paranoia is contagious. As I fumble for my key in the dark, a guy strolls by with a four-foot axe. I freeze, sizing him up. I'm upside down with no perspective. *Should I be scared?* Exhaustion wins. With resignation, I let it go. I hope he works for the hotel.

I put all my equipment on the charger and go to bed.

In the middle of the night, I am up again. I never adjusted the time on my computer or my cell phone and I'm unable to figure out the conversion, plus or minus daylight savings. I don't feel like making journal notes, so I lie awake until close to dawn before drifting back to sleep.

Shouting crowds, humming from a nearby street, wake me. *Are those riots or a celebration?* It's impossible to distinguish, though I try to tune in. Newly elected President Kabila is in town. *Must be a rally.* I listen for a long time, as if listening closely enough could filter my first day through a sieve and give me the definitive answer I'm craving to the question, Is it safe here?

People said that once I got to the hotel, I would make fast friends. Over a breakfast of fruit and toast with strawberry jam (exactly like my mom used to make), I sit between an officious French woman and the Congolese Army commander with his women. A few other guests are scattered around in groups. No one here talks to each other. Everyone must have a story, but they don't seem interested in getting into it with others. I don't feel like getting into it either. Instead, I watch the helicopter take off from a landing pad by the water. It belongs to a mining company headquartered here on Orchid's grounds.

I've made many calls for a guide and translator but they've all been dead ends. After breakfast, I meet Jean Paul, a UN staff member. He's booked on UN business, but he brings his brother Maurice, a mild-mannered man in glasses who wears a spotless, pressed T-shirt tucked into ironed, belted jeans and polished shoes. Maurice teaches English in Rwanda and has a gentle aura; he is more soft-spoken and understated than his brother. His school is on break, so he's available. They've also brought a driver. Serge is more of an un-tucked guy's guy—stocky and bald, with an understated cool. He doesn't speak English, or at least won't admit to it. I hire them on the spot. Maurice and Serge will be with me every day of my journey in Congo, and along with Hortense, will be at my side to translate every story, every moment, every interaction I have in here with non-English speakers—and in this French and Swahili-speaking land, that's almost everyone. They'll work for US$10 per day. A steal.

But first, I have to do an errand. I ride alone with Women for Women's staff driver to Bukavu's main drag; we pull over across the street from a cell phone shop. We both sit in the Range Rover, unmoving. I need phone minutes. One of us has to get out of the car.

I haven't seen a westerner on the street. One of us has to leave the bubble. If the driver goes, I'll be left as the lone guardian of the Range Rover. If I go, I'm walking alone, exposed, across the street, without an escort, without security, out of compound bounds. I feel like I've been asked to strip and go grocery shopping naked. I motion to the driver, hoping my broad gestures will help overcome the language barrier. "You go or I go?"

"You." He can't leave the car unattended.

I finger the door handle, feeling like I did in middle school, when I stood on the high-dive for the first time. I stared down at the water as friends jeered, egging me on while I measured the social cost of retreat. I remember wondering if they would see my flaming cheeks, prickly with humiliation, if I slinked back down the ladder.

Each moment that slips by fuels the awkwardness of the moment.

What's the big deal?

I don't move.

Just get out of the car.

I unlatch the door, step out on the road alone and dash across the street.

CHAPTER EIGHT

Souvenir

I'M SO WRAPPED up in the sea of virgin-faced killers on my first morning at Bukavu's child-soldier rehabilitation center, *Bureau pour le Volontariat au Service de l'Enfance et de la Santé* (BVES), I don't notice Noella in the crowd. It's a flurry of activity as half of the boys get ready to depart for home after their two-month stay here. Boys collect their parting gifts—a blanket, a soccer ball, and some tennis shoes—before heading for the vans that will drive them south to be reunited with their families.

Noella's shaved head blends in with the ninety boys' faces in the group. Her skinny eleven-year-old frame swims in her oversize pajama bottoms. Perhaps that's why I missed her; she doesn't look like a girl. Or perhaps her history has made her expert in being invisible.

She comes to my attention because of her younger brother, Luc. He is the youngest here, only nine years old. I notice him, in a man-size T-shirt that hangs to his knees, dodging in and out between the older boys as they pack up the vans. *How could a kid that age be a former soldier?*

I ask the staff. He's not. Luc and Noella were picked up on the road by aid workers who found them wandering, lost in the forest. They only speak

Kinyarwanda, the language of Rwanda. Despite their ever-changing story, in South Kivu that means one thing.

It is not the first time the center has aided Interahamwe children. In fact, the influx of Hutu refugee children was the catalyst that started the center, in 1995, when an earlier program split into two projects, one for unaccompanied child refugees and the other for 650 former Interahamwe children.

The center director, Murhabazi Namegabe, whom I met in Portland a year ago, is an intense man with a serious temperament that commands respect.

I ask him, "What is it like bringing children together from rival militias?"

"In Eastern Congo, children were raised with the idea that someone who is not of your tribe or ethnic group is an enemy," he says. "There was conflict between Hutu and Tutsi children staying at the center."

Murahbazi explains that the center was home to children from the Mai Mai, a homegrown Congolese militia known for its use of witchcraft, as well as kids from Rally for Congolese Democracy, or RCD, militias backed by Rwanda. "The children from Mai Mai were dirty, and children from RCD were clean and tidy. The clean children considered the others witches because Mai Mai practice sorcery. When they were playing cards, if the Mai Mai won, immediately a fight began with, 'They won because of witchcraft.' If the RCD won, the fight began, 'They had intelligence from Rwanda! They had modern technology!'

"The key message is, You are children. There is no difference between you. You must live together, share together. We ask the children, 'Is there someone who has chosen to be born in Rwanda, Burundi, or Congo?'

"No one among the children raises a finger to say, 'I chose to be born here.'

"This causes a change in consciousness. After one week, they become friends."

THE VANS DRIVE AWAY, leaving the remaining boys to file back inside the compound. As the dust settles, their focus shifts to the only remaining source of entertainment: me.

On long runs, I fueled myself for miles by contemplating this moment, rehearsing what I might say. As the boys crowd around asking questions, the moment has arrived. I step up onto the front steps, reach back into my mental file of talking points rehearsed on the trail, and launch into a speech about hope! And caring! And healing! And choices! And "You are not alone!"

One boy yells from the back, "Blah! Blah! Blah!"

They all laugh.

Another one steps in, "White people always say they care, they want to help. But where is the help? They never do anything!"

That went well. Nothing like teenage boys for a little straight talk. Let's call it "open dialogue."

There's an old stock photo trick that always worked with kids. It's cheesy, but it's worth a try. I ask, "Can I take your photo?"

The boys crowd around, posing. I snap the shot and show them the viewfinder. "Shanella!" they cry—an apparent Swahili hybrid for Lisa Shannon. They are all shouting, "Take my photo!"

Vanity. Works every time. After they are warmed up, I talk with a couple of boys privately.

I SIT IN A PRIVATE classroom with Junior. He is seventeen, clean-cut, and seems like a good kid, one that in a different context might be found buried in a book or taking college prep classes.

"Can you tell me about your family?"

"Even though my family was very poor, I chose to live with them. It was by force I was taken. What the chief made us do was not good. Because I was to kill, to make sex and violence on wives and children. It upsets me now."

I'm surprised we're getting straight down to it. "What was it like the day you went to join the Mai Mai?" I ask.

"I was a pupil. That day, the Mai Mai came and asked us to join . . . there was no alternative. You must join or you will be killed. Once in the mountains

. . . I became ill. Only after I recuperated, I became a Mai Mai. I knew how to write, so they made me the secretary of the group. What they made me do still upsets me. We are not welcome in our village because we made violence against the civil population."

"They made you attack your own village?"

"I think the village population will understand it was not our will, but the will of the chief. Sometimes we avoided making violence in our own village. It is in other villages we made sexual violence against women. The real problem was sleep. We slept without anything, no blanket, just on the mountain. There was nothing to eat. Bad food. Bad sleep. No sanitation. We lived like savages. This led us to sexual violence against wives and to loot villages for food."

I find it remarkable he has brought up sexual violence, all on his own, several times, as though I am his confessor. "Did they force you to rape?"

"This was a kind of revenge. Whenever we saw a girl or a wife, we had to attack her immediately. For me, it was a kind of safe defense, to reject the problems I had in the army, to forget."

"What do you hope for in the future?"

"Even though I am poor, studies can change my situation. I hope I get my diploma, that I can be a VIP, a very important person."

PAI PAI IS CLEAN-SHAVEN, wearing a white tank top that shows off his muscles. He has the kind of toughness that comes from having nothing to prove. He's seventeen and though he is mild mannered, I can't imagine anyone giving him a hard time. Something about him radiates, "Don't mess with me."

"I was in the government army. The salary was very little. Twenty-five dollars a month."

"How old were you when you joined the army?"

"Twelve."

"Five years in the army."

"Yes, five years."

I'm not going to get too far with 'yes' and 'no' answers. I try to prompt him, "Why did you join the army when you were twelve?"

"I was taken by Rwandan soldiers to the forest, to carry things of the soldiers. Once there, we were formed by RCD. Eventually, because of bad treatment, I changed to the government army. I hoped there would be a change, but the conditions were the same.

"In my mind there are remnants of violence I have done to people. Now I would like to do something to erase those souvenirs, to forget things I did in the army."

"You had to do violence? Can you talk about that?"

Pai Pai crunches up his face, ticking his tongue. "Ugh. The problem is that I killed a lot of people. But it was not my will. I was under orders of Rwandans; because of this, I had to kill my own brothers, and sometimes this makes me feel ill at ease."

"Can you tell me the story?"

"I had a lot of cases. Once, at the village of the president, the Rwandese asked us to erase the village. We had to take people in their houses, lock the houses. We poured petrol on the houses and burned them. If you tried to escape from the house, you'd be shot immediately."

"How many people do you think you've killed?"

"People I myself saw dying? Around three thousand."

That must be a translation error. I clarify, "Three thousand?"

He emphasizes, "Three thousand that I saw myself. We had to take dead bodies, I had to put them in rivers or the lake."

"Did that include children?"

"What?" He looks at me like, *yeah, duh.* "Children, babies. . . ."

"What made you decide to leave the army after five years?"

"It was only because of my age. They asked me to leave, but I was happy to. The souvenirs of what I did in the army are very bad. I do not think I will be able to study. I have a problem in the mind. I want to be an apprentice for manual work.

"I feel sometimes in my mind I am very different from other children my age. Because now I continue to think about violence, what I have done. Maybe I will practice violence in the future. I can't behave that way now, but I have to fight the images in my mind."

I WANT TO TALK with little Luc. While staff members round him up, I notice two girls. The littlest, around eight years old, wears a skirt. Noella, eleven, hangs close to the other girl, clinging to her like a life raft. I'll talk to the three together.

We climb a steep wooden staircase, accessible only through the director's office, to a little room perched on top of the center. The girl's room feels like a princess's high tower, albeit a worn-down, African-war-zone version. I look out the window to the hills and fields of Rwanda.

I squeeze in between Noella, Luc, and the other little girl, then show them photos of my family, postcards from New York City and the Oregon Coast. Our driver, Serge, speaks Kinyarwanda, so he translates. I show them a photo of myself running in the forest, which I use as a lead-in. "Does this forest look like the forest where you used to stay?"

Luc says, "Yes, but I don't know where . . ."

Noella takes over. "We are only angry and upset about the absence of our mother. We would like to be back with her."

"What about your father?" I ask.

"We love both parents."

"Do you want people in America to know something about you?" I say.

Noella plays with her hands, while Luc laughs, "The white man can help us to eat well and when we know something about our parents we will say 'bye-bye' to the white man and go home."

"Do you know anything about Interahamwe?"

They whisper to each other, then Luc speaks up. "We don't understand talk about Interahamwe. But whenever we passed, we saw men with hammers looking for precious metal, like diamonds." Noella elbows him, gives him a hard stare. He continues, "They must be in the mountain because I hear people search for these metals . . ."

The two whisper to each other, conferring. Serge points out, "They are discussing what to say and what to avoid saying."

I try to soften them up by saying, "Sometimes people tell little kids to not tell the truth, but it's always better to tell a safe adult. You might feel better to tell the truth."

Noella furrows her brow. She's one stressed little girl.

The staff member jumps in. "Sometimes they say they came from Rwanda, they were arrested by police on the road. Sometimes they say they came from the mountain. Some days they say they came from the village. When we separate them, they change the subject. They were found in the forest, so their parents must have a link with Interahamwe. They are not allowed to talk about it."

Maurice adds, "If they say they are from the forest where they have parents who are Interahamwe, they will jeopardize their own lives. That's why they emphasize they are from Rwanda. But we know Rwanda, we work there. They have something to hide. These children are specialists in secrets."

Another staff member says, "Those children come from the forest. They come with a message that must be translated to a member of their family, if the situation is quiet, to come here or something."

The littlest girl excuses herself to go to the bathroom.

"I want to go out," Luc says, startling me with his English, but continuing in Kinyarwanda. "I want to pee."

That leaves only Noella. I sit down next to her on the bed. "My niece is like you, your age," I say. "She's thirteen." I show her Aria's picture. "I hope you find your parents very soon."

She looks indifferent, moves with the slow, defensiveness of an animal under threat.

"What do you hope for in the future?"

"I want to be a child forever."

Outside on the steps, the boys again crowd around me as I show them photos and postcards from home. Maurice translates, "They encourage you in your job. You are doing a good thing."

One boy points to a photo of my niece, taken when she was ten years old, and says, "What about her breasts?"

"I don't want to talk about that," I reply curtly. "Clean your mind."

Then I look at Noella.

The next day, when I come back, her little girlfriend is gone; she's been sent home to reunite with her family. Noella is now the only girl here. She holds Serge's hand as we wander around the compound. While I take photos and look at boys' sketchbooks filled with drawings of guns and military uniforms, I note the paths to the bathrooms, the little corners of the compound, and I keep checking back in on Noella, tracking her on the periphery of the crowd.

I ask Murahbazi, "Do you really think it's safe to keep a young girl with all those boys?"

Those boys with the habit to kill, among other, um, *habits*.

From Murhabazi's long pause and stare, it is clear I've overstepped. "She has a separate room. We have female staff. She's okay."

CHAPTER NINE

When I Cry

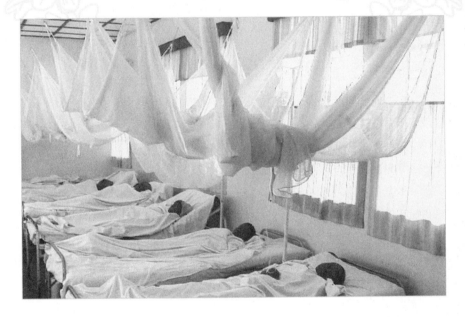

MARIE, A GIRL about seven years old, with kinky braids bent like wiry antennae and a big gap in her toothy smile, sizes me and my camera up from across the walkway. She is standing among the scraggly rose bushes that line the corridor, with the women in bold African print dresses, waiting. She seems oblivious of the gravity of this place and of her status in it as Panzi Hospital's youngest victim of fistula from gang rape. For a moment I contemplate filming or interviewing her. I conclude, *No way.* I hide the camera. The little girl returns to bouncing around in her party skirt, visiting with the nurses.

If Congo is the worst place on earth to be a woman, then Panzi Hospital is sexual-violence ground zero. Kelly has joined me to visit this high-profile treatment center for traumatic fistula, which occurs when the wall separating the vagina from the bowels or urinary tract is punctured and cannot heal. The damage creates a steady, uncontrollable leakage of urine or fecal matter. The victim smells bad, causing her to be rejected by her family and community.

In most of the world, fistula can occur as a rare complication during childbirth. In Congo, traumatic fistula is a common form of sexual torture, inflicted with guns, tree branches, or broken bottles.

I do notice a bad smell, now that we are standing outside the fistula ward. Dr. Roger, a slender man in a white doctor's coat who carries himself with a quiet elegance, has led us through Panzi's outdoor walkways and neatly cut lawns, past the "bad fed" (malnourished) children, the rows of male patients with bandaged gunshot wounds, the maternity and C-section wards, and finally, here, to the fistula ward. An unmistakable odor—like that of a long-neglected urinal—wafts out into the open-air corridor.

The air here is weighty, like the wailing that filled the parking lot when Serge shut off the engine. I spotted a girl in the corner, doubled over, crying out some Swahili lamentation over and over again between her sobs. I averted my eyes, watching the rain collect on the windshield, as we sat quietly listening to her cry.

Dr. Roger calls Marie over, explaining that she was gang raped when she was five years old. I try to make friends. "Marie is my sister's name." I tell her. "Dr. Roger tells me you've been to my country."

Marie disappears for a minute, returning with a photo book, the home-designed kind printed at Kinko's, apparently made for her by "American friends." Someone in the United States heard about her situation and sponsored her to come to the States for treatment, accompanied by her grandmother. A church? A family? Someone in Texas? I can't tell.

I flip through the pictures of Marie in someone's suburban home, her grandmother in an American kitchen, Marie in the hospital. She stayed for months, undergoing multiple surgeries and receiving the highest standard of care as they rebuilt her insides.

A year after her return to Congo, she is back in the hospital with complications. The American operations were unsuccessful. Everyone knows why she is here. I don't ask her any more questions.

A haunting silence hangs in the fistula ward, like the gauzy netting that hovers above each patient. In the dingy yellow room with twelve basic metal hospital beds, women lie flat, shrouded in white sheets that they pull up to their chins. Only their heads peek out. They are recovering from fistula surgery and watching us with a reserved curiosity.

The nurse prompts me, "Would you like to say something to them?"

I look over at Kelly, who motions for me to take the lead. Even with hundreds of letters to my sisters behind me, now that I'm facing a room full of women who have been tortured, I feel impossibly insignificant. I scramble, trying to remember the speeches I rehearsed mentally on all of those long training runs.

There is no choice but to stumble through whatever bits and pieces come to mind. I tell them about what we've done through Run for Congo Women, trying to get to resilience and beauty and inspiration, the part about them being my heroes. "All of you . . ."

I can't. I am at a loss. Blank.

And worse, I choke. I start to cry.

I have their attention now. They sit up, watching me keenly.

I can't say anything else.

The nurse says something to them.

I ask the translator what the nurse just said.

"The nurse told them, 'She feels very sorry for you.'"

Not heroes. Not beauty. Not resilience. Pity. The opposite of what I wanted to say.

The nurse coaxes them into a weak round of applause. *Should I take a bow?*

I vow that I will not cry in Congo again.

We are ushered into the open warehouse space that serves as the hospital activity center, where hundreds of women are crammed along the tables like sardines. They form a beautiful mosaic of headscarves and colorful dresses, yet it feels like a holding pen on a factory farm. I recognize it from Lisa Jackson's film, in the scene where she asked, "They were all raped?" Her guide responded, "All of them."

The nurse explains the program. "Each day, they start with prayer and Christian songs. Then they are taught literacy and numeracy and different skills." She holds up plastic bags and mats the women weave in fluorescent yellow, pink, and orange. "They sell them. They sew as well. Before they had any activities, they were very, very sad. Many psychological problems. You would find them sitting off to the side, just weeping. But when they are doing this activity, they seem to be very happy—very pleased."

I stare at the viewfinder on the camera, watching them. Journalists have made a habit of filing in and paying their respects here at this warehouse. Somewhere in the back of my mind, I hear my friend Anne's warning: "So many journalists show up in Congo saying, 'Show me the raped women!' Be human about it. Be a woman about it."

They know they are being studied. I wonder if they have agreed to be filmed, and how often they are asked. Do they feel herded, transparent, with their deepest humiliation on broad display, simply by virtue of sitting in this warehouse? I scan their eyes. They look indignant, numb, suspicious, exhausted, angry, bored, defensive . . . but *pleased?* I don't see it.

I want to prep my speech this time. I want to get it right. I turn to Maurice and ask, "Can we work on this 'heroes' thing?"

"Yes, hero . . ."

"Like someone you look up to. Do you understand? Someone you admire."

I'm not sure they get it.

I turn to Kelly, "I feel embarrassed to make a speech, but they've been waiting a long time. It's expected. You should talk too." Yet Kelly stands back, as though an unspoken rule was made a long time ago, maybe in D.C.: I'm the one who does the talking.

"Okay!" I turn to the crowd, puffing myself up with a strained cheeriness. I almost flinch at how much I sound like a cheerleader, one who is calling her troops to attention. I try to gauge the crowd. Some are focused on weaving plastic baskets; others are looking at me skeptically. "I'm happy to be here to visit Panzi Hospital. Thank you for waiting for us."

The gregarious nurse, clearly used to rallying the troops, knows the right tone—the "how-you-talk-to-rape-victims" tone. Maurice translates English to Swahili, and the nurse adds the extra filter, a safety net.

"In the U.S., I learned about Congo when I was watching television one day, and my life changed . . ."

As it's filtered through two translators, I scan the crowd, wondering how this is going to land. I suspect not well.

The crowd claps and I catch a few smiles. Emboldened, I speak more passionately, using broad hand gestures to minimize the language barrier. "I know you probably feel really alone here, but more and more and more American women are learning about you and they're trying to help. You aren't alone, because we care and we are doing everything we can."

They applaud. I smile at Kelly. It's working.

"Thanks for the applause! But I want you to know Congolese women are my heroes, our heroes, because to live through what you have lived through takes so much strength and inner beauty. I can look around at every single one of you and see something beautiful that no militia can ever touch."

They cheer!

I hold my hands up and join the clapping, pointing back at them, declaring, "We're clapping for you!"

No translation necessary! They *love* that! Erupting into applause, smiling, some even shout out, *"Ndiyo!* Yes!"

The translator leans over to me. "Your presence really affects them."

As the crowd settles down, I ask them, "Is there anyone here who feels strongly about saying something to American women?"

A modest young woman with a raw aura, wearing a bulky pink sweater and headscarf, steps to the front and speaks directly to the camera.

"I do. Thank you for the two of you who came to visit this place. Please tell other American women to continue thinking about our bad situation. And that program you have for Congolese women, don't let yourself fall by the way, but continue up until the end."

She clasps her face, trying to hide the oncoming eruption, then bursts into tears.

I put my hand on her shoulder, trying not to choke up. She keeps talking through her sobs, repeating "Mama Ah-meh-ree-kaah."

The translator simply says, "She's crying for help from American women."

She cries out through the tears. "We came to be cured because we were raped! But if we go back to the village, we could be raped a second time by four men, five men, six men!"

Instinct takes over and I embrace her, cradling her while she cries.

The nurse interrupts and says, "In order to get out of this psychological problem, let's sing a song to make us happy."

The girl retreats to her place as the nurse beats the table as a drum, leading the women in a song, repeating a word even I could make out: "Amen."

A MEMBER OF THE STAFF ushers us to Marie's private room, off the fistula ward, to talk with the raw-faced girl in pink who spoke at the meeting. She is twenty-two and unmarried, soft-spoken and shy.

"How was it you came to Panzi Hospital?"

"To be cured," she answers.

"Of what?" I ask in a tiptoe tone of voice.

"Urine."

"How did you come to have a fistula?" I ask, as gently as possible.

"I was sleeping in my house when those negative forces came. They woke my parents and brothers. In a family of eight, I am the only girl. So they beat the boys and my parents."

She starts to cry, "Then they started having sexual intercourse with me in front of my brothers and my parents. When they finished they took metal and introduced it into my vagina, so the metal tore my vagina."

"How long ago did that happen?"

"June 2004."

"How long have you been at Panzi?"

"Those two years. I live far away, so I've had no communication with my family, only nurses and doctor take care of me. I want to see my family, but I'm scared to be taken again by those negative forces."

"You say 'negative forces.' Who raped you?"

"Hutu."

"Interahamwe?" I ask.

"*Ndiyo.*" Yes.

"When you think of the future, what do you hope for?"

"Only that I will recover. About the future, I'm waiting for God's plan."

She looks out the window, tears wetting her face, "Up until now, my mind hasn't recovered. I'm still in a very unstable situation."

The door opens and someone comes in to get Marie's toy frog.

The young woman continues crying, wiping her eyes with her scarf. "I am living, but I do not consider myself a human being. When I think about what happened to me, I feel as if my mind is far away. I think of the five men who had sex with me and I feel as if I was killed. Please think of me when you go back to America, because I don't expect to get out of this situation. I feel as if the Panzi Hospital will be my home forever. I have many difficulties . . . many wounds inside my vagina."

How do I gently wrap this up? I follow the nurse's lead by asking, "Would you sing a song for us?"

She sings in a sweet, intimate voice: "When I remember the suffering I've had, I really weep. When I cry, I think about how I was suffering, because it was suffering in a true way."

As I'm packing up my things, I notice a wiry braid and a party skirt peaking through a crack in the doorway. A little hand rests on the latch. Marie inches her head in for a moment and rubs the wall. She smiles and retreats behind the door, leaving only her hand to linger.

I call out to her, in a singsong voice. "Helloooo, Ma-rie . . ."

Her fingers creep back and rest on the crack in the doorway.

"Ma-rie-eee, where are you?"

I pull out the camera and find her hiding behind the door in the hallway. I flip the camera monitor toward her so she can see it. She squeals, delighted and intrigued. She follows the camera, watching herself as I record her. Maybe I'm playing with her, maybe I'm doing it for the sake of my own memory, but this is footage I swear I will never show anyone.

CHAPTER TEN

The Peanut Girl

WE STOP AT the market to buy peanuts and bread. I'm in the backseat, buried in my notes, waiting for Serge to return. When I look up, a girl, perhaps eleven, stands by my window staring. She doesn't hold up her hand, but she still appears to be a beggar. I drop my gaze back to my paperwork. As I look down at the paper, the image of her face registers. Hollow cheeks, closely shaved head. Thin. I look back up and survey her boney shoulders and arms. She is Ethiopia thin. Holocaust thin.

I ask Maurice to buy two extra pounds of peanuts. He hands me the bursting, soccer-ball-size plastic bag. The girl has abandoned her mission and retreated a few feet, so I turn to her and we lock stares. I invite her with a slight nod. Her eyes bulge for a second when she sees the nuts.

I unroll my window and slip the peanuts into her hands. As she grabs the bundle of protein and calories, Maurice almost squeals, giggling with delight. We pull away into the crowded Bukavu street and we are approaching the traffic circle when I think, *She's starving, and what do I give her? Peanuts.*

Let them eat peanuts. . . .

A moment later, we swing around to head back to Orchid and I see her again. She stands on the traffic median, grasping the bag of peanuts like it's a precious baby doll, digging her hand in and stuffing the nuts in her mouth by the fistful.

CHAPTER ELEVEN

Militias in the Mist

I'M CARSICK AS I step out of the SUV following the thirty-mile drive on the bumpy, dusty, pothole-ridden, "jog-bra roads" (as one friend calls them). It has taken us an hour and a half to drive the thirty miles from Bukavu to the gates of Kahuzi Biega National Park with Eric, a local conservationist. We are in Congo's eastern forests, where Dian Fossey *(Gorillas in the Mist)* began her primate research; later, she was forced across the border to Rwanda, due to (surprise!) instability in Congo.

A Canadian environmentalist friend asked me to check out Eric's programs for potential carbon-offset initiatives. The Congo basin forest is the second largest tropical forest in the world—only the Amazon is bigger—and the Democratic Republic of the Congo holds 8 percent of the world's carbon stores, making its preservation essential to solving the global climate crisis.

Eric is only three years older than I am, and his glowing, everyone-is-my-friend African smile shows no trace of war. In 1992, when he was twenty, Eric founded a small nonprofit dedicated to protecting gorillas and easing tensions between the park and his native community, which lies just outside the park gates.

I'm standing next to Eric in his field office just outside the park, in front of the first memorial I have seen in Congo: A wall lined with framed eight-by-ten photos of gorillas. "These are the gorillas killed in the park," says Eric, and he speaks about each of them with the kind of affection people typically reserve for a beloved pet dog. "Ninja, killed April 1997 by rebels. Maheshe, 1993, poachers killed. Soso killed with her baby by rebels in 1998."

A larger-than-life mural of gorillas graces the opposite wall, each animal with a name painted underneath. Shelves are lined with hand-carved elephants, rhinos, and chimps created in an initiative launched in Eric's first year—an art program that trained poachers to carve souvenirs for tourists. The idea was that if these locals had another way to make a living—through ecotourism—they would give up poaching. The problem: Most of the tourists coming to the forests were being routed through Rwanda. In April 1994, tourism evaporated. Eric simply says, "The carving program went down."

In July 1994, a flood of refugees came to these forests from Rwanda. Eric describes that time: "Three big, big, big camps were set up three kilometers from the park. The United Nations High Commission on Refugees helped facilitate them, in cooperation with the government. Not only did they come and stay in camps, they started cutting down trees in villages. Poaching activities increased; they were cutting trees from the park to make charcoal. Those people were looking for stuff in villages, like bananas or sticks or something. At first, they would say, 'Please help, I am a refugee.' Second, 'Do you have some work? You can pay me a banana.' Sometimes they would steal. Most were respectful. We had respect for refugees. They were here under UN law.

"The camps remained for one and a half years.

"We knew them only as refugees under the UN structure, not as anything else. Then, in 1996, Kabila came with the Rwandan Army to fight President Mobutu and to chase refugees from the camps. The soldiers said, 'Those are not refugees. It's Interahamwe, those who killed in Rwanda.' We were confused: Are they refugees or Interahamwe?

"The camps were in our village, so when they were chased, we were chased together. It was nine in the morning. I was in my village, home with my parents, when we heard 'Ta, Ta, Ta, Ta.' Bullets. We took what we could—little bags. I put mine on my back, my parents got theirs, and we went in the direction of the park, thinking we'd hide out in there. But when we went that way, we heard bombing ahead of us in the forest. We said, 'No, no, no. We'll die there.'

"We went north, along the border of the park without knowing where we were going. Somewhere. We were tired. It was a whole day walking. It was getting dark. By that time, we were not with refugees. Everybody was saving himself. If we went in the park, they would be bombing. If we went down to the village, they would be fighting. We said, 'We'll stay here. If we get killed here, we accept it.'

"The next day, the fighting continued. We knew they were hunting refugees and soldiers, not Zairians, so three friends and I decided to try going home. When we arrived in our village, there were plenty of soldiers. We met some of them who said 'You. Stop.'

"We put our hands up. 'We are Zairians.'

"They said, 'Where are you going?'

"We told them, 'We are going home to get something for our families.'

"A Rwandan soldier asked us to show where we lived, to show them the key. They made us open the door. They said, 'Tell your family they can come back here. We are not against Zairians. We are against Interahamwe and Mobutu soldiers.'

"That evening we returned to the forest and told everyone we could to come back home. Many people were killed, though. They said, 'I'm Zairian, I'm Zairian!' and the soldiers said, 'No, you look like Interahamwe. We will kill you.'

"In my village, nine guys were killed by the men of Rwanda or Kabila."

"Did you see the Rwandan refugees again?" I ask.

"They were gone."

It's a stunning thought. For a year and half, two million refugees were camped out in Congo. Then, overnight, they were gone. "You have no idea where they went?"

"I heard on the radio they were killed or something."

The cement visitor's center at the park entrance displays a plaque that reads UNESCO World Heritage Site. Inside, the place is empty except for a few plastic chairs, the static video looping on a monitor in the corner, and two souvenirs for sale: one T-shirt and one book. I buy the book.

I walk into a room filled with skulls piled up to my chest: They're the skulls of gorillas, elephants, and antelope, all killed by poachers and militia. According to Eric, 450 elephants were killed between 1998 and 2003. The park's gorilla population has been cut in half since the war started, from 260 to the 130 remaining today.

"The Second War, the RCD war, was more destructive," Eric tells me. "Many people were killed, not because they were Interahamwe or soldiers, but just because they were businessmen. You know, you would be killed because you had studied. It was like an operation to remove anyone who could have any influence."

Eric is quiet for a moment. "Yeah. So many people died."

He continues: "Since that time, insecurity began inside the park. Our access was very difficult because of many scenarios: looting in the park, people passing through the park and saying that refugees now are in the forest. [The refugees are] not well located, they need food; they are killing people, looting mines. Then they started attacking rangers in the park, even killing them, and going to surrounding villages to rape, loot, kill and return to the forest.

"Our work went very, very . . . down. We were looted, lost many things. We were afraid, a bit stressed. We developed a kind of cohabitation. When you knew there was a new *commandant* in the area, you could see him and try to make friendship to avoid any problem.

"Once, I went with two journalists to collect information on coltan mining. Theoretically, the RCD wasn't there. But everyone there was in Rwandan formation."

The Rwandan army in charge of a coltan mining site? Hmmm.

Whenever I speak to groups about Congo, some keen person in the back of the room always raises their hand and asks, "So who's making money off of all this?"

The Democratic Republic of the Congo is among the most mineral-rich countries on the planet. It has vast stores of more than 1,100 minerals, including diamonds, gold, copper, tin, cobalt, tungsten, and 15–20 percent of the world's tantalum, otherwise known as coltan, an essential semiconductor used in electronics like cell phones, laptops, video games, and digital cameras.

The United Nations has accused every nation involved in the conflict of using the war as a cover for looting. According to some estimates, armed groups make around US$185 million a year from the illegal trading of Congo's minerals. Countries like Rwanda have made hundreds of millions of dollars off of their Congo plunder. (For instance, Rwanda's primary tin mine produces about five tons per month. Yet over a six-month period, Rwanda reports 2,679 tons in tin exports.) According to UN reports, when Rwanda seized control of eastern Congo in the late 1990s, they smuggled hundreds of millions of dollars worth of coltan, cassiterite, and diamonds into Rwanda. *The New York Times* quotes one Rwandan government official as saying, "I used to see generals at the airport coming back from Congo with suitcases full of cash."

Eric continues his story. "The RCD were in control of the airport as well. They arrested me and the journalists and took us to the airport. We paid six hundred dollars, but they didn't release us. They kept us in a small room. My wife called a partner in Kigali. The partner called London, who called the embassy in Kinshasa. The embassy called the UN. The next day, the UN came to release us."

"Has anyone been attacked or killed in the communities you serve?" I ask him.

Eric smiles broadly, presumably at the naiveté of the question, and answers. "Thousands of times."

In January 2001, Laurent Kabila was assassinated. His son, Joseph Kabila, took over as President of the Democratic Republic of the Congo. While the conflict technically ended in 2003, and many countries' soldiers or their proxy militias returned home, the Interahamwe remain in the park. Appropriately, locals throughout South Kivu still refer to them as the Interahamwe, given their unbroken, fifteen-year campaign of killing together.

"Officially—theoretically—the fighting finished," Eric says. "But behind the scenes, other things are done. Our park rangers were allowed to get back their guns so they could take control of the park like before. At some points, park rangers meet Interahamwe in the park. Park rangers are armed. Interahamwe are armed. They are enemies. So they open fire on each other. It's a military thing. There's going to be a fight."

"How many park guards have been killed by Interahamwe?" I ask.

"Six."

"Have you ever met Interahamwe?" I press him.

"Two years ago. I was studying for my degree in rural development. I did research on coltan mining in the west highland section of the park in 2005. I had hiked three hours to reach the mining site where the villagers, the miners, have a camp. I had a questionnaire. I was talking to miners, collecting data, when suddenly I saw men coming with guns. They didn't have soldier uniforms; they were just civilians with guns.

"The miners said, 'Don't worry, they are Interahamwe. We have to pay some taxes.'

"I asked them if that was who collects taxes here. They said, 'Sometimes, yes.'

"The Interahamwe asked the miners about me, saying 'Who is this one?'

"'He is a student from Bukavu,' they answered.

"And the Interahamwe asked me, 'Are you meeting park rangers here? Are you some kind of official?'

"I said, 'I'm sorry, I'm a student. I'm confused . . .'

"They said, 'You don't need to know, just ask the miners.'

"I was afraid, but fortunately I was presented like a student. They collected money and they went. The Interahamwe were not violent, they were not pressuring the community. It was like it was not the first time, like they have an arrangement. After they went, I asked the Congolese, 'Why do those people come here? What is the linkage?'

"'This mining camp belongs to them,' they told me. 'We have an arrangement to give them a percentage of income from the mines we dig here.'

"I asked, 'How do you do that?'

"They said, 'There are mining sites that are ours and mining sites that are theirs. Their mining sites, we just dig. Say, for example, we have ten kilos. We divide down the middle—they get five, we get five. But at our mining site, we just pay taxes to them.'

"'How much?' I asked.

"'It depends, but we can negotiate.'

"'How do you negotiate?'

"'We negotiate like . . . We hide some quantities. For example, if we dig a hundred kilos, we show ten kilos and pay like ten dollars. But we don't want you to ask us about that.'

"'Yes,' I said, 'But I'm just a student getting information.'

"'Where will you bring this information?'"

Eric smiles at this point. "I told them, 'Just to school.'"

MILITIAS CONTROL MINING TERRITORIES. They mine and export the minerals themselves or they "tax" the locals who do the work for them. Everyone seems to be in on the action: Corrupt government officials who orchestrate shady contracts; foreign militias; foreign governments who back militias; the Congolese army; the Mai Mai and other homegrown militias; and of course, the Interahamwe, who control the majority of mines in South Kivu.

The New York Times will later run a report on an operation run by a renegade Congolese army brigade that controls a remote, mineral-rich area. The brigade, journalist Lydia Polgreen writes, is the "master of every hilltop as far as the eye can see." Unchallenged, they employ locals at ultralow wages to mine and lug loads of ore via remote forest trails to the nearest road, where the goods are trucked to a stretch of road that serves as a landing strip for Soviet-era cargo planes that fly the minerals to Goma or out of Congo.

How much does a guy make if he carves out his own slice of this pie? One official estimates that this operation makes US$300,000 to US$600,000 in "taxes" alone. This operation is estimated to be worth as much as US$80 million a year.

The goods are illegally exported to countries like Rwanda or Uganda and are in turn shipped to processing plants, primarily in Asia. Eventually, large corporations buy them and distribute these "conflict riches" around the world in the form of our favorite consumer goods: diamond engagement rings, Sony PlayStations, sleek new MacBook Airs, or our ever-precious CrackBerries.

But rebel groups can only control the minerals if they control the territory. And they can only control the territory if they control the people. And there is one age-old way to control the people: terror. As one Harvard researcher puts it, there seems to be a "competition among armed groups to be the most brutal."

As we continue on, Eric recounts story after story of conflict in the area. Their office attacked and looted. In 2004, Nkunda's militia came to his home. "They attacked my home, with my wife and three kids. They said, 'Nkunda's people sent word for Eric.'"

"They know you by name?" I ask.

"Yeah. Most of them were working at the airport and around. They demanded US$10,000, saying otherwise you are killed. They found my wife. She had all our money on her, hidden under her clothes. After pushing her, they found the money. While they were counting and distributing the money, she escaped through their legs and hid.

"All these women were raped. I don't like to remember. Fortunately, we were saved. Everyone hid us by saying, 'I don't know where he is.' I hid two weeks in one house. I saved my passport, car, and family. Everything else was gone. I saw myself dying, you know. After that, I moved to Bukavu."

These days, Eric commutes to the park.

I ask him, "What is the solution?"

"Interahamwe are the priority of priorities. They constitute the center of the problem. You know, Lisa, it is easy to say, 'This is a Congolese problem.' But the Interahamwe were brought here by the UN."

They were brought here by the UN. We gave them bananas.

I ask him, "Do you think about giving up the work? It's so dangerous."

"My country has lost five million people. I'm not better than them. I've been doing this work since I was twenty years old. I've worked in hard conditions, poverty, whatever, I don't see what can stop me. I know what environment is. I have to assist my community."

"Are you scared?" I ask.

"I can find a solution at any time. I was attacked at home, in my village, so I moved my family to Bukavu. If I go there and they arrest me, I can negotiate. I can a find solution to any problem, if I'm not killed."

He smiles. "Yeah, if I'm not killed. If I die supporting my community, I go well."

And I pat myself on the back for recycling.

CHAPTER TWELVE

Sugarcane

LITTLE HEADS BOB and weave their way through the manicured tea plantation, heading in our direction, as Eric gets out of the SUV to guide us to the Pygmy village on the edge of Kahuzi Biega National Park.

Children emerge. Yep, they're short. But they don't seem that short, especially when they're standing next to each other. We follow a long, winding path to a collection of small, crumbling mud huts some might call a village, standing like an island in the middle of a sea of scraggly tea bushes. Men and women track me, intrigued. Eric has been visiting this village since he was a child, so I am welcomed and ushered into a tiny round hut made of straw and sticks. As men pack into the space, I'm introduced to the chief, who is dressed in pleated pants and a grungy T-shirt. At first we speak in generalities about the impact of war on the village: looting, rape, and the budding sense of security post-elections. The chief is blunt, "If you have sugarcane, you can leave it for us."

Gimme a little sugar, huh? As in, cash please.

"I don't have any sugarcane," I tell him.

Most people would stop there. Eric is far too polite to imply a donation is expected, so I'm free to do as I please, even offend. Maybe it's the clean forest air, but I'm feeling emboldened, so I add, "I could give you sugarcane, but then I would be taking your dignity. I believe in self-sufficiency."

Uh-oh. They are soooo not impressed.

The chief signals an abrupt end to our meeting. I emerge from the hut to find the village women sitting on the ground, glaring at me. Who knew? A little travel tip, apparently lost in some early 1990s printing of *Lonely Planet Zaire:* When visiting Pygmies, never refuse the ritual love-offering of sugarcane.

I ask Eric to find an older woman who might remember life in the forest. Within a few minutes, two women settle together onto a small bench on the periphery of the village. Sifa, fifty, and Cecile, sixty, each have a scar running from their foreheads to the center of their noses. I turn on the video camera, then I ask about it, "You both have a mark here?"

"It is for beauty," Sifa says in a gruff voice. She launches in, "Life was wild. We didn't have food. We were living just like animals. The white man named Adrien conducted us out of the forest. He promised to put us in better conditions. We came here, where we are not as comfortable as we were expecting."

Sifa is one decidedly salty lady. She rages against the white-man machine with a long list of grievances, clapping her hands in time with each item, almost rhythmically. "We have no farms. Nowhere to cultivate. We still live like wildlife. We have no source of income, no animals. He didn't give us a place to stay because the houses are not enough for all of us. He didn't keep his promise because we don't have our own village. We cannot live with Bantu people because they cannot accept the mixture. We spend our days here. To get food, we work on Zairian farms. We have no other people we rely on. We are not protected in our houses. We need money to start small businesses to get animals for husbandry. Look at the way we are skinny," she says, pushing up her sleeves, grasping her thin arms. "It's because we have a wild life. Poverty."

I love Sifa's sassy, direct approach. "We also have the problem of clothes," she says. "We thank Eric's organization so much for thought of our children's education. We are grateful the park has given small jobs to our husbands. But that's not enough. Up until now, we women are still idle. We would like to start small businesses, just like other women around. Like in Kavumu, women go to sell. We also need to go for supplies to sell like other people. We would be very happy to be active like other women in Kavumu or Bukavu."

"What is stopping you from doing that?" I ask.

"Only Eric comes to visit us. Other people don't think of us."

"I'm planning to give you each twenty dollars," I say. "Let's get that out of the way. Have you had problems in the village because of Interahamwe?"

"We were in serious trouble because people were being killed. Sometimes they were coming. . . ."

"When was the last time?"

"Yesterday they visited the other side," she says pointing away from the village toward a hill.

"The Interahamwe? They were there yesterday?!"

She nods. "On Monday. Five houses. They still live in the park."

They shake their heads in disapproval. Sifa claps her hands together again as she says, "When they get in the house, they take dishes, clothes, they even sleep on somebody."

"How many Pygmy women have had the problem of Interahamwe 'sleeping on them?'" I ask.

"They go for Zairians. Only one of us was raped and she caught it. She was infected with HIV. Then her husband died from HIV."

"Have they ever killed anyone in the village?" I say.

"They have never killed any of us, but when they kill your neighbor, you can be sure one day they will reach you and kill you. They've never killed any of us . . . so far."

"Do you remember the very first time you met Adrien?"

They argue with each other before Sifa answers. "He came just like a guest. He was hunting birds. When he went back to Europe, he came back the second time with a weapon. He started shooting elephants. The white man was killing elephants and gave us meat, so we had to go in the village to Zairians, to exchange it for a cluster of bananas so we can also eat food like common people. Then he said the park had become his own property. He told us there was a potential war. That we would escape or we would be killed.

"He said he would look for another big piece of land where we would stay, so we would leave him the park. We left in 1972. Cecile already had two children. We crossed two big mountains to join the other people. Our grandfathers and fathers died. They didn't see the land as promised.

"We came here. The Zairians refused for us to squeeze them. They wanted us to stay in the bushes. We were given this place to live.

"We beg you to help us so our voices can be heard by other people. Your presence helps us think we are remembered, that other people care about us. It raises our hope."

I turn off the camera. I tell them about my great-great-great-great-great-grandfather, George Harkins, who was chief of the Native American Choctaw tribe in 1831. At the time of the Trail of Tears, the so-called "Five Civilized Tribes" abandoned their homelands and walked more than a hundred miles to newly formed reservations. My ancestor wrote a famous letter of protest. I describe it to Sifa and Cecile from memory in paraphrased shreds.

"We, as Choctaws, rather chose to suffer and be free than live under the degrading influence of laws, which our voice could not be heard in their formation. . . . We found ourselves like a benighted stranger, following false guides, until he was surrounded on every side, with fire and water. The fire was certain destruction, and a feeble hope was left him of escaping by water. A distant view of the opposite shore encourages the hope; to remain would be inevitable annihilation. Who would hesitate, or who would say that his plunging into the water was his own voluntary act? Painful in the extreme is the mandate of our expulsion. We regret that it should proceed from the mouth of our professed friend. . . . The man who said that he would plant a stake and draw a line around us . . . was the first to say he could not guard the lines, and drew up the stake and wiped out all traces of the line. . . . Let us alone— we will not harm you, we want rest . . . and, when the hand of oppression is stretched against us, let me hope that a warning voice may be heard from every part of the United States, filling the mountains and valleys . . . and say stop, you have no power, we are the sovereign people, and our friends shall no more be disturbed."

I can see their minds churning: This has happened before, they are thinking, in other places, to other people. They're curious. Trying to digest the new information, Sifa asks, "Were there Pygmies on this walk?"

"No." I find a photo of a Tibetan woman that's saved on my camera and tell her, "Native Americans look a little more like her than like you or me. It's just that white people have behaved the same way all over the world. But then my great-great-great-great-great grandfather's daughter married a white man, then her child married a white person, then their child married a white person and so on. So now, I'm white. That was all before I was born. But you're not alone. In the United States, we did exactly the same thing to Native Americans: We gave them land surrounded with nothing, gave them nothing."

Astonished, they nod emphatically. "It's just like we were treated."

They study me for a moment, pensive.

Sifa adds, "It is as if we are the same."

CHAPTER THIRTEEN

A Friend from Far Away

LIKE A BRIDE on her wedding day, I peek out of the second-story window of the Women for Women office in Bukavu, watching for the guests to arrive. Today is my first meeting with my sisters! As women trickle into the courtyard, I don't recognize anyone and I'm not sure I will, since all I have is a tiny photo of each of them. I return to the coffee table piled with bright green gift bags, each stuffed with carefully selected trinkets: stickers, sparkly pencils, balloons for the women's kids, pastel-colored plastic head-bands, little journals. I look to Maurice for reassurance. "Do you think the gifts are silly?"

"No," he says. "It is only to show you are happy to meet them for the first time. You send them money every month, so they'll be happy."

I get up and go back to the window again. Three women in the courtyard look at me, point, and wave.

"Is that them? Are they my sisters?"

"Yes," a staff member says.

I can't wait. I rush downstairs to embrace them. Within a minute, I am surrounded by Women for Women participants, all getting in on the group hug—even though most are not my sisters! I give them each a warm embrace in honor of their sponsors who will never make it to Congo.

My sisters and I slip inside a meeting room. Much to my surprise, I recognize them all from their photos. We show each other the letters we've kept and together survey their sponsorship booklets, which contain passport-size cards that list their names, monthly slots where they sign for their money, and a line that reads, "Sponsor: Lisa Shannon/Run for Congo Women."

The woman sitting next to me has a baby strapped to her back. "Who's your beautiful little one here?" I ask.

Maurice translates her answer. "When she bore the child, she was on the rolls here. She named her after you. The child's name is Lisa."

I take the baby from her mom and hold her on my lap. This little Congolese Lisa was not named after me because of Run for Congo Women, but simply because I wrote her mom letters from America when she was pregnant.

These twenty women have just finished the education part of the Women for Women program and await vocational skills training. They are all from Bukavu. The first sister introduces herself. "I became a seller of firewood, but the children were ill, so I spent all my money on medicine."

· I ask her, "So you had to stop selling wood, but now that they're better you can sell wood again?"

"Yes, I can start to sell wood again. If I have money. . . ."

"You have nothing left from your sponsorship funds?" I'm concerned, and it shows.

And so I've opened the door, setting the tone for the remainder of the meeting.

"With eight children, I was selling maize flour and wood. But now it's difficult after paying the hospital bill," she says. "Now it is difficult selling wood also, because my children got ill. I paid sixty dollars and that was all the money I had. Now I have no income."

Oddly, every sister seems to sell firewood or fish or clothes, and every sister just spent her sixty dollars in graduation seed money on emergency medical care for her kids and can no longer work . . . unless she gets more seed money.

Ugh. This is not what I was expecting to hear.

I'm sinking. As we go around the room, the conversation is all about angling for more money. I realize I've failed to meet a basic expectation. The term "American sponsor" seems to imply "unlimited source of cash." But with more than two hundred sisters, I can't afford even five bucks each. I know it was naive to expect otherwise, but I did, even after one policy wonk in D.C. warned me, "Don't go there expecting it to be all sunshine and roses."

Plus, corruption is baseline here. Suspicion is ubiquitous. The feeling that you're being ripped off is as inherent in the Congo as are women carrying loads. Why wouldn't it be? The Congolese people have been ruled in a nearly unbroken lineage of kleptocracy. After the Belgians left, in 1965, Mobutu Sese Seko, the quintessential corrupt African dictator, came into power. Mobutu siphoned off at least US$5 billion from Zaire into his personal coffers during his rule from 1965 until 1996. People here don't trust those with power or pass codes to big bank accounts. That includes charities.

The pervasiveness of suspicion here registered the other day when I had tea with Jean Paul, my friend from the UN. He leaned in close and announced, "I would love for you to expose Women for Women!"

Bewildered, I asked, "Expose them for what?"

"The sponsors send a hundred dollars each month. But the women only get ten dollars! It is being stolen! It's criminal!"

Jean Paul is wonderful; he's naturally passionate about his country and protective of his people. But I had to stop him right there. "No American sponsor sends US$100 per month to one sister. Women for Women is transparent about funds. Sponsors give twenty-seven dollars per month. Each sponsored woman gets ten, which is confirmed by signatures of two staff members and the participant. Then five dollars a month is put in a savings account, so that she gets sixty dollars when she graduates. The remaining money is used for her education, the letter exchange, and program costs. There are no secrets or intrigue."

Jean Paul was quiet for a moment. I changed the subject and the conversation drifted to the Interahamwe, where he continued down that slippery slope of zero-credibility conspiracy theories. He claimed one of the top Interahamwe leaders was his good friend when they were both students in Rwanda. They stay in touch. While Jean Paul railed against the Chinese, I got the funny feeling he actually thinks the Interahamwe are A-OK. "The story of the Rwandan genocide as it is told is not what I saw," he says.

If he is leading up to saying that the Interahamwe are the victims of the Rwandan genocide, well, I'm not joining him for a stroll down that country lane. I cut the meeting short. The next morning, I ask Maurice, "Is Jean Paul sympathetic to the Interahamwe?"

"Yes, Lisa. Very sympathetic."

Sweet. So I've hired the brother of an Interahamwe-sympathizing Women for Women hater. I'm off to a great start. . . .

I'm taking nothing for granted, so I decide to keep an eye on Maurice, to make sure he's not showing any bias.

A SISTER, FURAHA, slips into our meeting late, the last to arrive. She hasn't picked up on the tone of the meeting, the cues to join the campaign for more cash. She begins to talk, but starts weeping. "I came from Ninja, a village eighty kilometers from Bukavu. They killed most of my family. It was done monthly—one month they come and kill some members, another month they come and kill other members. The last member was killed in November, three months ago."

"Furaha," Maurice says, noting the irony in her expression of devastation. "In Swahili, it means joy."

I had imagined that presenting gifts bags—mostly for my sisters' children—would be a fun, lighthearted moment. But I feel only dread as I drag out the green gift-sacks adorned with stickers, cringing as I make excuses. "I wish I had more to give you."

They smile and dance with gratitude. I give each of them a big hug and we say goodbye.

I ask the four sisters that my mother is sponsoring to stay after the meeting. We call my mom in America at two in the morning, her time. She picks up, foggy but delighted. We put each of her sisters on the line; in an awkward attempt to connect, they speak into the language-barrier void. Maurice steps in to translate. A heavyset, earthy grandma, who looks remarkably like my mother, takes the phone. She repeats something emphatically, keeping it clear and basic with one word. Maurice does not translate. I ask what she's saying.

He translates, "Money! Send more money!"

CHAPTER FOURTEEN

My Own Private Sister

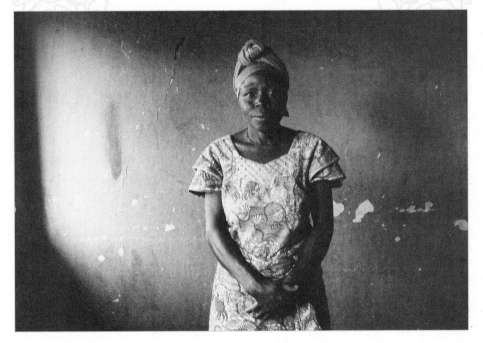

I HAVE A confession to make. During the first year my first sister Therese was in the program, I did not write her. I was so busy running and speaking and trying to build a movement, I let it slide. Maybe it was because I had only received one letter from her. Maybe it was because I assumed the important part was putting a check in the mail. Maybe I just didn't know what to say.

Since I've been in Congo, I've learned that the assumption "They don't care if I write" is dead wrong. In my spare moments, waiting in the Women for Women courtyard, I regularly find myself surrounded by participants who dig out plastic pouches from around their necks or under their blouses that are stuffed with letters from their American sisters. They shove their sponsorship booklets and letters my way, asking, "Do you know my sister?"

I'm so sorry. I don't know Susan Voss from Illinois or Patty Philips from Little Rock or Teisha Johnson from Atlanta. (Amazingly, in two cases I do happen to know their sisters.)

I've found myself animatedly explaining the details of American life that the women's sponsors have written about. I give spontaneous yoga demonstrations; tell them what it means to put a dormer on the house; describe

Disneyland (a place with giant, magic talking mice and roller coasters, where people pay to get scared—for fun!).

For the Congolese women, getting a letter from an American sponsor is kind of like an American woman getting a personal note from Julia Roberts. Even if she told you about her fabulous time at the Oscars, would hearing about her life make you jealous or depressed? No! You'd frame it and put it on display. Or at least tack it up on the fridge, so you could tell your friends, "Oh, yeah, Julia and I are tight. I'm totally on her Christmas card list."

I am not the only sponsor who hasn't written. It turns out that not writing is more the rule than the exception. For every one letter sent by a sponsor, three are sent by program participants—exactly the opposite of what I would have guessed.

A few days ago, a lone woman approached me and showed me her sponsorship booklet. "I've been in the program eleven months with no letter," she said.

I fessed up to her. "At the beginning, I didn't write to my sister either," I said. "But she was still very important to me." Then I ripped off a sheet of colorful stationary (I've learned to always keep it on me for these occasions), and fired off an inspirational note to the woman standing in front of me, announcing, "You are officially my adopted sister." I stuffed it with a couple of postcards and photos of my family.

Therese, my first sister, had noticed I didn't write. When she was just about to graduate the program, I received a batch of three letters she had posted nine months before. (The surge of new sponsors after the *Oprah* report created a massive backlog of letters.) She wrote, "I used to write to you, but you never reply. I wonder why."

Oy vey! I scrambled to write her a long note in a greeting card, continued it on legal paper made folksy with flower stickers, and stuffed it in an envelope with postcards and family photos, scrambling to compensate for the months she waited for my reply that didn't come. I posted my letter to her on her last day in the program. I have no idea if she ever received it.

I vowed to be better about corresponding, and in the past year I've written each of my sisters four letters.

Today, I'm meeting Therese in person. I'm embarrassed, but I'm hoping the fact that I've traveled all this way will exonerate me for not writing. My meetings with women's groups have been nonstop, and no meeting has been like that first hard-charged campaign for cash, after which I slinked upstairs to the office, depressed. Jules, head of the sponsorship staff, approached to ask, "How did your meeting go today?"

I told him.

"Lisa, we could have told you this would happen," he said. "It is why we don't pass on email or postal addresses. They are poor and they are city women. Of course they will ask you for more money. It's a matter of survival. In rural areas it will be different."

In fact, it hasn't happened again. All of my subsequent meetings have been ebullient celebrations. I tell the women I meet about *Oprah*, my run, the movement, all the women who support them from America. Then we go around in a circle and each tells me about "the trouble I got from war."

The war stories are endless. But so are the success stories. And the thanks.

I've learned a couple of Swahili words, just from hearing them so much: *Aksanti*, thank you, and *Aksanti sana*, thank you so much. And again, *Furaha*, meaning joy or "I am happy." *Furaha sana*. So much joy. I am so very happy.

"We no longer rent. We got our own land. I pay them to work on my farm."

"I lost all things, burnt. I lost dignity. You dignified me."

"I regained joy."

"The help you are sending helps us to be human beings, really."

"Today I can really breastfeed my baby because I am eating well."

"If only you could open my heart to see how happy I am to see you. I am buying hens. Whenever I am hungry now, I slaughter one."

"If I was a bird, I would fly and meet you in America."

"If my kid grows up, it is because of support from you."

"I don't know what measurement I can use to measure my joy."

"I feel somehow a person in life, a woman in life. I didn't think I would feel like other women."

"You have to continue up to the coming of Jesus."

"Thanks, thanks, thanks."

"May God bless and bless and bless and bless."

"It doesn't arrive every day to be in this kind of joy. But I am really happy."

WE'VE DRIVEN FORTY-FIVE MINUTES up the long, winding road that hugs the hillsides above Lake Kivu. With Congolese military hanging around the ramshackle shops at the village crossroads, I emerge from the SUV. Squishy clay mud sucks my flip-flops under.

The women who have been waiting burst into song. The men and children stand back. It's a women's party today and they are not invited. Singing and dancing continues during their long procession to the Women for Women compound. The reception today seems almost surreal, the women in saturated colors against the lush landscape dampened with morning rain. Two women lead the group in an impromptu call-and-response chant of endless thanks.

"My kids couldn't go to school, and now they have education because of you."

"We were hungry. Now we eat because of you."

Twenty minutes into the reception, Hortense leans over to me and says, "The woman in yellow is your sister Therese."

She is a modest woman, perhaps early forties. She wears a traditional African dress, crisp and precisely wrapped, in vivid yellows and purple. I tower above her. (My friends will later laugh at me in the photos. "You look like an Amazon next to her!")

"Did you ever receive my letter?" I ask, hugging her.

"I got one letter." She says, "I had already finished the program."

"Did you get photos?"

"I love them," she says. "I told my husband you were coming. He wanted to meet you too, but this place is only for women."

"You said in your letter that your husband had been taken to the bush. Is it the same husband or did you remarry?" I ask.

"I have many, many things to tell you."

We file into the cement classroom with eight other sisters, whom I greet individually. I kneel down next to a sister in a leopard-print headscarf and a dress with puffy sleeves and shiny embroidery. I look at her booklet.

Beatrice. Her sponsor line reads: Kelly Thomas.

Though it would have been easy to schedule this meeting on a day that fit Kelly's needs—just a minor coordination via email—her plans prevented her from making it today to meet her own sister. She entrusted me with a letter and photos to pass along to Beatrice. "It's probably better if you don't tell her I traveled all this way, but didn't make it to see her," she told me.

Why on earth would I want Beatrice to know that?

Gesturing to Beatrice, I tell Hortense, "Don't mention that Kelly is in Congo."

"Beatrice was called here to meet Kelly," Hortense says, "I've already told her Kelly didn't come."

Ouch. Beatrice keeps her eyes cast downward to hide the awkward, sinking look of someone trying to hide disappointment. I pull out Kelly's packet, tied with a bow, and say, "Kelly was so sorry she couldn't be here today. She wanted to meet you so badly. She asked me to send you her love. It just wasn't possible."

I snap a shot of Beatrice holding the photo of Kelly and her husband.

We move on with the meeting, while Kelly's sister holds a half-smile, fingering the photos and letter quietly. Still, she looks like a person who's shown up at the wrong party, like she wouldn't mind disappearing.

We begin with "the trouble I got from war," but conversation quickly shifts when one of my sisters says, "Some children died."

That's one of my talking points. I ask, "How many have children who have died?"

Six out of nine raise their hands.

"How many of you have had more than one child die?"

They hold up their fingers. A couple of them hold up two fingers. One of them holds up three fingers. Another woman raises four. "Four children died."

Another explains, "The twins died, and a baby after."

They each launch into their own one-line explanations, "The baby was tired after birth and didn't breast-feed."

"My 13-year-old daughter died from anemia, after she had four packs of blood."

"Two babies, both died at the clinic. I remain childless."

Therese adds, "One child died because of bad living conditions in the bushes. We buried her in the yard."

These stories always shock me, though they shouldn't. I've been citing the statistics for years. Congo's child death rate is twice that of sub-Saharan Africa, which is already the highest in the world. Fifteen hundred people continue to die every day as a result of the war. In fact, less than one-half of one percent of the war-related deaths in Congo are violent. The vast majority of the deaths are due to the war's aftershocks, primarily easily curable illnesses. Almost half of the deaths are children under the age of five.

We get so wrapped up in the discussion about everyone's lost children that the meeting time flies by. I hear almost nothing from Therese, who remains quiet and unassuming. When it's finally her turn to speak, she says, "I escaped with my children. It was dark, but I saw them take my husband away."

The Interahamwe took five girls and eight other men that night. "The abducted girls escaped death, but the other eight men were tied on crosses and killed, except my husband."

"Did your husband become an Interahamwe soldier?" I ask her.

"He was a slave, cooking," she says.

"He was sent to get firewood the day he escaped," she continues. "When he came back home, they sent letters. They say they will come for him one day.

My husband is a good cook, so they say they want him back because they can't find someone else who cooks like him."

"Can't you move to Bukavu and open a restaurant?" I ask. "Do you still live in the same house?"

"We're still there."

Sadly, we are out of time. We take a few group photos and I give Therese a big hug. We wave to each other as I pull away, and I call back to her, *"Kwa heri!"* Goodbye.

On the drive home, as we peel around corners that reveal soaring views of Lake Kivu, the meeting feels like a letdown, as much for Therese as for me. After her months of waiting and wondering who Lisa Shannon might be, and after my years of thinking about her fuzzy, dark photo while I ran miles on the trail, rehearsing what we might say to each other, I've met her in person. I've embraced her. But we spoke for less than five minutes. We exchanged only a handful of sentences. I know almost nothing more about her.

CHAPTER FIFTEEN

Gift from God

SO THESE ARE the Walungu sisters, whose black-and-white photos radiated damage. Here in Walungu, an hour from Bukavu, the town itself is secure. It's crawling with Congolese Army and UN officials, but it attracts Women for Women participants from villages neighboring "the forest" (a.k.a. Interahamwe territory), like the notorious Kaniola, five miles down the road. That is plenty to account for the shell-shocked looks in their photos.

Wandolyn sits close to me and weeps. She hasn't cracked a smile since we met a few minutes ago. I try to break the ice. "Did you get my letters?"

She ticks her tongue, looking away.

I show her the letters she wrote to me. "I saved them. When I was running, I had your face in my mind, sometimes for hours. I saw in your photo, in your eyes, that you've been through difficult things."

She covers her mouth, mumbling something. Hortense says, "She remembers her difficulty. That is why she is weeping."

"Would you like to talk about it?" I ask.

It's a smaller group today, only the four sisters, so we have the luxury of time.

"Congolese soldiers came to our village and raped me," Wandolyn says. "At the hospital, they asked why I had kept silent. It was then I knew I was pregnant from the rape."

I keep my hand on her shoulder.

"How old is the baby?" I ask her.

"One year, eight months. I didn't think I could accept it. Whenever I saw it, I was only seeing a sign of my bad life."

I give her a little hug.

She smiles. "I'd like to keep you near me."

Then Wandolyn starts crying again. "You are the only one who takes care of me and knows about my situation. The money helps me take care of my baby and my children at school."

"I consider you my friend," I respond. "I'm happy to do it."

"I am extremely happy to see you," she says. "My mom died when I was four. You are my mother. Even my husband is proud of my new mother. My children always say, 'We have a grandmother who takes care of us. We are studying because of our grandmother.' Every day my children ask me to show them your photo. They ask, 'Can we see our grandmother someday?'"

A grandmother! I'm only thirty-one!

I'm stunned. A couple of postcards, letters, and photos have given me near mythic status in this family and transformed me into a kind of magic fairy godmother.

Wandolyn continues. "My husband encourages me. He says, 'In the past, you wanted to put an end to your life, but now you've found a mother and that mother helps us. You should be happy.'"

I ask her, "You wanted to end your life?"

She looks me in the eye and says quietly, *"Ndiyo."* Yes.

There is no way I can live up to the impossibly personal role that Wandolyn has cast for me. But there is also no way I can dismiss her at the end of this meeting, after only a ten-minute exchange. She has staked her claim.

Despite Women for Women HQ's warnings that these visits only cause problems, I cannot leave without meeting my sweet little "grandchildren."

Wandolyn's son greets us as we emerge from the car on the outskirts of Walungu. He shakes my hand shyly. I follow Wandolyn up a long, winding path through the rural countryside, past banana trees, and pigs and calves munching on underbrush, to her home compound—a perfectly round African straw hut.

If I had dreamed this scene a few years ago, how absurd it would have seemed! Me, meeting my half-grown African grandchildren in their tribal compound, something straight out of a storybook but tense with the weight of war around us. I would have woken up and thought it impossibly bizarre.

The turns life can take.

I announce, "Grandma's here!" and embrace each of the children. Wandolyn's husband is fourteen years older than she is and he is frail, clearly in bad health. He shakes my hand with a gentle formality. I peek inside their dark hut. Scrawny white rabbits stumble around in the dark like ghosts.

Wandolyn holds her baby daughter, Nshobole, who is a stoic child. But little ones are often shy around new people, so it's hard to measure the impact of the event on her psyche. "May I hold her?"

I take her in my arms, searching her eyes for evidence.

Neighbors gather, and I know that can mean trouble after I have gone. It starts to rain and it's best not to stay, so I say goodbye.

Yet it isn't enough. Not nearly enough. I ask Wandolyn, "When can I meet you again?"

A few days later, we meet at the program center in Walungu. Her neighborhood has been abuzz with my visit. They're saying I've come to take her family to America. Demands for money are sure to follow.

Wandolyn brings Nshobole with her. The baby sits on my lap while her mom talks.

"I was coming from fetching water in the valley when I heard gunshots," Wandolyn says. "When I got home, men were in the compound. They were

Congolese, speaking a local dialect. My husband had been at home with my kids, but they hid on the farm. Tutsi soldiers had invaded Bukavu and Congolese government soldiers retreated here to Walungu.

"I tried to escape, to run, but they caught me and told me to go in the hut. I asked them to enter the house and take what they pleased instead of taking me. They said they would take rabbits and the cassava flour I had just gotten from the mill. They didn't. They said, 'From you, we need only yourself.'

"The commander told me to lay down.

"I said, 'I don't need to do that.'

"They threw me down and began cutting me. They slapped my ears, so I couldn't hear. They stabbed one of my buttocks. It was so painful, I cried. They laughed at me and told me they would kill me."

Wandolyn spaces out, rocking; her breathing is labored. Hortense says, "She's having emotional flashbacks from reviewing what happened to her. It's as if this is the first time she has told the story."

"They laid me down and started to rape me. They used a piece of cloth to wipe. When one finished, he wiped with the same cloth. Then the other would introduce himself. When I cried, they said stabbing my buttocks was nothing compared to what they would do. They told me they would stab me in the neck, they would kill me. I felt dying was better than suffering like this. There were so many, but while I was conscious I only saw three. I lost consciousness."

She folds over, collapsing her head and hands on her knees, crying.

I approach and hug her, interrupting. "You don't have to talk."

She sits up and continues, seemingly determined to get it out. "They folded the cloth and passed it, wiping."

In my best attempt to usher her through the story, I ask, "Did your husband know about what happened?"

"When he came back, he found they had split my legs. I was lying in pain. He knew because he was the one who treated the injury. When I started to tell him, my husband said, 'Keep quiet. Don't say more. Don't tell to anybody.' He kept silent.

"It was June. I hid myself until December. I wouldn't go out. Only my children did housework, went to farm. As days went by, I felt woozy. I would fall down because of the level of infection. My husband pushed me to go to the hospital. I was ashamed to go to the doctor, because it was taboo to speak about rape. After six months, I accepted to go to hospital because my wounds were so infected that flies were getting in the house everywhere.

"The doctor was angry to see they kept me at home so long. The infection was high. A nun stayed close to me, to take care and wash me.

"The day the doctor told me I was pregnant, I felt dying was better than remaining with that pregnancy. When I went into labor, I was revolted.

"I delivered a baby girl. They brought the baby to me. The nun counseled me, 'The baby is innocent, the baby needs love.'

"I said, 'Keep it away.' I didn't even like to hear about that baby. I didn't even like to see that baby. I considered it the source of my misery and suffering. I said, 'I won't even look at that baby.'

"The next day, the nun asked me to breast-feed. I said there was nothing inside.

"They had to ask other women in maternity to give the baby some milk. After two months, the doctors told me they were tired of asking for milk. They asked me to take the baby. I said no.

"I was worried about my husband, who was sick, who I had been looking after. I was the only one looking after my kids. Now they were suffering from malnutrition because I was in the hospital. The doctor promised to take care of my husband and me.

"The nun sent for my husband. She told him I delivered a baby girl. When my husband heard, he said, 'You are not guilty. I won't say anything against the baby.' My husband told me to take the baby, because it was a gift from God to us, even if it came from suffering and pain. That's how she got her name, Nshobole, which means 'Gift from God.'

"My husband was suffering malnutrition; he couldn't walk. But the doctor took care of him. He started standing up. I regained hope, little by little.

"My husband developed a friendship with the doctor. My husband told them we would take the baby home, but we didn't have the means. The nun told me I would only have to help with breastfeeding, but on all the other counts she could be responsible. They even gave me baby clothes. Everything for the baby came with us when we left the hospital.

"I was careless with the baby. I left the baby to the father. When I had babies before, he wouldn't touch them. He said he didn't know how to take care of them, but this one, he was taking it each time she cried. Of my children, that was the one my husband loved the most. He couldn't accept the baby crying.

"My husband loves me so much. He is sad when he finds me unhappy. He said he would never separate with his wife. But even if I were to be infected [with HIV], he would rather be infected with me so we can die together or live. He said only death will separate us."

"How do you feel about your husband?" I ask her.

"I love him so much," Wandolyn says. "When I'm angry and I quarrel with my husband, he keeps quiet and asks me to cool down. He never speaks when I'm angry. He is grateful because I suffered in order to take care of him, and I didn't tell anyone we were living separate lives because of his health."

"How do you feel about the baby?" I say.

"He loved the baby so much. He tells me the baby is my own blood and I have no right not to love the baby. He was even angry because I told the doctor the baby is not his. He needed me to tell everyone it is his. With his support, I love the baby, because I love him so much. Even today, he never once speaks about the event that led to the baby. I didn't choose to have this baby, but the baby is mine. The baby is the profit of our misfortune."

Hortense says, "You must give her something to care for the child."

It's not a suggestion. It's mandatory. I scrounge around my bag and pull out US$40, slipping it to Wandolyn with the uneasy feeling I've just paid her to relive all that.

Wandolyn's husband joins us later. I speak to him privately and ask him about the event. "How did you feel when Wandolyn came home with injuries?"

"I prayed to God for her to heal," he says. "My father advised me to take another woman, but I said it won't be possible." He wags his finger. "I made a vow to live with her in good and evil, only death would separate us."

"What would you say to men who want to reject their wives?" I ask.

"I can advise them about mutual forgiveness, show them it didn't happen willingly," he says. "We were faithful; we were living a Christian life. That's when the event happened. I kept it a secret. I wouldn't reject her because we were faithful to each other. We have mutual acceptance. We share everything. She loves me. She hides me nothing. She respects me. And I feel she makes me happy."

Wandolyn and I sit outside a church compound, in the shade under some trees. Nshobole perches on her mom's knee. I snap a photo. The mother, with her child, looks like a living religious icon. An African Madonna.

I give the baby a sheet of sparkly heart stickers. The little girl is mesmerized. Wandolyn peels off stickers and sticks them on Nshobole's wrists and arms. Nshobole pulls one off, then she reaches back and sticks the sparkly heart on her mother's cheek.

CHAPTER SIXTEEN

Generose

OF ALL MY sisters in Congo, the one I've most been looking forward to meeting is Generose. Her letter describing the way her leg was cut off, though it was only a brief sketch, was the most awful incident any sister had written about. Her photo intimidates me, for sure—she looks so shell-shocked, even angry. But I felt we were working as a tag team when her letter helped me lobby.

Our meeting was scheduled for this morning. She didn't show.

I'VE SPENT ALL MORNING on the veranda at the Women for Women ceramics studio, lazily sipping soda in the shade with the other twelve sisters in her group. I watch them all walk away together under the trees, laughing and chatting. They look a little fatter, dress a little smarter and smile a little wider than most Congolese women I see around Bukavu. We've had a lovely time, but as they glance back and I wave goodbye, I'm trying to conceal my disappointment that Generose was not among them.

One sister lingers, sick with what she believes is malaria. We drive her to the neighboring Panzi Hospital to get checked out. Doctors shortly confirm that this young, unmarried woman's "malaria" is actually a pregnancy.

On the way out of the hospital in the parking lot, I work overtime with a pep talk: "My American sister is a single mom. It happens all the time. I've met so many Congolese single mothers who thrive all on their own. . . ."

As we are saying goodbye, someone calls my name.

I look up. A woman on crutches approaches me, smiling warmly and wearing a traditional dress under a Puma sports jacket. She says, "I am your sister. I am Generose."

I look closely at her. She's much heavier—and happier—than she looks in her photo. But it is her!

I embrace her. "How did you know it was me?"

"I saw you walking down the corridor and recognized you from the photos you sent me."

Unbelievable! "I was so disappointed you didn't make it to the meeting," I say. "Of all my sisters, I had especially looked forward to meeting you."

"I know," she says. "You wrote me sometimes when you didn't write the others."

Generose is in the hospital with a life-threatening bone infection—her leg is rotting where the Interahamwe cut it off. We find a quiet corner in the back of the building and I ask her about that day.

"I was in my house preparing food for my husband when they came," she says. "They made me prepare food for them, then asked me to wake my husband, who was asleep. They demanded money. I had one hundred and thirty dollars, and I gave it to them, but they didn't care. They said, 'That money was the nurse's participation. The husband is head of the school. He has to make his contribution.'

"My husband said, 'I have nothing.'

"They started to beat him, so I cried for help. The Interahamwe shot him immediately, killing him.

"I continued to cry to alert other people. They said, 'Shut your mouth. Put your leg on the chair.'

"They took a machete and cut off my leg. We had six children at home;

one was my sister's child. The Interahamwe cut the leg into six parts and burnt them in the fire. They gave each child a piece of my leg and commanded them to eat.

"One of the children said, 'I can't eat a part of my mother. You already killed my father, so you will have to kill me.'

"They killed my child.

"They tried to burn the house. The children got us out. They took me to the garden outside. Because of the burning of the house, because of despair, because of the loss of blood, I was like a dead person. The next day, I found myself at the hospital in Walungu without knowing how I got there. The UN and the head of the neighborhood had taken me."

"When was the next time you saw your children?" I ask her.

"Two months and a week," Generose answers. "It was painful when they saw me with only one leg. They ran away, saying they would wait until the leg grows back before they would talk to me. I could only cry.

"I approached them, and told them, 'You need to thank God. I am alive. I only lost my leg. Not like Mama Annie.'"

"Who's Mama Annie?" I ask.

"The Interahamwe began the attack that night with our neighbor Mama Annie. They killed her husband. She was pregnant. They cut off her eyes, nose, and mouth. They cut out her pregnancy. I met her in the hospital. She died after four days."

Generose stops for a moment. "Neighbors came to visit us and they told us about the wedding. . . ."

The wedding. So here it is, and I sense it before she even begins the story.

"After us, they went to another neighbor's. They took the bride to the forest, where they raped and killed her. They burned her compound where the wedding feast was supposed to take place. Forty-six guests were inside. They burned them alive.

"I would not stay one day in my village. There was no husband there, no house.

"I can't go back, I can't see the souvenirs. I asked for help from a neighbor who had a car. He drove us the forty-five kilometers here and dropped us with a relative, a cousin I knew well. We grew up in the same house. We arrived, she prepared cassava. Her husband said, 'I'm sorry, there is no place. I don't have enough money to accept another in my charge.'

"We went to a parish, where we were welcomed. They fed us dinner. They needed to know if I was really an internally displaced person, so they called a woman to vouch for me. We ended up staying with them for two months. Then the priest rented us a house, paid for it six months in advance, and gave us food for a month.

"I spent a month begging. People gave money, clothes, food. By chance, I met an employee of Women for Women who knew the story from Kaniola. He saw me begging. He lent me twenty dollars and told me to go to Women for Women.

"When I had my leg cut off, I felt I was not a human being. But when I enrolled, I was accepted unconditionally. I began to feel like a different person. I was told I had a letter. Your letter made me very, very happy. To know there was someone thinking about me. I was a nurse in a hospital there in my village. I became a seller with money from Women for Women, and already the benefit has been more than a hundred dollars, which I used to buy a cow. I sent it to my village. Maybe in a few years, it will have babies that I can sell and buy a house here in Bukavu."

"How are your children now?" I ask. "Are they okay mentally?"

"They are traumatized," she says. "They passed a year without eating meat."

We are silent.

Eventually, Generose begins again.

"I can't find exact words to say thanks for what you did. A person can't forget someone who does something for them. That's why I recognized you. Since getting your photo, you've stayed in my mind."

Generose's bone infection requires a two-month stay in the hospital and two successive surgeries. The price tag? Three hundred dollars. She doesn't have it. The surgery has already been stalled due to lack of funds.

I offer to pay. She's over the moon and showers me in thanks as she leads us through Panzi's maze of corridors to her ward. When we reach her bed, she asks, "Can you accept to look at my leg?"

She shows me her amputation scars, mid-thigh.

"Is it painful for you?" I ask.

"Of course," she says. "It hurts."

That's when I notice her low-end, make-do prosthetic leg sitting off to the side. She has painted the toenails.

GENEROSE IS DESPERATE to get home to check on her children. We catch up on the ride. I show her my notebook with her photo and letter, which I read back to her: "'War is a very bad thing.'"

"If you compare my photo, I have changed terribly," she says. I think she means good-terrible. "I was thin and pale. Today I have become big and brighter. I'm fat with joy."

She does look in good spirits.

"How's Ted?" she asks.

I hold my two pointer fingers together, tip to tip, then split them, and tell her, "Life in the U.S.A. isn't perfect."

"Are you still running?" she asks. "I felt bad to see someone suffer for me, to run."

Is she kidding? There is no trace of sarcasm in her voice. All I did was go for a run. I do a quick mental scan. What did I say in those letters? Did I complain? Was I melodramatic? God, I hope not. My poor friends; I whined for months about the mustache tan and losing my boyfriend and my toenails. All I can say to Generose is, "It was a privilege."

We pull up next to a steep hill overflowing with makeshift wooden huts, the Bukavu slums. Generose invites me to meet her children, an offer I can't refuse. I follow her down a narrow corridor between shacks, with thick mud squashing around my flip-flops.

Her little ones come up and greet us on the path, *"Karibu!* Welcome."

The twins, around ten years old, smile shyly and offer a handshake. I carry Generose's sweet four-year-old daughter, who's wearing a polka-dotted dress and has big baby-doll eyes, to their dark stick-and-mud hut.

Generose introduces a matronly, officious looking woman who is lurking in the doorway with her hands on her hips. She says, "This is the proprietor of the house."

I sit down, ignoring the woman.

Generose continues. "The problem I have is, I'm at the hospital. The proprietor is chasing the children from the house. We do not pay at the moment."

I'm doing my best to ignore what she just said; I feel like I've walked into a trap. "Right," I say. "Which of the children is sick? The little one?"

Generose reiterates. "The proprietor is chasing us."

Is this posturing, some kind of act?

"Who stays with the children when you're in the hospital?" I ask her, forging on.

"They stay by themselves. Sometimes the proprietor takes care of them."

Generose pulls out a small bundle of my letters and photos. She has tucked them in between her only remaining photo of her husband. "I want to show you my husband who died in the war."

In the photo, they stand together casually at the hospital where she worked. "The request is, as I don't have a husband, I'd like to have a small house of my own. If possible, I can live quietly if I have my own house."

Mercy. I have to nip this in the bud. "I can't do that," I say. "I'll pay for the surgery. But I have so many sisters. I can't build everyone a house. It wasn't even my money that sponsored you. I asked other people to give money."

"I don't know what to do," she says. "The children are being chased from the house. I have a debt of sixty dollars in back rent."

"Sixty dollars?" I say. "The problem is, every sister has told me they have problems. I don't have enough money to give every sister sixty dollars. Do you understand? If I give it to one sister, every sister will expect it. They'll be angry with me."

I do the calculation in my head: 200 times US$60 equals US$12,000. "I don't have that money."

"*Ndiyo. Ndiyo. Ndiyo. Ndiyo,*" she says. " I understand. Thanks for what you promised to do for the surgery."

"It's a special case, because it is life or death," I tell her.

Fellow slum-dwellers have piled up in the doorway. It is exactly what HQ warned: If you visit sisters in their homes, all of a sudden they are tagged as having money. Nothing but harassment will follow—demands for money, theft—unless I can address it publicly, right now, head on. For the benefit of onlookers, I speak loudly and clearly. "The other problem is, if I left money with you, you would have problems with neighbors coming. So it would be dangerous."

"I thank you," Generose says. "I would like for you to take this photo."

She hands me the photo of her husband. I can't believe she would offer it to me. "This is your only photo of your husband, isn't it? You keep that one."

She thinks the better of it too. "Yes, okay."

The landlady hangs around. I look back at Generose after we say good-bye and her expression—apprehensive, strained, disappointed—says it all.

That was no act. Her kids are going to be thrown out.

CHAPTER SEVENTEEN

The Road to Baraka

"YOU'RE GOING TO drive us through 'treacherous rebel territory' today?" I ask Moses, Women for Women's field driver.

"Yes!" He bursts out laughing.

"Do you think the drive is safe?" I ask.

"No problem."

"We're driving through Mai Mai territory?"

"Yes."

"Will we see the Mai Mai?"

He smiles. "We hope we can."

I laugh. So does Kelly. I'm actually not sure why we're laughing. It isn't that funny. But it is nice to have someone from home to giggle with, even if we are only half amused, half feeding off of each other's hunger for adventure.

Kelly is joining me for this leg of the trip. She surprised me a few days ago when she came to visit me at Orchid and told me she has run out of money. With only US$300 left, she doesn't have nearly enough to make it through her last week, even with the homestay. She asked if I could float some of her expenses, offering to pay me back once we make it home. This is no place to run out of cash, so I agreed.

Fortunately, the Baraka leg of the trip is cheap. Christine has called in favors so we can stay at the UNHCR guesthouse, which is only US$25 per day, including food. I'm happy to have the company.

One thing I've figured out thus far: Congo is safe—as long as everything goes according to plan. Still, when I quiz Congolese, they seem to confuse "I've never had a problem" with "It's safe." Half of the women sponsored by Run for Congo Women live in the small town of Baraka, eight hours south of Bukavu. That war-affected region has been flattened by conflict and is known for mass killings. Most of the locals abandoned it years ago for refugee camps in Tanzania. These days, most foreign militias have fled the region too and it is now a stronghold of the Congolese militia, the Mai Mai.

With the area stabilized in recent months, the UN and other aid organizations like Women for Women have established outposts in Baraka to serve the returning refugees. Though there's been fighting this week in the mountains west of Baraka, Christine has spoken with the UN. They said we'll be fine.

As we load up the Range Rover, I ask Hortense the question anyway. "What's the security situation there?"

"The security is good," she says. "No problem."

"What about the Mai Mai?" I ask.

"I've had seven trips to Baraka with no problem," she tells me. "The Mai Mai are very kind. We will see them on the way. The general is a good man, taking care of them properly. They do not bother people."

The Mai Mai don't bother people? They must have a stellar spin machine, because that's not what I've heard in the conversations I've had with former child soldiers. Initially formed as a community-based defense force to fight foreign rebel groups, the Mai Mai are widely known for mass atrocities against the very people they claim to defend. As one Congolese told me in strict confidence, "The Mai Mai do everything any other militia does. But if you speak against them, they will come to your home at night and kill you and your family."

At present, the Congolese government is attempting to engage the Mai Mai in what's known as "brassage," a process of demobilizing combatants and integrating them into the Congolese Army. But tensions are brewing as some among the militia's leadership grow agitated at being left behind in Congo's emerging post-election political scene.

The Mai Mai do have one unifying thread: their use of witchcraft. The translation of "Mai Mai" is literally "Water Water"; the name comes from their belief that if they douse themselves with an herb-infused potion prior to battle, no bullet can penetrate them. By magic, whatever they encounter in battle will pass through them like water. Codes of Mai Mai behavior are based on traditional beliefs and range from wearing lucky sink plugs, to maintaining abstinence or committing rape prior to battle, as a source of power.

The pro–Mai Mai sentiment strikes me as more of a cultural courtesy. I've noticed Congolese rarely criticize other Congolese.

Maurice and I slip away to the market to stock up on Marlboros and a case of beer—emergency love offerings. We divide the cigarettes between us and tuck them away in our bag so they're ready in the event that we have to make quick friends.

Hortense sees the beer and shrugs. "I don't understand why you think of problems."

We hit the road about four hours late and cut over the border into Rwanda to borrow a good stretch of road. Meanwhile, Moses blasts Shakira's "Hips Don't Lie." I can think of very few songs that are less Congo-appropriate. Thank God they don't understand the English lyrics. When it's over, he rewinds and plays it again. And again.

A couple of hours later, we cross back to Congo and a different landscape: miles of flat, wide-open plains covered in grass and shrubs, with cloud-capped blue-green mountains in the distance. Tiny children spot us and leap to their feet, delighted. They run after us pointing, waving. To four-year-old Congolese kids, every white person must be with the UN. They scream, *"MONUC-ay!"* which is the children's name for MONUC—the French acronym of the UN mission in Congo.

They also yell, *"Muzungu!"*

"What does *muzungu* mean?" I ask.

"White person," Kelly says.

"Sometimes you can also call a Congolese a *muzungu*," Hortense adds.

"What is a Congolese *muzungu* like?" I say.

"They are an important person like your boss," she says. "Someone who will take care of you, give you money."

When we are outside the city of Uvira, we pass our first militia. The Mai Mai attempt to flag us down for a lift. Fortunately, this is a common issue with a common solution. All charitable vehicles display a special sticker—a gun with a red *X* through it, like a No Smoking sign, but with a gun instead of cigarette. It is a universal symbol indicating that the vehicle is for humanitarians only. No guns, and hence no militias, on board. It is surprisingly well respected. We breeze straight past the hitchhikers. Within a few miles, I lose count there are so many Mai Mai around. We make it into a road trip game, watching out for them like wildlife, trying to guess who is Mai Mai and who is Congolese Army.

"What about that one?" I ask.

Maurice and Hortense alternately answer, "Congolese Army."

"What about those guys?"

"Mai Mai."

I don't have a clue as to how they can tell the difference. To me, they look exactly the same. You could argue the Mai Mai look a little scruffier and occasionally wear red, but the Congolese Army is pretty ragtag too. Even after passing more than fifty Mai Mai, I still can't tell which is which.

We pull up to a gas station in Uvira, about halfway to Baraka. It's already past four in the afternoon. The fill-up takes forever. Hortense chats on the phone.

My cell phone is out of range, and I can't say I'm sorry. My mom has been calling twice a day, giving me anxiety-ridden pep talks, as much to calm herself as to soothe me. I've tried to keep my reports lightweight and clean, partly for her peace of mind, but also because she takes notes and likes to broadcast "what Lisa said," peppered with editorial embellishments, to the whole Run for Congo Women email list.

Hortense approaches Kelly and me with some news. "The UN advises no travel after dark," she says. "We will need to spend the night here and make the rest of the journey in the morning."

We check into a grossly worn-down motel with open corridors and balconies. I bypass the Presidential Suite, with its crusty patchwork carpet, for a smaller, more basic room. I peek out of the sliding glass doors to the panoramic view of Lake Tanganyika, the longest lake in Africa, which is swarming with mosquitoes. I retreat and lock the sliding glass doors. Double check the locks. Triple check the locks.

I lug my camera bag onto the bed, tuck in my mosquito net, snuggle up to my prized equipment, and spend the night spooning my camera bag.

I dream that a man breaks into the room and looms over me in my bed.

CHAPTER EIGHTEEN

A Separate Peace

I OVERSLEEP. By the time I scramble to pull it together, the others have been waiting for me outside for quite some time. Today is my thirty-second birthday.

Outside of Baraka, the landscape tells the story of the past decade. It's obvious the region was abandoned for years. Villages are mostly ruins, their mud-brick huts, roofless and crumbling, are overgrown with weeds. Hortense says, "In the next village, there were only four civilian families left."

We slow down as we drive through a village. I notice a large cement slab, painted with a mural: huts burning, soldiers hacking people with machetes. It reads: MASSACRE DE MAKOBOLA/BANWE, 20/12/1998.

Hortense points toward the hills and says, "They buried them up there."

We pull off the main road and drive up narrow grass tracks. In a clearing above the village, a stone monument marks the site. A local villager tells us the story, which Hortense translates: "People hid along the waterways to escape war. Then those people came and called out that peace was recovered. Soldiers gathered people, telling them there was peace already. Once the people got here, they killed all of them."

I follow Hortense behind the memorial. "They buried them here," she says, pointing to a wild patch of yellow cosmos. "Seven hundred and two people were killed. They buried them in four graves."

Three more mass graves, overgrown with weeds taller than I am, are just beyond the sunny wildflowers. Hortense repeats the story, boiling it down to basics. "They told the people there was no more war, gathered them, and killed them all."

As we continue down the main road, spanking new huts on freshly cleared plots, paid for by refugee resettlement projects, are beginning to creep into the landscape.

We pull into Baraka, which has the distinct feel of a Wild West frontier town. Its wide main drag is a dirt road lined only with NGO offices. Congolese soldiers with guns linger on every corner, bored, just hanging out.

We dump our stuff at the spotless UN guesthouse. It is decorated in UN blue and white, with spare, utilitarian furniture; it feels like the kind of austere vacation cottage you might find on a Greek island. When I ask a group of UN staffers about security in the region, a young European woman answers. "The FDD [a Burundian militia] and other foreign militias are gone," she says. "There is a Mai Mai general on the peninsula who's been making threats, but just rapes and looting for the moment. No attacks yet."

I sit quietly for a moment in the spare, whitewashed community room, balancing my gratitude for a clean place to stay and the generosity of my hosts with the implications of what she has just dropped into our conversation. I contemplate this young, wild-haired woman, with her slightly sweaty, disheveled look and the crusty demeanor of a seasoned European aid worker. As a staff member of the UNCHR, her task is to encourage refugees to return from Tanzania. She is currently working on a video project she can use to convince people it is safe to return home.

"You don't consider rape a security threat for returning refugees?"

"Rape here is so common," she says. "It's cultural."

Wow. I say nothing but allow the weight of her comment to settle in the room.

NEXT, WE HEAD out for our meetings.

As we pull up to the Women for Women center in a village south of Baraka, we are greeted with an archway of flowers. I'm presented with a little bouquet of marigolds, gathered in a rusty can, and a goat. A goat! That's what—forty dollars? I've gotten lots of chickens and eggs, but this is remarkably generous. This may be the best birthday celebration I've ever had. Just one little snag: I'm a strict vegetarian.

I joyfully receive the squealing, upside-down little gal, grabbing her bound feet. I set her down. "Thank you so much for this wonderful gift! I am so grateful for your generosity, so proud of you all, that I am presenting her back to your group as a celebration of our friendship. I have only one condition. You must never hurt the goat. The goat is blessed. The goat is sacred. Never, ever kill this goat."

One of the participants leads the group in a cheer and dance. We settle into a large circle, shaded by ancient trees, and shoo away eavesdropping teenage boys. Almost all of these sisters have just returned from Tanzania, where they lived in refugee camps from eighteen months to ten years. Freshly resettled, the women boast about buying new plots of land every month with sponsorship funds. "We can buy a farm of twenty square meters for twenty dollars," one says.

I've developed a quick survey to take at these meetings. How many have suffered a violent attack on their home? Had a relative killed? Lost a child? The women are always open. But I have never asked about rape directly at these forums. Maybe if I'm nonchalant, it'll put them at ease. I try to slip it in as part of my survey. "How many of you have been raped?"

A few hands go up then quickly retreat. It's a group of fifty, but only three women keep their hands raised. They stare at the others defiantly, stretching their hands higher. This is why oft-quoted statistics on rape in Congo are ridiculously low. Even in a group that's all women, including Western women who have supported them financially, Congolese women won't talk about sexual violence in public, at least if no one else does.

Hortense shrugs. "They are hiding themselves."

They stare at me blankly. Okay, that was tacky and insensitive. I shouldn't have asked such a personal question in a public survey. I try to rectify it, take them off the defensive. "In America, we believe if a woman is raped, it is never her fault. She has nothing to be ashamed of. So if any of you know someone who has been through this, I hope you will support her and let her know she didn't do anything wrong."

I'm ready to call it a failed experiment. I'll just leave it alone.

We begin with "The trouble I got during war."

Like most groups I have met with, these women are open about violent attacks. But an hour or so into our meeting, no one has mentioned rape. We land on the participant who led the singing earlier. She shifts on the edge of her wooden bench and speaks with a defiant tone. Even with the language barrier, I can tell by the others' body language—they are folding their arms, rolling their eyes, or adjusting their dresses—they find her brash. Hortense translates. "When you asked about it earlier, we were not honest. Even if the others are hiding themselves, we were all raped. All of us."

She continues with her story, motioning to her lap, slamming her fist between her legs, as she describes the attack. Some snicker with discomfort.

I thank her profusely for her courage to speak up and tell her story.

Later, others open up.

"They treated us the way they wanted. They met us in houses. They did what they needed."

"When in the field, they were beating us with sticks, chasing us, doing whatever they were doing, downgrading us through raping."

"They obliged my husband to have sex with my daughter. He refused. They killed him immediately."

"All of my clothes, including my underwear, were torn to shreds."

"My womb was seriously destroyed."

"They tried to make my older brother rape me. He refused and was killed. So they raped me. They took my husband and raped him. He died from that incident."

"We were sleeping in water, in a marsh, with so many mosquitoes. It was so cold. The FDD came at night. They made so much trouble. They took all our clothes. I was eight months pregnant, standing naked in front of my daughters and my husband. They inserted money and did the same to my daughters who were twelve and fifteen. They raped me. My husband ran away. We were left naked. I fell ill. I didn't know where he was. People in the village found me naked in the forest. They took me to the hospital, but there was no one there. They took me to Lake Tanganyika, where they put me on the boat to Tanzania. I don't know where my husband was. I delivered a baby there. The girl is six years old today. I came back in April. I found my husband, now old and poor."

I ask, "How many of you have been attacked since you returned from refugee camps?"

About half raise their hands. A woman in her thirties explains, "Peace has not really been recovered. They are still raping women. When we go to our farms, we are stopped on the way to the fields and raped. Especially in the bush. In the center of Baraka, no. But when we go to the fields . . . it's like me with my age, they ask me to stop."

Another woman adds, "It was said the war ended, we were called back here. But since being back we had an attack from FDD."

"Who has raped you since you returned?"

They all chime together: "FDD."

This confuses me. The UN staff verified there are no longer foreign militias in the area, including FDD. I recall Maurice explaining, "A Congolese woman can never say she was attacked by another Congolese. It is not culturally acceptable. It is not safe."

I think of the main drag running through Baraka, the armed young men standing idly on every corner, the innumerable Mai Mai along roadsides. The Congolese Army is in large part comprised of former militias. In the disarmament process, brassage, militia members are integrated into the Congolese Army and promised US$20 monthly. But they are rarely paid. They are expected to take what they need—food, money, supplies—from the locals. In the process, they rape.

"Peace" and "stability" here seems to mean that people are no longer slaughtered by the hundreds (mass killing is at least one activity from which the Congolese Army refrains). But women, well, they have to feed their children. If that means the long daily walk to farm their fields and risking rape on the way, the alternative is watching their kids starve.

One woman asks, "Do they also rape women in America?"

I answer, "Women are raped all over the world. It is not as common in America as here. But a number of American women who have been raped have run to raise your sponsorship. Because they know that in some ways, you feel the same. They asked me to especially extend their love to you."

They nod.

One woman raises her hand and asks, "What can we do to manage and improve so we can support other women?"

CHAPTER NINETEEN

An Odd Paradise

KELLY AND I shoot each other looks as if we are kids on a remote corner of the playground, hoping to not get caught.

"HQ will not be happy we did this," I say, as we step through leaky canoes onto the rusty, faded, red and teal motor-powered fishing boat. I decide to think of it as charming, well art-directed. A weather-beaten skipper and his first mate await us on board, disaffected guys who walk around barefoot and in swimming trunks. They barely say hello.

There is a Mai Mai general on the peninsula who is resisting disarmament and threatening a fight. Christine was clear: *Under no circumstances are we to go without the UN boat. We need it for security.* The UN speedboat is also fast, while local boats are notorious for capsizing. A few months ago, two Japanese visitors took a local boat and when a storm hit, it sank a short distance from the port. They had to be rescued by the UN.

When we arrived at the port a few minutes ago, Hortense announced, "The UN boat is booked on other business." She smiled and gestured as though she was revealing a big birthday surprise. "So we'll take this one, a local boat."

Cancelling is not an option. We sponsor women in two villages on the peninsula, which is a two-hour boat ride from Baraka—twelve new sisters in one village, five in the other. Hortense has already notified them we are coming. One of them, Fitina, is on my short list to interview. Her enrollment form indicates that seven of her children have died.

It is a stunning day as we roar across Lake Tanganyika—clear, blue skies; calm water. I feel dorky for wearing a life jacket, especially next to our barefoot crew. We sit on wooden plank benches on the boat's deck, munching on rolls and peanuts, taking in the scenery. Hortense tries to brief me, yelling over the engine.

"When we did our assessment in this village . . ." She trails off, something about rape. I can't make it out.

"What?"

"Ninety percent."

"Ninety percent what?"

"Yes. Ninety percent of the women in the first village have been raped!"

The sleepy fishing village is an odd paradise with a crystal-blue lagoon and a pebble beach, backed by cascading forested hills and terraced plots hosting mud huts. It's a last little slice of paradise not mapped and quartered by Lonely Planet, a place that would be high-end vacation property if it were anywhere but in Congo.

The village women gather to greet us, waving flowering tree branches and palm leaves in the air, dancing in time. As the crew shuts down the engine and we drift to shore, the women's ebullient singing takes over. They throw cloths on the ground to welcome us and initiate a procession through the village, one that gives me a piercing headache because I'm smiling so wide for so long.

The two celebrations today are nearly identical, as are the villages.

I don't bring up rape. Neither do they.

Kelly is quiet through the first meeting, as always. I encourage her to join in, but she keeps it to a couple of brief sentences. On the way to the second meeting, I ponder out loud. "I wonder if I say the right things to them."

"What you say is too complex for them," she says. "Keep it simple. Just say, 'Your sisters love you. You're good dancers.' Stuff like that."

I am wearing thin. I hang back during the second procession, focusing on the children who have joined in. I touch their clean-shaven heads or hold their hands, which elicits smiles. When we reach the center, I slip to the sidelines and let Kelly take center stage.

I scan the crowd for Fitina, or anyone in bright pink, on the off chance she would wear the same headscarf and top shown in the photo that is stapled to my paperwork. I can never pick out my sisters in these crowds.

Then a heavyset woman lumbers up the path, wearing a bright pink headscarf and top. It is Fitina! She looks exactly like she does in her photo.

Our twelve sisters give stiff before-and-after speeches that feel more like testimonies. I ask Fitina to stay behind.

She sits alone on a wooden bench. I join her and pull out my notebook. "Mama, this is the intake form I received about you. Is it true you have had seven children die?"

Fitina looks a bit lost, but she searches her memory, counting aloud. "Nine . . . Ten . . . Ten children have died."

"How many children are living?"

"Five."

"I would like to visit your home and talk with you more."

Hortense is already anxious about time. "Make it quick. The port closes at dark."

It is late afternoon, but I don't care. I want to talk with Fitina. Nothing else is on my radar.

Kelly and Hortense enjoy a traditional Congolese feast of fu-fu (a variation on cream of wheat), greens, and meat, while Maurice and I slip away to follow Fitina through the village. Villagers stare at a polite distance as we pass compounds of brick huts with thatched roofs and gardens lined with rickety homemade stick-fences. Cooking smoke is rising in the late afternoon sun.

Fitina leads us to her lakefront property on the far side of the village. Her family's mud hut is flanked with pecking chickens; sardines are laid out to dry on warped metal sheets. The hut sits next to an empty plot where their former house stood before a militia burned it to nothing. Now the same land bears eggplant and vegetables with African names I can't follow. For a brief moment, I picture this plot in an alternate universe, as a perfect spot for a modern prefab home, straight from the pages of *Dwell* magazine.

A neighbor laughs and teases Fitina; she is trying to get in on the action. Children linger. I won't be able to talk with Fitina privately.

A few minutes later, we head back through the village with a troop of children escorting us like bodyguards. British radio emanates from one of the huts. I look up towards the forested hills. Mai Mai are out there somewhere, threatening to attack.

"Do you feel embarrassed?" I ask Fitina, hoping she is okay with being followed around by an American who is flashing an expensive camera.

We round a corner. Three men with guns stand in our path.

Uh. . . .

I go blank with shock.

The men meander past us, and one sizes me up. I glance at them, catching their backwards glances at me. They are young and have mismatched uniforms. One wears a bright yellow beret. Their weapons look second-rate. I ask Maurice under my breath, "Are they Congolese army?"

"Um . . . yes."

Then we're fine, I reassure myself.

I turn around and see another soldier standing in front of a hut with an older couple. He stares at me and beckons.

"What did he say?" I ask Maurice.

"He wants you to film him."

Under other circumstances, I would probably find this amusing, a scene straight out of the movie *Blood Diamond*. Everyone's a sucker for the camera! Instead, I move slowly, like someone approaching a strange, haggard dog that's been found roaming the streets. I don't know if he bites.

I'm tense, fumbling. "You want me to film you?"

He's intrigued, but not friendly. He knows he's in control. I flip around the viewer so he can see himself, an attempt to break the tension. This always works with children.

"Nice," he says, nodding. "Good."

"Are you visiting your family?" I say.

Maurice translates, but the soldier looks at me vaguely.

"Okay!" Hortense approaches from behind. "We really must hurry! It's going to get dark soon."

I am not willing to leave without interviewing Fitina, so Hortense ushers us back to the compound. "Try to make it short, eh? We will run into trouble at the port."

I grab a chair and find a quiet spot where we sit on the edge of an open, unfenced field, with the forested hills just behind us. Fitina holds a young child on her lap and another little girl, about six years old, clings to her. They are her grandchildren.

"Can you talk with us for a minute about your experience of the war?" I ask Fitina.

"We didn't go to Tanzania," she begins. "We went up to the hills and stayed in the bush, where we stayed in bad conditions until the end of the war."

I ask about her children.

"Five of my children are alive. Two among them are in school in Baraka."

"How many children have you given birth to?" I ask.

"Fifteen. I gave birth to fifteen. Five are alive and ten have died."

"Can you tell me how they died?"

"From illness."

"What were the names of your children?" I say. "How old were they when they died?"

Fitina's voice grows thin, "Maribola . . . Makambe . . . Maribola died from illness. She was a teenager. She only had a headache and she died. Makambe died when she was a few months old. . . . All died from illness."

Fitina has a remote look in her eyes. But I am feeling the pressure. Military in the village. Port closing. Long boatride home.

I press Hortense to translate again. "Can she just list the names and how old they were when they died?"

"Liza also died," she says. "Ruben also died. Na . . . Na . . . Nape also died."

She struggles. "Some died when they were two, some others were a few months old, a few more than three years old. Maribola died just after the war. She already had breasts. She was a teenager."

"But can she list their names and how old they were when they died?" I plead again. "Just a list?"

My pushing does not strike me as inappropriate in the moment, but she is swimming in her own thoughts, not listening to me. And Hortense does not translate; I take note of her cue.

"The others . . . I don't remember their names because I never want to talk about them."

"Is it difficult?" I ask. "Would you prefer to not talk about them?"

With a crack in her voice and desperate, evading eyes, she ekes out, "I feel grief when I talk about them."

We sit in silence for a long while.

Then I try again. "Do you remember other names, or do you want to just forget?"

Hortense snaps. "She has already given you five names. She has forgotten the names of the others because she never wants to talk about them."

Fitina fiddles with her hands. An exasperated, pain-soaked smile spreads across her face. She strains to say, "They were all so young."

Another long silence. The child still hangs on Fitina, resting her head on her grandmother's shoulder, watching me like I am the enemy. Even with the language barrier, the child sees what I've missed. My push to reduce Fitina's losses to a list has shut her down completely. There is nowhere to go.

Finally, I ask, "Is there anything you would like to say to other mothers in America?"

Fitina smiles shyly. "I send my greetings. If you are strong, it is my happiness."

CHAPTER TWENTY

Water Water

WITHIN MINUTES OF wrapping up with Fitina, we load onto the boat. The motor revs up and we are off.

Cruising along the edge of the peninsula, Maurice, Kelly, and I sit outside on the wooden benches, exhausted from the day. I ask Maurice, "Were they Congolese military?"

"Ah, no. They were Mai Mai," he says, as he leaves to retire inside.

Fear chemicals surge through me and I start to shake as I describe the soldiers to Kelly.

The boat slows down suddenly. The skipper and first mate are throwing on their life vests. This is not a good sign. They've been barefoot and shirtless most of the day.

I look ahead. A few miles in front of us, rain pours from storm clouds onto the lake; it looks like a steel wall.

"What's happening?" I ask Hortense.

"They are turning the boat around. We will spend the night in the village."

With our new Mai Mai friends?

I ask rhetorically, "The Mai Mai . . . Do you really think it's safe?"

She flashes a big, tension-diffusing smile. "Safer than drowning trying to cross the lake, yes?"

The canvas canopy covering the deck flaps wildly, while the first mate grasps the canopy frame, trying to keep it from flying off. He maintains a tense gaze forward, anxiously blowing a plastic whistle as if to a drumbeat. I can only imagine that he's poising himself to send out a louder, high-pitched call for help should the boat capsize without warning.

So these are our choices tonight, more only-in-Congo choices. Would you rather be raped or watch your children starve? Drown, or camp with the militia?

So be it. We're sleeping over with the Mai Mai.

I grab my camera and try to capture it all on video. By the time the boat rocks to shore, slate-gray clouds blot out the remaining evening light, leaving just enough for my eyes to adjust and glean detail, but causing my video camera viewfinder to go black. I wobble back down the wooden plank.

I notice a little girl I walked with earlier today among the handful of women waiting for us. I touch her shaved head affectionately and say hello while the others disembark and Hortense talks to the women on the beach.

"They are glad we have returned," she says. "They knew it would rain and were concerned." (Much later, Maurice tells me what he overheard the villagers muttering to each other. Tension between the Congolese Army and the Mai Mai is at its peak, they were saying; it could erupt into gun battle at anytime.)

I kneel on the pebbled shore and grope around putting my camera away. The first fat raindrops hit, warning that a downpour is moments away.

"We must hurry!" Hortense calls back to me, chastising me for dallying.

I don't understand why you think of problems.

I look up. The others are already halfway across the beach.

The girl lingers, her reedy frame draped in a tattered white dress with a faded strawberry print, a rounded collar, and buttons up the back—the kind of dress American girls wore in the 1950s with Mary Janes. She stares at me with her thin dress flapping in the wind.

I take her hand. We walk across the beach, squinting in the wind and pelting rain. I glance towards the lake and see another girl walking beside us. I'm not sure where she came from, but she must be my little friend's twin. I can't distinguish her features in the dark, but she wears an identical flimsy white dress—open in the back—over her thin frame, and she has the same shaved head.

I offer her my other hand.

The rain is immediate and heavy. The instant drench of a monsoon washes over us. By the time we reach the narrow footpath that leads to the village, the others have disappeared completely.

My flip-flops slip and grasp at the mud.

I stop, lost. We've reached the main path, but everything is black and blurry with rain. I can't see two feet in front of me. I don't want to do this. I want to retreat to that familiar cocoon: *I'm an American. They won't touch me.* But then, the Mai Mai are a militia that attacked the UN. Took twenty-five foreigners hostage. It is one thing to stumble without warning across unidentified guys with guns; it's another to do so knowing who they really are. And it's quite another to know they are here, in the dark, in the rain, after they've seen me wagging my oversized camera around.

I'm still clasping two small, wet hands.

The girls continue ushering me forward. I'm at their mercy.

I take slow, hesitant steps. I imagine men with guns must be just beyond the blur, waiting. The girls walk in front, patiently guiding me. All I can see is the dim glow of their white dresses and their eyes peering back at me. Wide-eyed African angels.

A lantern appears in the distance and floats across the path, then disappears.

We follow in its direction.

A wooden door opens and unseen hands shepherd us into a dim cement room. Maurice, Hortense, Kelly and a few villagers stand against the walls of a small storage room, weakly illuminated by a kerosene lantern that casts colossal shadows around the corners of the space. The children stand next to me as the rain pounds the corrugated metal roof and leaks down the walls, pooling on the floor, making it impossible to sit down or lean against anything. We stand still and listen to the rain.

One of the girls inches towards me and stands close. I put my hand on her shoulder. Someone offers her a shawl. She lifts it to share, draping it around my shoulders. Am I comforting her or she is comforting me? I put the shawl back around the two children, patting their heads dry. We are waiting for the rain to subside, unsure of what is next.

But the rain continues to pour, with no signs of letting up. It feels like we've lingered here at least a half-hour. We make a mad dash outside, then run to another door. We settle into a living room, furnished with a few wooden benches, in a half-constructed cement house with no inhabitants. We dry off and the girls sit beside me. I can see their faces better by the kerosene lantern. I dig out my gift bags and divide stickers between the girls and another child. We plant big blue daisies on each other's faces, ignoring the world.

Kelly and I take underexposed snapshots of the room with our digital cameras, musing that the blurry, out-of-focus quality will give them a high-art vibe.

The rain softens. An older woman comes to the door to collect the children. They go home for the night.

I would feel secure, cocooned away in this house, were it not for one problem. I need to pee. So does Kelly. The house has no toilet, so the nearest place to go is about a hundred yards away via the main path through the village.

I scramble through my bag and dig out the two flashlights Ted packed. One for Kelly, one for me. After all the resentment toward my Congo work and what it cost our relationship, he still meticulously packed my camera bag for every eventuality.

We step outside onto the empty mud path, still dripping from the rainstorm. My steps are quiet and self-conscious. I am trying not to think about the Mai Mai, or words like *exposure* or *bait*. It's like my dad used to tease me when I was a kid: Whatever you do, don't think about elephants. I try to steer my thoughts away from calculating our risk factor in a village where 90 percent of the women have been raped. I fixate on the flashlights. They seem like the most romantic gift ever, making up for all the skipped birthdays and Valentine's Day presents. I feel the way I did after my first 24-mile training run, when I descended the last hill and saw him, my one-man cheering squad. This is love.

We arrive at the outhouse on the remote edge of the village, backing onto fields and forest. I step inside. Its rough wooden slats go only as high as my shoulders. It is full of gaps and holes; mosquitoes are circling. Still, it feels like security. I turn off my flashlight and pee, imagining I'm invisible.

When we return, we meet a man sitting in front of our hut, wearing rain boots and a slicker, a machete and ax at his side. Two men, husbands of program participants, have been assigned guard duty for the night.

Back inside, someone delivers foam pads for us. Somewhere in the village, a family is having a far-less-comfortable night's sleep because we are here. The run supports twelve families in this small village. Is that why we're getting special treatment? Or is this simply a Congolese welcome they would extend to any stranger stranded for the night?

We decide to sleep. I stretch a small cloth over the old foam pad, drape my sweater over my shoulders, and position myself for sleep. No one mentions the fact we wouldn't be here right now if I hadn't taken so long in the village earlier today. Instead, we listen to a squeaking bat climb around somewhere up above. Hortense assures us the animal is not inside with us. Kelly and I both know she's lying, but we prefer her version of the story and decide to go with it.

Listening to the bat squeak, I wonder what the protocol is when someone fails to return from a day-outing in Congo. I picture our UNHCR hosts filing through the buffet, lounging in the living room, nursing beers. Would they notice? Would someone say, "Where are those girls?" Would they make phone calls? I imagine the call to headquarters in D.C., or worse, to my mom, igniting hysteria: They didn't make it home.

"At least it will be a good story for the grandkids," Kelly says from the opposite end of the room.

As though today's events weren't enough, I add in my best movie-trailer voice, "They clung to the tiny boat for their lives, as the gusty winds and waves threw them to and fro, bringing the young American girls ever-closer to the menacing rebel forces lurking beyond the peninsula's looming cliffs. . . ."

We bust up laughing. *Yeah. We're fine. This is no big deal.*

We spin embellished, melodramatic versions of the day's events, and Kelly and I laugh ourselves to sleep, or at least the pretense of sleep.

With my camera bag propped under my head like a pillow, I wait all night for the knock everyone in eastern Congo dreads: the knock of a militia outside your door.

In the middle of the night, I hear men's voices out front. I strain to hear. Someone is talking to the guards. *Who else would come calling at this hour? It must be the Mai Mai.* I brace myself, grasping the straps on my camera bag like the emergency strings on a parachute.

The voices disappear between intermittent rain and the foggy angst of an adrenaline-infused attempt at sleep. The knock never comes.

A soft, blue, early-morning light appears in the cracks under the door and around the windows. Hungry and edgy, I step out of the house. The guard still sits out front, awake. He's been up all night.

As I wipe my eyes, adjusting to the light, the Mai Mai I met yesterday, the one who wanted me to film him, saunters by with a Kalashnikov strapped to his back. He greets me with the casual air of a neighborhood shopkeeper. *"Muzungu, habari."*

White girl, good morning.

CHAPTER TWENTY-ONE

The Long Drive Home

AT DAYLIGHT, we don't waste any time. Fitina, along with a few others, escorts us to the boat without ceremony. We wave goodbye and I dash into the cabin in search of the rolls and peanuts I left on board last night. I'm hoping to quell my acid stomach and edgy bad mood induced by no sleep, no morning caffeine infusion, and no food. I find my plastic snack bag. Empty. The crew, who slept on board last night, devoured every bit of bread, every remaining peanut.

My empty stomach proves an asset. On the ride back across Lake Tanganyika, there are no raging storm clouds. It doesn't even rain, but the wind is strong, splashing water over us, and waves swell dangerously close to the lip of the boat. Agitated by all the talk of sinking boats, I cling to the railing as if we are about to sink, calling on every in-flight, bad-turbulence ritual I've developed over the years. Measuring my breaths, muttering prayers, I run through a series of complex rationalizations, closing my eyes to imagine how much worse I would feel if I was being tossed around like this on an airplane. It's not the best fear-control strategy since it leads me to recall the rationalization I always use on planes: It may feel scary in the air, but I am much more likely to die in a car crash or on a sinking boat.

Rescued! I think as we approach the port and I spot a UN vehicle waiting for us. Haggard, I climb into the SUV, and I've never before felt so soothed by that new car smell.

At the UN guesthouse, I walk down the hallway with wet hair, my feet bare on the smooth cement. I'm wearing clean clothes after my head-to-toe scrub down, but I'm still reeling from the adrenaline hangover.

I hear Kelly's voice drifting from her room, muffled laughter. Her cell phone is still in range, so she's called her husband to tell him about our night. The door to her room opens, she walks out into the living room, and catches me tuning in. I must wear something like a craving expression because she motions to her phone, offering for me to use it next.

When she gets off the line, she offers again. "You're welcome to borrow my phone if you want to call. . . ."

Call who?

If you feel like taking stock of your life, ask yourself this basic question: If you were stranded in a thunderstorm for the night, on a remote African peninsula, with a militia, and just made it home safely, who would you call? Not to double-check the minutia in your life insurance policy, but just to say hi? Mom is not a possibility, given the inevitable public hysterics that would follow. Perhaps pulled by the ambiguity that stretches months or years past the last time you share a bed or say "I love you," I think of Ted. I think of his hand on the back of my neck and I consider calling him. But I'm certain his tone will tell me I shouldn't have, and that isn't something I can deal with today.

Nonchalance is the easiest response. I play it off like I've officially earned my bad-ass credentials, like I'm check-in-with-no-one independent. "I'll just wait until I get back to Bukavu."

I return to my little blue and white room with its wooden wardrobe, pull the mosquito net around me, and lie down, still spinning from last night and fruitlessly attempting to sleep.

ASENDE, A SISTER I met the other day, has been on my mind since our meeting, when she spoke of surviving a massacre. Her story involves a higher body count than any other I've heard firsthand. We track down her mud hut in a quiet neighborhood and wait for her to return from work in the fields. She approaches; her austere eyes and modest manner give her a simple, nunlike presence. She carries a straw basket filled with rusty farming tools. Surprised to find us waiting on her doorstep, she invites us into her spotless mud row-home. It's furnished with a couple of wooden benches, a calendar on the wall, a pile of plastic tubs and pots in the corner, and a curtain marking the passage to another room.

I begin the conversation by asking about the slaughter.

"Around five hundred of us escaped from the fighting and hid in the bush," she begins. "The FDD militia found us and began killing people. They shot me three times before I fell down. They went around killing wounded persons with knives and taking everything they found on the dead bodies. I was wounded, but they couldn't tell I was alive. Finally, they left. When I opened my eyes, I saw a person wearing white, who secured me. It was then that I realized I was alone among the corpses."

"What was your life like before the war?" I ask.

"My husband abandoned me for other wives, so I was alone to care for my children," she says. "During the war, we escaped to a place where I met my mother, who had three children left in her charge by my younger sister, who was a prostitute."

Up until now she has maintained a plain, direct affect. While Maurice translates what she says next, Asende wipes her eyes with her skirt. She is crying. What could be worse than the massacre she just described?

"My mother became ill and went to Bukavu to be treated. She died."

I'm surprised. She is reduced to tears not because her husband left, not because she was shot or buried alive among hundreds of bodies. Her mother's death, from illness, makes her cry. Why? It raises such a basic question about the human breaking point. Studying her, I wonder if losing her mom marked the end of all support, beyond which she was utterly alone.

"So I took care of those three children."

"What is it like for you raising orphans in addition to your own children?" I ask.

"I consider those children as my own," she says matter-of-factly.

"What do you hope for in the future?"

"It is very difficult to have any thought about the future. I am living, but I have a bad life. About the future, I don't have any hope."

No party spin or testimony here.

Trying to nudge her towards the positive, I ask, "What gives you happiness in your life?"

"When I am angry or sad, I feel ill. So I try to consider life normal."

We are all silent for a moment. I sit here and look at my new friend. There is something this woman has—a simple open manner, a quiet dignity—that I have yet to find for myself.

"I wish you could see what I see when I look at you," I say. "I see one of the most beautiful souls I've ever met."

Her face lights up with a toothy smile.

THE NEXT MORNING, Kelly and I watch Mai Mai cut trees for firewood. They hack down branches and drag them along the dusty Baraka back road where we are stalled, waiting, passing the time as many do. We complain. Hortense is running late again. We were both packed and ready to go at eight o'clock sharp, as instructed. Hortense has left us in the car for close to an hour while she takes care of one last piece of business before we hit the road on the eight-hour return trip to Bukavu. Kelly leaves tomorrow and she's stressed about getting ready for an early boat to Goma, where she will catch a flight back to Kinshasa.

Hortense finally emerges. Smiling as always, she announces her triumph. "A participant's baby is sick. We have secured treatment!"

I sink with embarrassment at the ugly *muzungu* routine. While we've been sitting in the car griping, Hortense was saving a baby's life.

I stop complaining.

Kelly mutters, "Just hope we make it." Hortense doesn't catch it, or at least pretends she doesn't.

We hit the road, cruising up the long, flat stretch of road running next to Lake Tanganyika, and I'm cramped in the back of the SUV between Hortense and Maurice. As always, they are cheery.

The car slows and stops on a muddy patch. A UN jeep is tipped sideways, entrenched in road mud, blocking traffic. The road is quickly backing up with vehicles from every imaginable NGO operating in Congo: War Child, UNHCR, Caritas, The Red Cross, Save the Children, and more. Hortense laughs. "Forget Run for Congo Women! You need to Run for Congo Roads!"

We are stalled for a long time as crowds of men try to rig the car to a truck while dodging the deep pools that fill the road. Kelly is wound up. If she misses the border, she misses the boat, and if she misses the boat, she misses the plane . . . and no one wants to be stuck in Congo. I get that. Anyone would be tense about missing the boat. I want to make it back quickly too. It's just that we are tagging along on Hortense's business trip. She's not getting paid extra to have us along. She owes us what, exactly? I shrug off Kelly's complaints.

Finally the road clears. We continue on to Uvira, where Hortense rushes off to take care of more business. Meanwhile, we grab a lunch of french fries and Coke at a dive with plastic tables, laminated tablecloths, and a caged monkey for entertainment. Kelly continues griping about how Hortense is wasting time. I try to comfort her with a worst-case-scenario analysis. "Even if we get back late, even if the border does close and we were stuck in Rwanda for the night, you'll still make your boat in the morning."

Kelly protests. "I don't know what time the seamstress's shop closes. I need to pick up my dress."

Is that what the grumbling is about? Welcome to my limit, Miss Kumbaya. I lean across the plastic table and snap, "A dress? We're late because Hortense was saving a child's life."

Kelly's face turns pulsing, patchy red (and mine might be looking that way too). "I don't understand how you're all of a sudden so high and mighty," she says. "You've been complaining too."

She's right. But people change. I had my epiphany *hours* ago.

I'm sure an international border is open twenty-four hours and to prove my point, I turn to Maurice and ask, "Does the border ever close?"

Maurice stares at the tablecloth. He doesn't seem to appreciate being dragged into the middle of a *muzungu* girl-fight. He answers, "Six o'clock sharp."

Whoops. I'm wrong and embarrassed for the unfair lashing. It's 2:15 PM and we are four hours from the border. If we gun it, there is a slight chance we could make it. We abandon our lunch, find Hortense, and hit the road.

Kelly and I don't say much for the rest of the ride.

CHAPTER TWENTY-TWO

Orchid Safari Club

DESPITE THE NAME "Orchid Safari Club," I've never seen anyone here actually wearing safari gear. So someone must have sent out the wrong dress code memo to a group that has shown up on the terrace decked out in deep-bush khakis. I noticed them peripherally last night at dinner, when I was dropped off here just after six o'clock, having narrowly made it over the border before closing time. I saw them, but at the time I was backed into an extended debate with a white man who was raised in an African colony and is now a maintenance guy for the Red Cross. He took a little too much pleasure in lecturing about women like me who clearly know nothing about the conflict, yet have the gall to fundraise and mobilize.

Tonight I'm exhausted and want to be alone. I arrive on the terrace in the early evening, before the hordes descend, and stake out my spot in the far corner. It's buzzing with mosquitoes, but there is a soft breeze off the lake. I order chips and tea, the watered-down kind that tastes like it's been run through a hotel room coffeemaker. I plug in my earphones and power up my laptop, as much in an effort to avoid tiresome conversation like last night's as to appease my roaming desire to tell someone about my run-in with the Mai Mai, even if that someone is only a blank Word document.

But apparently I'm going to have a new lounge companion, as one of the would-be Dian Fosseys interrupts me and asks permission to take over a neighboring lounge chair. It's one of those moments when life knocks on your door in the form of an annoying stranger and you just want to say, "Will you please go away? Can't you see I'm trying to brood in loneliness here?"

In a disengaged fashion, I remove my earphones. "I'm sorry, what?"

"Mind if I join you?"

I don't answer, but I motion approvingly to the seat, plug my earphones back in, and crank the volume, thinking, *As long as you don't talk.*

The terrace fills quickly with NGO people just off work. The next cluster of chairs is packed beyond capacity. What a collection of people lands here on the shores of Lake Kivu! There must be a common thread connecting us, an emotional through-line explaining how we would all find this, of all places on Earth, the best place to spend our time and money.

A man with choppy, cropped silver hair walks across the terrace. He might be in his early fifties, perhaps a creative professional; clearly he's one of the safari-goers given his ill-informed outfit. But he carries himself with the smooth stride of the ultraconfident. The head-to-toe khaki can't contain his movie star cool. His is not the ho-hum handsome of Ken-doll stock models. His bold features give him a larger-than-life aura. Do I recognize him? There's something familiar about him.

He stops to socialize with the aid workers already filling up the chairs nearby. I can't say why he catches my eye every time I scan the terrace. Or I catch mine catching his, leading to an exchange of glances that's a little too obvious for comfort. He is not my type. I've maintained a longtime preference for quirky, pensive, super-smart artists, so the regal, uberhandsome persona is like steak and eggs to a vegan. Not my thing. I dive back into my notes, trying to end this most-inappropriate man-interest. It's not on my Congo agenda.

The safari crew takes over the remaining chairs surrounding me, so I know he's not long behind. Within a few minutes, he joins his group in what I still choose to think of as my seating area. I try to concentrate on my notes, but can't thanks to Mr. Wonderful's companion, a wild-haired, wild-eyed, bandanna-wearing fellow who seems to me like a modern incarnation of Henry Morton Stanley, the kind of bloodthirsty disaster tourist you might expect to land on the shores of Lake Kivu. He loudly drones on with manufactured sophistication, critiquing the cheap knock-off African masks sold at Orchid's front gate as though he's discussing the finest of wines. I give up. Abandoning my attempt to write, I pull out my earphones and interject myself into their conversation. "What brings you all to Congo?"

His companions fill in the blanks. They are a conservation group that's just spent the day in Kahuzi Biega Park. Though decked out in trekking gear and prepared for hours of off-trail bushwhacking in search of great apes, they stumbled across a gorilla after a ten-minute stroll. As I'm introduced to D, he makes it clear he is only tagging along on this group's trip; he is not part of their organization. He hands me his card: founder and CEO of an environmental nonprofit. His voice, with indistinguishable accent, seems so familiar. I'm convinced I know him. I must have heard him speak. Maybe in a video podcast from one of those global-ideas forums? He asks me to join them for dinner.

"That would be lovely," I respond.

"Yes, that would be lovely," he says.

Uh-oh.

We take a seat. D leans over at every opportunity, offering me his tomatoes and bread as we try to talk over Modern Stanley, who sits between us. Conversation turns to the subject of risk. D points to me as an example. "You see, Lisa, your being here in Congo is a major risk, but you must get something out of it. Something bigger than your potential regret for staying at home."

D gets a call and excuses himself for a moment. Modern Stanley leans over to me, unable to conceal his pride as he informs me how truly Big, Important, and Rich their traveling companion is. He lists D's credentials: his stint teaching in the Ivy League, his role as founder and CEO of a multinational software corporation that serves half of the world's banks, the number of zeros in his bank account. Mr. Stanley's boasting makes me cringe with embarrassment—he is grasping for status by osmosis—but I am even more pained for D. Though we have never exchanged a private word, as D returns to his seat and briefly looks at me, his bulletproof persona seems transparent. I know what people say about him when he leaves the room. When I look into his eyes, the weight of isolation seems clearer to me than their color.

He tells me about befriending malnourished kids in a village today. They were hungry, so he bought them eggs. Then more kids wanted eggs, so he bought eggs for them too. Then everyone wanted eggs. He bought every last egg the sellers had and before you know it, kids were laughing and eggs were flying, falling on the ground and cracking. Beautiful egg chaos. Here's a guy who would seem more in his element skiing in Vail or sailing the Mediterranean, but he's in Congo buying eggs for hungry kids. I think of his Egg Kids to my Peanut Girl, and I can't help but smile and remark, "That's the kind of thing I would do."

Still, I do what any rational woman would do upon meeting an intriguing man in an exotic locale; I excuse myself and go back to my room. Sitting on the edge of my bed, I hold the phone in my hand. I contemplate a call to Ted to tell him about my night with the Mai Mai. I wonder if it is worth the leap.

I dial.

Long calls from the Congo to the United States would eat up all my phone card credits in no time, but they have special rates for calls from the States to the Congo. So if I want to talk to someone back home, I always ask them to call me back. Ted picks up, so I say, "Hey, can you call me back?"

I'm met with silence. Finally, with a distance far greater than any crackling phone line, Ted says flatly, "I'm working."

All I can eke out is, "Oh."

We are quiet for a long time.

In his English way, he cuts it off. "I need to get on and do."

THE NEXT DAY, I join D's group for dinner again as they go out on the town for their last night in Congo. We drive across Bukavu to a restaurant that sits above the lake, sprawling and empty. In the old days this place must have been grand and happenin', complete with swimming pool, but tonight it is obvious those days are long past. We are the only group in the restaurant all night. The power goes out, leaving the worn room to be lit with dim, buzzing florescent lights powered by a generator; we wait two hours for curried mush. In the meantime, D gives a talk to the group, explaining his vision for future projects in Congo. As he returns to the seat next to me, he quips, "Now you know the truth. I'm just a glorified used-car salesman."

We talk with ease. He mentions he's heading to Zanzibar after they leave Congo tomorrow. With a vague recollection of flipping through Africa guidebooks many months ago, I say, "I meant to do something like that when I was here."

"Why don't you join me?"

Run away to Zanzibar with a man I just met in Congo? I laugh.

Modern Stanley steers conversation towards the Mai Mai, making boisterous jokes about their strange rituals, from wearing sink-plug necklaces to raping farm animals. Tonight, even lighthearted mention of the Mai Mai makes me uptight. I squirm, then interrupt him, as if firing a warning shot. "I just had a campout with the Mai Mai."

The table quiets down, perhaps due to my tense, shut-the-f———-up delivery. Almost uncontrollably, I blurt out the whole story of my night on the peninsula. An uncomfortable silence settles over the table. D leans over the table, looks me in the eyes and says, "You're very brave."

We sit next to each other on the ride home, cramped in the back of the SUV as it bounces and shifts along Bukavu's crumbling streets, around bends and past hills dotted with kerosene lanterns glowing on top of streetsellers' wooden crates.

With surprising insecurity, D asks, "Did you have a good time tonight?"

"Yes."

"Really? You're sure?" His hand creeps over and touches my arm, then retreats.

"I had a great time."

For the rest of the ride back to Orchid, he holds my hand.

I'm staying in a cottage on the far edge of the Orchid compound now and my nightly walk back to my room is creepy. So when D offers to walk with me, I don't hesitate to accept. His company is a comfort on the dark, lonely trek. We barely speak as we pass the guestrooms with armed men lurking out front, the gate marked PRIVATE: NO ENTRY, the Last Belgian's private porch, the ax-wielding security guy, guard dogs, and a hanging orchid garden. We arrive at my cottage, the last on the edge of the compound. The only barrier from the outside world is a rotting bamboo fence, with its own little terrace perched on a cliff above Lake Kivu. He kisses me.

The whole walk across the compound, I was thinking, *Whatever the question, the answer is yes.* So imagine my surprise when I hear myself telling him, "I need to say goodnight."

He launches a fresh campaign for me to join him in Zanzibar, but I decline.

A dog's rabid growl comes from behind the cottage. We scramble inside my room.

"It's dangerous for you to be here," I say. "I like you more than any guy I've met in a long time." I might be trying to convince myself as much as him as I offer reasons why he can't stay. "I'm just not a casual-hookup kind of girl."

"I didn't think you were."

Good answer.

I add, "It's just that I don't know you very well."

"In fact, you don't know me at all," he says. "You've only heard me give a speech."

We look at each other for a moment, an unspoken exchange. What are the odds, the momentary chances in life? He doesn't push; he politely asks to trade numbers and leaves. I go to bed churning. *Did I really just dismiss him? Am I out of my mind?*

I don't see him again in Congo.

CHAPTER TWENTY-THREE

Mama Congo

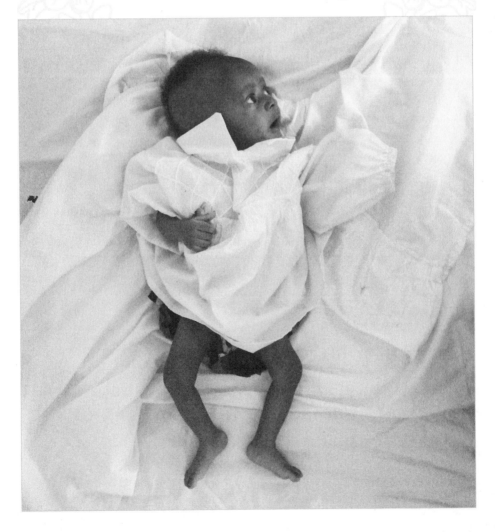

GENEROSE'S LANDLADY MEANT every word of her threats. She has confiscated all of Generose's things and thrown the children out. They are scattered god-knows-where. With friends? Relatives? Generose doesn't know. She is distraught and dazed from the post-op medication when we briefly visit Panzi. My only comfort is a little secret. My mom has put out the word back home and we've raised US$1,500 to buy her a house. We say goodbye and head out to house-hunt.

Real estate shopping in Congo proves to be the strangest business experience I've ever had.

We start with the basics: Location, location, location. Maurice and I have brainstormed and narrowed our search down to the Panzi neighborhood, next to the Women for Women ceramics studio. Houses here should be in our price range, and Generose will already have welcoming friends and neighbors since several from her women's group live nearby. It's close to the hospital and, best of all, it is right next to a UN compound. As we get out of the car, I notice sandbag watchtowers on the periphery of the UN property, which overlooks a field and the neighborhood—you can't beat twenty-four-hour security. Maurice asks around about houses for sale. After a few minutes we have a lead: a house for US$1,200.

We follow a narrow path away from the road. I'm already sure this place isn't going to work—Generose can't navigate the path on crutches, especially the footbridge made of tree branches and tire rubber. But we will at least look for the sake of comparison shopping.

The little house with blue shutters sits in a tidy enclave of mud huts surrounded with gardens. We greet the owner, a woman about my age who's surrounded by a flock of young children who are just different enough in size to make me imagine this Mama has been nonstop pregnant for the past ten years. Maurice says, "They are selling because they do not have the means to survive."

We duck inside and tour the dark, smoky cottage. In the living room, wood-framed couches draped with crocheted orange doilies, photo displays, and a tattered buffet give the place a make-do dignity that would make any Midwestern homemaker proud. The kitchen is filled with smoky pots and piles of ash. The bedrooms are simple.

When I peek my head in the bedroom door, I barely notice a bundle of rags resting on the bed and a skinny, pale baby swaddled in them. I move to get a closer look at him. He's awake and quiet. Frail. But I know the look in his eyes, the way he's floating in and out; it's the familiar half-light of someone who is dying.

I feel the pull back to business, back to the hallway to talk with Mama about the house, to continue with the task of the day. It's sad, but it's not my problem. I'm busy enough today.

I look back at the baby.

It's like seeing a dog panting, sick and desperate, inside a sweltering car with the windows closed tight. You can look in at him and think, Well, it's none of my business . . . the owner will probably be back in a minute.

He's dying.

You can't save every baby in Africa.

Yeah, well, I'm not in the room with every baby in Africa. I'm in the room with this baby.

I have plans today.

I picture the identical scene playing out in suburban Minneapolis or Salt Lake City or San Diego, with a family going about their daily business unfazed while a baby is dying in the back bedroom. Unacceptable. Emergency.

But this is not the suburbs. It's Africa. It's the way things are, right?

I have plans.

I walk into the hallway and ask Mama, "Are you worried about the baby?"

"No, it's only the problem of illness."

"What did the doctor say about the baby being so small?"

"The doctor didn't say anything."

"That's a surprise," I say. "Is it normal for Congolese babies to be that small?"

Maurice jumps in. "It is not normal."

We move into the living room. His name is Bonjour. I rest him in my lap. He sweats, wearing a little polar fleece tracksuit. "Don't you think he's hot?" I ask Mama. Without waiting for permission, I peel off his pants, then his sweatshirt. It gets stuck on his head.

I say, "You can tell I'm not a mother."

Mama helps me pull it off. She looks stressed that I've taken such a keen interest in her son. I stare at his delicate little body, his bony legs, his pale little ribs poking out. He starts to cry. I've never heard a child's voice sound like this before. Not the pushy, insistent cry for a mother's attention, but slow. Thin. Desperate.

"Please don't cry," I say. Uh-oh. I feel it coming on. He pees. I grasp for something to absorb it, a towel a cloth, a doily, anything. "Oh, man! Right where it counts, too!"

"A real Mama!" Maurice bursts out laughing, "Like you are christened! You are really Mama Congo!"

I sit for a moment, shaking my head. *Anyway. . . .*

His mama takes him. She cradles his naked body while he nurses.

I'm tense, but I say, "I would like to take the baby to see a different doctor. The baby needs help. The baby needs food. The baby needs medical treatment. He's not normal. He needs to be rehydrated. The baby shouldn't be this small."

"Our doctor said the illness can't be treated at the hospital," she argues. "It needs local medicine."

"He's severely malnourished," I insist. "I would like to take you and the baby to Panzi Hospital."

"I took the baby to the hospital and the doctor told me to take him to traditional doctors," Mama says. "Since I took him, the situation is getting better and better."

To be clear, I get how totally, radically inappropriate it is for me to march into this woman's home and tell her how to take care of her children. I'm no doctor. I don't know this family. I remember my college seminar debates on the feminist empowerment model. It's just that I don't care about these issues right now. The baby is dying.

"How many children do you have?"

"Eight children."

"How many have died?"

"None."

She's annoyed. But she dresses him anyway, avoiding my eyes as she wraps him in a little white dress, then a ruffly white curtain.

On the way out I notice her next-youngest, a little girl with thin blonde hair, a snotty nose, heavy bags under eyes, and a balloon belly. As long as I'm shamelessly meddling in this woman's business, I ask, "Is this baby sick too? Does she need to see a doctor?"

"The malnutrition is due to the little difference in age between the two," Maurice surmises. True enough, with this many babies and Mama's already slender frame, milk is likely scarce.

Mama doesn't say a word, but wipes little Nina's face clean, undresses and washes her, and rubs oil all over her body, trying to give her child a healthy glow. She grabs a cotton party dress with faded yellow flowers and dresses the little girl. Nina is not amused.

Nina shoots me the death stare on the ride to Panzi. She looks like she hasn't cracked a smile her whole little life. I'm still waiting for the pee to dry—it covers my whole lap. At least I'm in all black today.

The nurse at the center for malnourished children is not impressed. They examine the kids, slinging them around—much to Nina and Bonjour's horror—and stretching them out on a board to measure their height while they scream and cry. Mama strips off Bonjour's angel outfit and the medical staff wants to put him in a hanging sack to weigh him. I hand him over, feeling jumpy. "Support his neck. Watch his neck. Gentle!" He's swallowed by the bag. It covers his face, while half his hip hangs out, as they drop him on the scale like a hunk of meat.

They hand him back to me. I rock him as he cries. He pees for a second time. I am truly, deeply soaked in malnourished-baby pee. Totally worth it.

"For this one, it is no problem to be treated," The nurse says, motioning to the girl. She wags her pen at Bonjour, "But for this one, because he was ill he became this way. It is only if the mother takes care of him, feeding him."

I'm dumbfounded. "They're not going to treat this child?"

"The problem is to be well fed."

"Yeah, I get that," I say. "That's why we came to the *center for feeding malnourished children*. How do we solve that problem?"

"The mother can find maybe milk from the breast."

I'm shocked. "So they can't do anything for this baby? 'Cause the baby's really small?"

He's really screaming too.

"Being small is the fact of illness," she says again. "The baby has been treated. We have nothing to do for the baby. If the baby becomes ill, we will treat him. But the baby is normal."

See? The baby's fine. Next time, mind your own business.

It's all I can do to not lunge across the table and strangle this nurse. "This is not normal."

The nurse gives me a "piss-off" shrug and moves on.

My phone buzzes; it's a text from Dr. Roger, who hosted our earlier visit to Panzi and today ushered us to the feed center between surgeries. "It's a good thing you do. I think you saved that baby's life. If you have any problem. . . ."

Dr. Roger meets us following a Cesarean. We breeze past a long line in the corridor into a private examination room. Dr. Roger introduces us to a woman pediatrician. She unwraps Bonjour from the christening gown and examines him as fat tears fall down his face. When she's finished, I re-dress him in his gauzy white outfit and ask, "What's wrong?"

"Complications from cutting something here," she says, pointing to his throat.

"His tonsils?" I ask.

"It's a traditional treatment for a cold," she says. "The action provoked a chest infection."

"It's serious?"

"The baby will die without treatment," she tells us. "Severe malnutrition, an infection in the chest. He will need to stay here."

Mama is exasperated. Maurice translates, "She wonders what will be the life of the other children at home if she must stay here."

I ask, "You still live with your husband, right?"

"Yes."

"Can he help?"

The look on her face says "no chance." She shakes her head. "My husband is jobless. I am the one who is working."

"Maybe the husband can stay here with the baby?" I ask. "She can stay at home."

She looks at me blankly, as though I'm speaking the absurd.

"It is very difficult," Maurice says.

"It is just not done, okay," I say. "She understands if she doesn't stay here, the baby will die."

Now I am staring at the real Mama Congo, facing yet another Sophie's Choice. I watch her make the calculation: *If I let this one go, the other seven will live.*

Dr. Roger adds, "He's very fragile, Lisa. The level of treatment he needs . . ."

"How long does he need to stay?" I ask.

"Seven days of treatment." Dr. Roger responds.

"Do you have friends or neighbors who can help?" I ask Mama.

"They can take care of the babies. But no one will accept to feed them."

"We'll buy the food," I tell her. "What do you need? Rice? Beans?"

She gives us the list: Beans, rice, fu-fu, salt, onion, lamp oil, vegetables.

Dr. Roger says something to Mama two or three times, something about *aksanti* (Swahili for thank you).

She smiles and quietly says, *"Merci."*

WE DASH ACROSS TOWN to the local market, where we pick up twenty-five-pound bags of beans and rice; piles of cauliflower, onions, potatoes; flats of eggs; bananas; and maize fu-fu ("the right kind for ones who suffer from malnutrition"). Neighbors help us carry the food back to Bonjour's home. I've tried to buy enough so that I can bribe the neighbor women to watch the children in exchange for food.

While we're in the neighborhood, we cram in some quick house shopping. Now all the locals are happy to show us their houses. They quote us prices US$2,000 and up, despite our repeated attempts to clarify that US$1,500 is the budget. There is no more money.

Finally, we look at land instead. We find a modest plot, about the size of a plot in Portland, for US$600. We ask the local real estate mogul to estimate the costs of constructing a simple wooden house with a cement floor, finished stone-stuffed walls, and a tin roof—built quickly. We ask him to show us a house he can build for US$900. He says it can be done in ten days.

It looks like it's doable.

I turn to one of the locals and ask, "Do you think it's a good deal?"

"Ask this guy to think about all of the material, write it down, and bring it in the morning," the local advises.

We do.

"The woman will be in the hospital for two months," I emphasize. "It needs to happen quickly, but it is more important that it happen exactly as we've talked about and that we stick to the price. And that Generose has the legal document to the property—that it is hers. We can't have anyone come back and say, 'Oh. Sorry. It's going to cost you more.'"

"Stone on the ground," the developer says.

"No—cement! She's on crutches." I laugh and say, "People who deal with real estate in the United States and the Congo are the same."

Sure enough, when we meet him in the morning, he brings a long, itemized list, with the new "after calculation price" of US$2,300.

"Ah. Then we have no deal."

"The problem is they saw only a *muzungu*," Maurice says.

Maurice offers to manage the construction, in cooperation with Generose's brother, for the stated budget.

BACK AT PANZI, Bonjour rests in his white dress on the hospital bed in the middle of the children's ward, while Nina shovels down a banana. We've just paid the US$50 for his one-week stay. I lean over him and say, "You're in a better mood. Already a little better." He cracks a smile. A smile!

As we leave, I ask Mama, "Do you have everything you need?"

She replies, "I need sugar so I can make tea."

I laugh it off, uncomfortably. "Maybe tomorrow."

CHAPTER TWENTY-FOUR

El Presidente

I'M IN A PACKED SUV, cruising along a rural road, Congo landscape flying by, sandwiched between a Congolese friend and a guy by the name of René. The front seat is occupied by another carsick friend, who needs to look out the front window. It doesn't matter where we are or where we are going. Why René is along for the ride, and who invited him, isn't the point. Sometimes questions of safety far outweigh the desire to spill all the details.

René speaks with a high-pitched voice that sounds like a woman's, but his baseball cap and sweater vest say "suburban dad." The whole ride, he's been touting his feminist credentials and long history working for a variety of international NGOs. He's angling for a job. "You should hire me to manage Run for Congo Women in Congo!"

I smile politely, but my mind is elsewhere. I'm unhappy with my friend and the "translation" issue at the meeting we've just come from, which involved talking with rape survivors.

As one woman spoke, I caught the words *Mai Mai*. I was surprised she was being so direct about a Congolese attacker.

My Congolese friend translated, "She says they violated her."

"Who?"

My friend added, "She said *Interahamwe.*"

"What did she say about the Mai Mai?"

My friend responded vaguely, "She did not say anything about Mai Mai."

What? I may know fewer than twenty Swahili phrases, but *Mai Mai* is one of them. "Yes, she did," I say. "Was it the Mai Mai who raped her?"

My friend was quiet.

I pushed harder. "Can you please ask her."

My friend asked again, then acquiesced. "Yes, she was raped by Mai Mai."

Now, fried after an exhausting trip on this long, bumpy road, I'm thinking about the meeting when I spot soldiers on the side of the road. As is now the routine, I ask, "Congolese Army or Mai Mai?"

It's quiet for a minute. Then my friend says, "I don't know."

They all stare forward, eyes on the road. "If you want to know about the Mai Mai, ask the man sitting next to you. He is the President of the Mai Mai for South Kivu."

There's no time to let it land, to shoot my friend a disapproving, "What the hell are you thinking?" look or to calculate the ramifications of what this might mean.

I feel the fear slip around inside me as I try to convince myself this is a great opportunity. The undeniable fact has settled into my stomach: In spite of all the paranoia floating around Congo, this guy really is dangerous. I need to tread lightly.

I flash a thumbs-up smile and say, "I'd love to talk with you more about the Mai Mai!"

As it slips out of my mouth, I think of the woman I just met, so frank about her Mai Mai attackers. *El Presidente* was standing right behind me when she said it. Then I pushed. Then I emphasized the Mai Mai raped her. Announced it. As if there is such a thing as "safe space" in Congo. As if after a few weeks here, I would know exactly how it works, fully grasp Congo's version of right and wrong, what needs to be said and what is better left alone.

I've only consumed rolls and Fanta so far today, so I'm wired on a sugar high and crashing fast. I raise my hand off my lap, trying to see if I'm shaking. It's impossible to tell on these roads. I try to ignore the murky, polluted feeling that comes when being deceitful, closing my eyes. The bouncing and bumping and pothole jumping feels like the worst airplane turbulence.

My friend graciously explains, above all else, that René is organized. He was brought on to help the Mai Mai develop into a proper organization, to raise their profile and their efficiency. To be their public relations machine. I work overtime to get him talking, forcing my tone of voice to keep it upbeat, to prove I'm on his side.

Just be Socratic.

René explains, "I am a Congolese patriot. I love my country. I love my forefathers' land. I am ready to say 'No!' to any kind of aggression against my country. Our army showed it was weak; some noticed bribery among political authorities. Soldiers were running away instead of waiting for the opponents. People gathered to discuss the weakness of our army. It was unable to face the war. I joined the other people who were ready to have some kind of manifestation of resistance."

"When was that?"

"The 1996 war."

"So you've been involved for eleven years? From the very beginning?"

He smiles boldly, hands cupped around his knee; he rocks back and forth, delighted but feigning modesty, like a housewife who has just been complimented on her cookies. "Ah, yes."

"It's no wonder to me that with your skill set, if you've been involved that long, you play a leadership role in the upper levels."

"I was appointed president of all of South Kivu province of the Mai Mai movement. I was appointed by my fellow Mai Mai to be a candidate for national elections. But they needed only five and there were three hundred of us running. It wasn't successful. I lost the election. "

"That's elections," I say, laughing anxiously, trying to get him to relax and speak freely.

"My work was, of course, focused on the political movement," he continues. "As the Mai Mai is a movement of action, it needed to be structured politically, ideologically. As they knew they would kill whoever opposed them, they needed an ideology about who to kill, because they must kill whoever along the way."

"So you developed an ideology of when it is appropriate to kill."

"I read different documents on how to behave in a time of war, books regarding human rights, such books as *The Battle of Solferino*. In the book they figured the soldier's attitude towards civilians and other opponents during the war."

"What guidelines did you develop?"

"In the books there are different attitudes to take, according to the circumstances in which we find ourselves. You can be, for example, with a civilian who has betrayed. These civilians . . . You see, it is during the war, there is not even any legal judgment, but you have proof he has shown where your positions are . . . These civilians can be killed, in order to demand that other civilians do not betray. So you understand? There are cases like that. What we have for an ideology is: We only kill the enemy. You do not need to arrest him because you don't have prisons or jails. So you must kill the enemy and protect the local population as much as possible. That's it."

"What about behavior typical to all militias—raping, looting—"

"The Mai Mai don't have to steal because they are local defenders. The local population gives soldiers what they need as support. Rape is a foreign practice. A foreign behavior the Congolese did not know before."

My carsick friend leans back from the front seat, clearly annoyed and determined to call him out. "What about child soldiers?"

I lean forward, subtly squeeze Carsick's arm and whisper, "Don't go there. It's a safety issue."

René leans towards the front passenger seat. "There is no need to abduct children. They volunteer. They want to be part of our fight."

We are all quiet for a moment. I think of the BVES boys I interviewed, who spoke openly about being abducted, and stealing, and raping any female they came across.

"I cannot say the Mai Mai are perfect, that they are like saints," René says. "Sometimes they switch to environments which are not their own. They feel hungry and go to farms to loot crops. But Mai Mai is a traditional movement; it has *hints* to follow. They are not to get drunk, smoke, rape, or do something bad because according to the elders, if they misbehave they will be killed on the front."

"Oh right!" I say. "There are some elements of superstition . . ." The second the word escapes my mouth, I want to grab it midair and stuff it back in. I quickly correct myself—"Beliefs, rather"— hoping to catch it before translation. It's too late. It's translated as superstition.

He smiles, strained, and rubs his eyes, "Madame. They are not 'beliefs' or 'superstitions.' They are *truth*."

I catch something about 'aspirin' and 'malaria' in his French. His wide-open, direct stare tells me I've stepped on his Mai Mai toes. I'm not even waiting for a translation as he speaks. I'm nodding and mumbling, *Yes . . . Right . . . Sure . . .* as he describes herbal mixtures used to treat malaria and fever or to make soldiers bulletproof. "A Mai Mai believes that when he washes himself with that herbal water prepared by midwives, and does no evil like rape or steal, no bullet can catch him."

Anxious to put him at ease, to get back on the same side, I enthusiastically offer, "It's like traditional medicine. There's so much interest in traditional medicine back in the States."

He rubs his chin. His voice grows strident. "It is exactly like traditional medicine. They had no medicine. They were dirty. They could easily catch diseases. They needed to use herbs, that which you call 'superstition' or 'beliefs.' They had to do it to protect themselves."

I scramble, trying to figure my way out of this apparently massive insult.

He adds, "What you call 'belief' is like faith. What you accept can manifest itself."

"*Faith*. That's the best word for it," I agree.

"Faith," he chuckles.

"Great. Now we're speaking the same language."

"A true Mai Mai respects the ideology of the movement, the regulations, the hints, 100 percent. He cannot die. A false Mai Mai is one who sinned against the hints. Such a person can be injured. The one who is caught by a bullet cannot be a true Mai Mai. He must have done something—raping, looting, even made sex with his wife before battle; they cannot make sex. It is as if he has dirtied himself. He is excluded from the ranks of the true Mai Mai. It is just like true Christians and false Christians."

"What is it the Mai Mai want?"

He spends ten minutes giving variations of the same answers, all beginning, "Mai Mai is a movement of resistance by local people . . ."

"Resistance to what? To whom?"

"Invaders."

"Why are invaders so interested in Congo?"

"Listen, we have a saying. If you have a pretty lady in your compound, the men will circle around for the treasure. The natural resources of Congo attract outsiders."

"When you talk about 'outside groups' or 'invaders,' are you talking about outside armed groups or people of other ethnic groups, like Banyamulenge Congolese Tutsis?" I ask.

"The Banyamulenge have been accepted by the structure, by the constitution," he answers. "They have been given nationality. But they cooperate with invaders: Rwanda, Burundi, Uganda. They are bridges for invaders' aggression on Congo. They are assimilated to their brothers. They are a path for invaders. We find them dangerous."

"So what is your take on the brassage process?"

"The Mai Mai are not convinced, so we've sent a group to listen to the ideology they are being given. They are the ears. But there is another group waiting at the backside, who will guard people, who will join resistance against a given attack."

My grandmother, a minister's wife, had a saying: Nothing is so tiresome as being insincere. And so it is. I'm exhausted, shaky, too freaked out to challenge a word. I feel like a coward. Especially with the faces of women raped by Mai Mai circling in my head.

Worse, I feel dirty.

I manage to say something to keep him friendly. "Of course. You want peace in your country."

"Yes, but peace at what cost?" He asks rhetorically, morphing into an amped-up, emphatic Citizen Congo, slamming his fist, gesturing wildly. "A true Mai Mai is someone who believes in a Congo for Congolese only! A true Mai Mai will never give up the fight!"

I smile.

He nods in approval. "You see, Lisa, *you* are a true Mai Mai!"

CHAPTER TWENTY-FIVE

Criteria

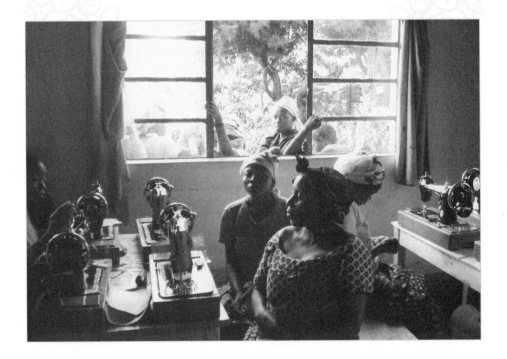

$\mathcal{I}$ THIS CROWD IS out of control! As soon as we pull up outside the church compound, a mass of singing and dancing participants runs up the road to greet me. I am surrounded in the biggest group hug of my life and my feet lift off the ground without warning. I'm bodysurfing above the crowd, struggling to hold my shirt down to keep it from coming completely off. Hortense grabs my foot and orders them to put me down. *Whew! That was the best public display of affection ever!*

I'm in Walungu again, an hour's drive from Bukavu. I have put out the word that I want to talk to women who have stories about recent attacks. I've come to the right place. The notorious village of Kaniola, about ten kilometers up the road, sits at the edge of Interahamwe territory. A handful of women volunteered.

I've asked for it.

Rachel: "One Thursday, the Interahamwe came and killed people. My brother didn't believe it. He wanted to rest in his bed when other people went to hide. He heard the sound of a gun. He didn't know it was his own son being killed. My brother went outside, they stabbed him, killed him, threw him in the bushes. They also killed my uncle. We found him. The same night, they broke into a church and killed a pastor.

"We went far away to feel safer, but I went back home after a few days. We are farmers. Kaniola is far from here. We were staying here, but we were starving. So we went back."

"Do you feel like that's the choice? Risk attack or starve?"

"We are not safe. When we scream at night, government soldiers are afraid of the Interahamwe. They do not come. For our security, instead of waiting for the soldiers to come, we run to them."

Sonya: "I am also from Kaniola. Once, at night, we heard screaming. I had just come from maternity; I had a little baby. We went outside and found they had killed my neighbors, a man and his wife, and threw the dead bodies in the fire. We ran away. We came to Walungu, where we stayed at a school. When we went back to our village, we heard screaming again. We thought peace was regained. When we went to see what was going on, we found that they had locked people in their house and burnt the whole house."

I ask, "The people were alive?"

"Yes. They burnt them alive."

"When did this happen?"

"February. This month. Just a few weeks ago."

The woman sitting next to her nods in agreement.

Antonia: "A few months ago, the Interahamwe took my younger sister away for slavery. She has never come back. They took me away and raped my mother. They took my husband away. I've never heard from him since."

"How long was your mother there?"

"They kept her as a sex slave in the camp for one week."

"How old is your mother?" I prod.

"Around sixty." She answers.

"When I came to get enrolled I was not accepted, even to this day I am not a Women for Women participant."

Hortense jumps in to say, "Today is enrollment day. She has not yet been enrolled."

My mind is fogging up with the weight of the stories. I need to shake off this malaise with an infusion of hope. As if busting out the defibrillator, I say, "I'll be your sister. I'll sponsor you."

Next.

Aksanti: "The war burst. We escaped, but they shot my grandchild who was on my daughter's back. Shot intentionally. The baby died.

"We ran away, left our village and came into Walungu, where we took shelter in a church for a month. We went back to Kaniola. We thought peace was recovered. It wasn't the case. Last Saturday they came to my village and killed two people, a man and a woman."

"Last Saturday?"

"Just Saturday. They wanted beer. He was a beer seller. When he said he had no beer to give them, it was finished. They killed him. They killed his wife. They poured petrol on the house and burnt it down. The dead bodies of that couple were inside. Mushisa is the name of the man."

I ask, "Interahamwe?"

No translation needed. She nods.

"Have you been hiding in the bushes this week?" I ask.

"We run away to the center of Kaniola to escape atrocities. There is a military camp where we can be protected by government soldiers. We are afraid. People are not stable. We cannot work as before. We are starving because we are afraid."

"There's a military camp in the village and Interahamwe are still attacking the periphery of the village?" I ask.

"We are in serious trouble," she says, nodding.

My colleagues in D.C. often frame Congo's problems as half solved now that elections have taken place. So I ask, "Elections have happened. Some people think the war is over in Congo. What would you say to that?"

She laughs, exasperated. "We have nothing to say. We are just like patients in a hospital, waiting to be healed. Even if they say war is over, our place is not safe. It is not over. We live in permanent fear."

Furaha: "They came at night, took my husband and me in the bushes. I spent three months there. They killed my husband. He was killed in my sight. I remember the way they cut my husband in parts. I saw all the parts."

She makes sharp, stabbing gestures with her hands towards her stomach.

They gutted my husband like a fish.

They cut him in parts.

I saw the parts.

I can't tell that story. It's not productive. If I tell that story, I'm a trash peddler. A gore-monger.

I smile supportively and look at them as they sit opposite me, on the edge of the narrow wooden bench, with their arms crossed. I feel cold and mechanical behind the camera. Something is off. This meeting has become an audition. An audition to become one of my talking points. I could have given them numbers and made a scorecard to help filter the information—charted their stories; rated them, on a scale of one to five, for *usability*. Which horror-nugget wins?

I'll just ignore this sinking feeling.

Since when am *I the enemy?* Stepping out of the car and into the rain outside Women for Women's Walungu vocational skills center, I am confronted by a crowd of women. They stand in the drizzle, huddle around trees, or crowd under the few umbrellas. At the sight of me, they run for the bushes, faces turned away, covering their heads with wraps and scarves and shooting me dirty looks. I ask Hortense, "Why are they hiding?"

Hortense, who has gone ahead, calls backwards to me. "They say you haven't written them yet. Why should they be filmed?"

They've been waiting hours in the rain to be enrolled.

When we get inside, the enrollment process is in full swing, with women hoping to join the program cramped between previously enrolled participants working on sewing machines and learning embroidery. Jules explains, "We cannot enroll all the women in the community. This time we can enroll 308 women based on the criteria."

"What's the criteria?"

"It depends on the project: internally displaced persons, killings, rape, refugees. The problem in this community is that all the women were raped, all are refugees. So here, we have to evaluate their stories. That's why those women outside are angry."

There is another, even larger crowd in back. I watch them through the rusty windowpanes, hoping they don't notice me. Women crowd around the doors, peering through. Forty or so maintain orderly lines under a plastic tarp. About fifteen more huddle under the eaves to avoid the rain, waiting their turn. Hortense explains, "These are the women who have been selected. They are waiting to be given forms."

In a few minutes, they'll be invited inside, where they'll take a seat at a long wooden table and squeeze the details of their lives into little boxes on a questionnaire that will soon be entered into a database, printed out, and stapled with a photo, taken today; in a few weeks, this packet will land in an American mail-slot.

Out front it's still a different story. Jules tells us, "We've told them that for today we have too many. Come next time. Go home."

They don't look like they are heading home. I walk outside and stand in the rain with them. "I'm filming so I can show Americans you are waiting. So they will sponsor you, okay? I'm trying to help you."

Hortense stands in the rain and translates while I slip back inside. A few minutes later, Hortense is still explaining. The women continue to argue; someone yells from the back, louder and louder. Everyone cheers. They are shouting, chiming in together. I don't understand a word, but it's clear they are going off. Even the babies wail, following the leads of their mothers.

Hortense walks back inside. "They've understood."

Really? They still look pissed off to me.

We dash out to the car. One of the waiting women approaches the window and says, "Call me. Call me."

As we're driving away, I call back, "I don't have your number."

She hollers after me, "Why?"

I AM WEARING THIN. On the ride back to Bukavu, I blast music on my iPod, trying to shut it all out.

Through dinner on the terrace at Orchid, my iPod is still blasting. It takes everything I have not to think. The phone rings: unknown number. I ignore it.

Minutes pass. I eat my daily staple, *plate de legumes,* and zone-out by staring at Lake Kivu. The phone rings again. I pick up. It is D, calling from the Nairobi airport. He's waiting for his flight to Zanzibar. "How was your day?"

"Sobering."

"Mine too," he says. "I spent the afternoon visiting genocide memorials in Rwanda."

We are both quiet.

"Do you feel like taking a break from Congo? Why don't you join me?"

I am not that girl. I mean, leave a war zone? Abandon Congo for a romantic weekend of R&R with a stranger? Come on. But I'm just fried enough to indulge the thought for a second, imagining another life where I *am* that woman— sitting in a luxury eco-spa overlooking the Indian Ocean. But that's not why I'm in Africa.

"It sounds like heaven. But I can't."

And that is that.

I finish my meal, then head back to my room for a doomed effort at sleep.

In the morning, I text D: "Is it too late to change my mind?"

CHAPTER TWENTY-SIX

Parentheses

FLOATING LANTERNS ON water, probably night fishermen making their way back to shore, are all I can see looking out the window from this small plane packed with Europeans on pleasure holiday. As we descend over Zanzibar, the bobbing lights lead me to imagine the island as a massive spa, full of tea candles and orchids.

It makes me tense.

I am already certain this was a huge mistake. I was sure of it earlier today, as soon as I stepped into the Nairobi airport, full of backpackers and safari-goers. I paced the main corridor, focused on breathing, trying to shake off my dis-ease. When I tried to escape over a cup of tea in the airport café, I sat next to a couple of leathery English women debating the affairs of the royal family. "Oh, never mind him," one said. "He's gay anyway."

A woman in a safari T-shirt invited herself to join me in my booth and initiated a chat about her volunteer work on a game reserve. She'd had a "shocking" visit to the local school, where the children wore dirty clothes and their school meal included only white rice. Don't get me wrong, I'm a whole-grain believer. Two months ago, I would have felt her white-rice pain. But I am ripe to crack. Half of me wanted to hurl expletives at her and everyone else in the terminal: "Are you f——ing kidding me? White rice? That's the most upsetting thing you've run across in *Africa*?!"

The other half of me wanted to find the nearest bathroom stall and cry. Instead, I was measured, even nonchalant, when she asked, "So what brings you here?"

"I've been in the Congo."

"On holiday?" she asked.

"Not exactly."

Clearly this is a risky little social experiment I'm undertaking. Slipping out of Congo for an exotic first date on a remote African spice island turns out to be kind of like going on a dream-job interview right after your best friend's funeral. Best avoided.

It's true, I could not have known how Congo would seep under my skin any more than you feel wet when you're underwater. But when you come up for air, well, that's something else entirely. I know the dating cliché: Just be yourself. But what if *myself* is *freaking out*?

To feel or not to feel, that is the question. If I start to cry, I'm afraid I won't be able to stop. I picture myself curled up in a five-star bathroom sobbing uncontrollably for two days, like D's hysterical sideshow. I hate to emote in public, and for all intents and purposes, D is the public. (After my dad died, even my mom and my sister were the public.) I've got to get it under control. Shut it down. Fortunately, over the last few years I've grown expert at this very thing. Then again, I am undeniably raw, more so than I've been in a long time. My new goal: just get through this thirty-six hours of self-allotted R&R without a major meltdown.

I spot D just outside of Zanzibar customs. My first thought: We glean so much about a person, albeit superficial things, through contextual clues— mutual friends, reputation, style choices in things like food, clothing, and home decor. He and I have zero context. The odds are high for us to stumble upon some deal-breaking fact and end up curled on opposite ends of the bed by tomorrow night.

He kisses me. I'm not sure what I find more awkward: the fact we know almost nothing about each other; my attempt to avoid eye contact, afraid he'll sense the fresh-out-of-Congo nerves; or a public display of affection in a Muslim country.

The taxi ride to the resort is long and meandering. It's late, close to eleven, and the cab driver doesn't seem to know where he is going. We pull over at a quiet crossroads and the driver leaves us to ask for directions at a local shop. With only a dim street lamp lighting the empty road, I engage D in a rush of fill-in-the-blank questions about family, work, and his background, all the while scanning the bushes, watching for movement. The paranoia has apparently followed me out of Congo like a stray dog. I remind myself: There are no militias in Zanzibar. No armed men lurking behind those bushes. No one is going to take us out on this abandoned road. My heart pounds anyway.

Entering his room is surreal. With Congo only a short hop behind me, here I am with a stranger in a modern, five-star palace where luxury oozes out of the walls. I look down at my feet and realize I'm still caked in road dust from Congo. It's sorely out of place here against the modern all-white decor. I'm exhausted from the mental combat I've been engaged in all day, all month, or much longer. I'm through with declarations about what kind of woman I am. I want Congo off of me, even if I can only shake it for a little while. I see D, who's standing across the palatial bathroom, as an escape route—or even just a temporary anesthetic. We're already warm from snuggling during the rest of our taxi ride, and there will be no tour now. It's straight for the bed—pushing aside the mosquito net and onto the six-hundred-thread cotton sheets.

It is not the first time I've been touched since Ted left, and I've already found that being with a new lover can prove far less soothing than expected. But this is something I have not felt in more years than I can count. There is no space for another thought or emotion. We take refuge in each other like we mean it.

I haven't slept in days. I still can't sleep. D asks if I'm having a hard time getting the stories and images of Congo out of my head.

I skirt the question and lie, "It's just the new environment."

While he sleeps, I stir over half-formed thoughts, recycling images of young men dousing huts with gasoline, straw catching flame, people screaming. As my thoughts inch towards lucidity, the title of a poem drifts to the foreground. I read it in high school; it was assigned in freshman English, in preparation for the visit from prominent American writer Yusef Komunyakaa, who later won the Pulitzer Prize for poetry. Though I haven't thought of the poem in almost twenty years, I remember it because I was confused by the title.

Later, I will look up the poem.

You and I Are Disappearing

The cry I bring down from the hills
belongs to a girl still burning
inside my head. At daybreak

she burns like a piece of paper.

She burns like foxfire
in a thigh-shaped valley.
A skirt of flames
dances around her
at dusk.

We stand with our hands

hanging at our sides,
while she burns

like a sack of dry ice.

She burns like oil on water.
She burns like a cattail torch
dipped in gasoline.
She glows like the fat tip
of a banker's cigar,

silent as quicksilver.

A tiger under a rainbow
*   at nightfall.*
She burns like a shot glass of vodka.
She burns like a field of poppies
at the edge of a rain forest.
She rises like dragonsmoke
*   to my nostrils.*
She burns like a burning bush
driven by a godawful wind.

IN THE MIDDLE OF the African night, I am haunted by the title. *You and I Are Disappearing.* When I was fourteen, I hadn't a clue how the title related to a poem about a girl burning in a napalm attack. During the Q&A period following Komunyakaa's reading, I asked him, "Who are the 'you' and 'I' and how are we disappearing?"

Who are the 'you' and 'I'? How are we disappearing?

I understand his answer now. I crawl out of bed and scrawl it down in my notebook. I know exactly who the "you" and "I" are. The burning girl is almost every person I've met in Congo, and me, or us, when we watch the Congolese burn "with our hands at our sides."

We wake up and stroll down to the sea. In the daylight, the whole resort is like a giant set for a stock photo shoot, no retouching required.

The day unfolds in a slow-motion haze. An elaborate breakfast buffet, a swim, iced tea on the jetty, massages at the hotel spa, a visit to a fishing village overrun with backpackers, a long nap. The resort is nearly empty. In the quiet moments, I occupy myself by mentally sketching a shoot here—casting, storyboarding, forming shot lists, framing shots. Otherwise, I continue to barrage D with intrusive personal questions. Nothing if not gracious, D obliges them all. I will do anything to keep the focus off me, off Congo, off cracking.

Alone at the resort's bar perched above the sea on a jetty, we gaze out over the ocean. I realize it's the first time I've looked at the night sky over Africa. D points out constellations he remembers from his childhood in South Africa. They're playing one of the Buddha Bar albums in the background, one we both own. Each of us loved it at first, we discover through conversation, then grew bored with it. It's just us and the bartender, who remains remote. I say, "I imagine you live in a place like this, modern, clean."

"Nope. I've lived in the same Victorian townhouse for the past twenty years, since I left academia."

I'm impressed. To build a global software empire and not upgrade your house? To use all of your resources—money, time, and influence—not for a better lifestyle, but to save the planet? Those are values.

We fall into a deep conversation about wealth as the great divider. We talk about two kinds of philanthropists: those who write big checks and those who doggedly work for something bigger than themselves. He tells me about acquaintances who fuss and send back a glass of water if it has four ice cubes instead of three. I tell him about my grandfather's work with Dominique and John de Menil founding the Rothko Chapel in Houston, an interfaith place of worship dedicated to human rights. Family legend had it Dominique de Menil, aka "Mrs. D," insisted on riding public transportation until she was in her eighties, when her staff finally had to talk her down: "You're *eighty*. It's okay to take a car!" Or the Vogels, who I saw on a segment of *60 Minutes* I watched with my Dad many years ago. They built an art collection worth hundreds of millions of dollars, yet still live in the simple two-bedroom apartment they bought when Mr. Vogel worked for the postal service. I comment, "Artists love them because they're in it for art, and not—"

"The commerce of art," D says, finishing my sentence.

"Exactly."

The more we talk, the more I realize he doesn't quite fit into the Big Important Guy demographic. He likes to secretly meditate in the woods, craves all things simple, and writes in his spare moments, scrawling down poetry to zone-out in board meetings. He's undeniably intense. Of all things, lurking under his thick persona is a quirky-pensive-brilliant artist. As we do that odd dance between foreigner and friend, I wonder if I might be sitting next to someone I will know outside of Africa.

We return to the room and, snuggled next to D, I sleep for the first time in days.

In the morning, we walk across a vast, pristine beach, arms stuffed with snorkeling gear. There's nothing commercial here, just African women in pastel dresses wading waist-deep in the ocean with fishing nets trailing behind them. D turns to me and says, "You could shoot here!"

"Too much seaweed on the beach," I blurt out, regurgitating Ted's predictable objection.

Did I just tell an environmentalist that Nature isn't good enough?

"The dark side of Lisa," D says, raising his eyebrows, "Part two."

There is nothing complicated about fish. They are beautiful, simple little beings in weird, wild shapes and neon colors, like eighties cruise-ship clichés, some with frills that remind me of war-era secretaries in black-and-white polka-dotted dresses. I squeal with delight, smiling so wide I break the seal on my mask. It floods with water over and over again, so I have to keep coming up for air.

We get back late, in a rush to make it to the airport. While the taxi driver loads my bags, D and I pause for a moment. We're too rushed for a decent goodbye, and I'm too worn down to drum up some witty, sexy, romantic endnote.

"I can't believe you're going back to that place," he says, kissing me goodbye.

I ignore the slow-creeping adrenaline buzz that comes when I think of Bukavu's gutted streets. My inner college-era feminist is tickled by the role reversal: powerful man kisses young woman goodbye on *her* way back to a war zone. He adds, "Don't do anything I wouldn't do."

Yeah, right. I laugh, and say teasingly as I climb into the taxi-van, "I'm already doing something you wouldn't do."

As the taxi pulls away, D stands in the driveway of the hotel watching me. I look down at my arms, which are getting redder by the minute. I press my fingers down and fixate on the white imprint that remains. My back smolders with my only Zanzibar souvenir: the worst sunburn I've ever had. It will blister and peel for the remainder of my time in Africa, aggravated by the daily thrashing from bumping over Congo's washed-out roads. Two years from now, the faint traces of the swimsuit I picked up in the hotel gift shop will still be burned onto my back.

CHAPTER TWENTY-SEVEN

Goodbye Party

THE WOMEN FOR WOMEN staff is abuzz with the imminent arrival of the organization's founder, Zainab Salbi, and the writer Alice Walker. Hortense called early this morning, letting me know in no uncertain terms that I am not invited to their arrival reception or to any of their meetings with women, including Generose. I don't know why and I won't lie: I'm disappointed. Especially after days of enthusiastically trying to walk the Congolese staff through every Alice Walker work I've read—from *Meridian* to *Possessing the Secret of Joy*—trying to remember all the key points I made in a twenty-five-page college paper comparing *Their Eyes Were Watching God* and *The Color Purple*. But as anyone who has engaged in the political minefield that is celebrity wrangling can tell you, this kind of thing goes with the territory. I decide to not take it personally and make plans to spend my day-in-exile following up with some of my new Congolese friends.

First up, Generose. Her brother has collected her children from various friends and neighbors, so they are now fine. It's time to break the news about the house. I sit next to her on her hospital bed. I don't want any of the other sisters in the neighborhood to be jealous, so I've made up a story.

"I've found an organization that provides small grants for people who are disabled because of war-related injuries," I tell her. "They are going to build you a small house."

For a moment, she sits quietly, absorbing the news. Then she lifts her hands up and cries out, *"Aksanti sana sana sana! Merci!"* Thank you very, very, very much.

On the way out, we stop by the baby ward to check on Bonjour. As I take him in my lap, shouting fills the room. We all watch, stonefaced, as a man yells at a crying child in the corner. The man moves on to the next bed, lays his hands on his next victim and launches into his routine once again, apparently egged on by the fact that the whole ward is staring at him. The new baby screams with fear while the man holds his hands above the child in some form of prayer symbol. Ah, he's exorcising demons.

I focus on Bonjour, touching his tiny fingers, looking in his eyes, trying to block out the Congolese exorcist. The little guy is getting better. His skin is darker and the half-light in his eyes is gone. He smiles.

I get up to leave. As I'm heading for the door, his mom asks, "What about sugar for my tea?"

I stop cold and look back at her, fed up with the *muzungu* routine. "You can live without sugar." Without waiting for the translation, I leave and don't look back.

HORTENSE CALLS. Zainab, Alice, and Christine will arrive at any time. The staff has cleared the compound completely, but my first group of sisters (*"Money! More money!"*) showed up three hours ago hoping for one last goodbye celebration. They refuse to leave.

We beeline it over there, load the women and babies ten at a time into the SUV, and take them to the vocation skills center down the road in the last harried minutes. On the main road, we pass the Women for Women SUV carrying Zainab and Alice.

At the skills center, we settle in and relax, drinking sodas. I notice I'm sitting across from little Lisa, so I greet her. The sister next to her holds a baby as well, her hair braided with pink ties and barrettes. "Her name is Lisa too," the mother says. Two little Lisas! I wonder how many Congolese babies are out there sporting American names like Ashley and Deborah because their mom was sponsored when she was pregnant.

Another sister presents me with her newborn. "I told you, if I deliver the baby while you are here, you will name the baby."

I've never had plans for children, so baby names have never been on my mind. I draw a complete blank. I stall. "Can I hold him?"

She hands him to me, wrapped in blankets. Yep, he looks brand-spanking-new, his face still pale and wrinkly. I ask her, "What do you hope he will be like?"

"Strong, responsible, someone who supports the family."

No pressure there. I stare at the little guy, at a loss. Strong, responsible . . . a lightbulb goes on. "I have an idea, but it's not going to sound like a Congolese name," I say. They all laugh.

"My father was strong and responsible."

They burst into applause, saying "Yes!" and "Amen!"

"My father's name was S-T-E-W-A-R-T. Stewart."

They look puzzled. They all try to rehearse it. It does not roll off the Swahili-speaking tongue. "Stu-ad. Stu-at."

The new mom tries to write it on her hand, but I jump in. "I'll write it."

I hand the baby back. They cheer, laughing, as I write STEWART in block letters on Mom's palm. She looks skeptical. "He was a loving, compassionate man," I tell her. "He worked with people to heal their war trauma."

"Yes."

"Are you going to change the name?" I ask, hoping my smile gives her visible permission to name her baby anything she pleases.

"I will keep the name."

They present me with a carefully wrapped gift. One woman, standing at my side, says, "We have nothing to give you as a present. But what we can do is thank and thank and thank you for what you did for us. May God bless you and increase your power to give and to give and to give and to give."

They present me with a woodcarving, a sculpture of a woman with a baby strapped to her back. One woman interprets it for me. "This is your image as Mama Congo. We are like your babies."

The expression of familial love is so sweet. I smile and thank them.

But the metaphor lands hard. I don't want to be their mother. Oh, how I wish we could let this "mama" stuff go. I have grown tired of the *muzungu* role. I just want to be their friend.

NOELLA HAS HAUNTED me for weeks. I've pictured her at the child soldier center, alone with all those boys. After I say goodbye to my sisters, I decide to make good on a promise I've made to BVES boys every time we've run into them on Bukavu's main road (which has been often). I pick up gobs of chocolate and soda, the sort of thing I would never feed kids at home, and head over to the center.

"Shanella!" They're happy to see me. Looks like we're buddies now. Luc is bright eyed, proud to be one of the boys now, and he can't be bothered with his sister. While the boys are feasting away on the treats, I slip away with Noella to her room. Two new girls have joined the center and share her room, but they are sharp edged and much older. They clear the space so I can talk to Noella alone. I present her with a matching, green-floral-print skirt and blouse. She puts it on and smiles. But her eyes are heavy. I instantly feel silly bringing her a trinket present, especially one that reminds her she's a cute little girl in a place where it is her greatest liability. I take her photo in the pretty outfit, which is barely large enough for her. It only fits when she stands still; every slight move of her arms pulls at the buttons or makes a sliver of her tummy protrude.

I look out the window, picturing her on her trips to the bathroom. Does a staff member escort her there? Certainly not. I hope she doesn't wear that dress.

"I've been thinking about you," I say. "It must be difficult for you here, the only girl with so many boys. Are you okay?"

She struggles to say something back, muttering, "It is no place for a little girl."

I'm at a loss. I look in her eyes, and struggle for any words of encouragement I can muster. "I don't know what it's like for you here. But I do know that whatever happens, there is a place inside you all yours, that no one can touch. Do you understand?"

Maurice explains to Serge, who translates to the girl. I suspect the translation wasn't exact. "What did he say?"

Serge says, "I told her, 'sometimes it's better to forget.'"

"That's not what I said," I tell him. "I would never say that to a child."

They look at me patiently, waiting for my anger to pass.

"Tell her that's not what I said. Tell her what I really said."

Maurice and Serge smile; Serge doesn't translate.

As we drive to the outskirts of town, my thoughts are flying like a fast-moving tennis match. Why didn't I offer to drive Noella and Luc to Rwanda myself?

International law.

Or take her with me back to Orchid. I could have been her foster mom for at least a while.

It's not your place.

Not my place? I could have pushed Murhabazi to place her somewhere safe.

You did bring it up to him. He said not to worry.

How stupid I was to listen. I could have protected her. I'm a grown-up. And I knew. I knew.

You did what you could. It wasn't your role. . . .

We park the car and start walking, winding our way past an abandoned warehouse, up the eroded paths on a hillside overlooking Lake Kivu, to check in with another sister who has sick kids. As we pass women carrying loads up the hill, I marvel at their efforts. If they catch me looking, I smile and extend a *"Jambo* Mama!" Some manage a vague smile under the weight cutting into their foreheads. But occasionally, one will flash a big smile and *"Jambo"* back, a reminder there is a woman under that load just waiting to be seen. When I pass one woman who gives me such a smile, I take it as an invitation for friendship.

"It looks heavy!" I say. "You must be very strong."

She pauses to wait for the translation.

"Ah. *Ndiyo.* Yes. Heavy."

"Is it okay? Are you okay carrying it?"

I don't know why I ask questions like this. Out of concern, I suppose. What is she going to say, *No?*

She smiles weakly.

I wonder how heavy it is. I want to help her. On an impulse, I say, "Why don't you let me take it. Let me carry it for you a while."

Maurice and my new friend laugh. "It is not possible."

But I love a challenge and I want to help, so I persist. "No. I'm serious. Let me take it."

Maurice is gentle but firm. "You will hurt yourself."

A few others have stopped to watch the spectacle. "Maurice, I can run thirty miles," I tell him. "I'm fit. Ask her if I can take it for a bit. I want to help her."

"Lisa," he says, "you will break your back."

But I have already started to move in on the load. She turns it towards me in acquiescence. I place my hands underneath her load, which is flour of some description. By the size of it, I guess it is about a hundred pounds. I try to lift it off her back. I cannot lift it one inch. It's that heavy. I reposition myself, remembering to lift with my legs. I muster all my strength and try again. It doesn't budge.

My new friend and I look at each other with resignation. She still smiles, amused, but struggling to hold the weight. Embarrassed for offering help I can't deliver, I offer the obvious explanation. "I want to help, but you are stronger than I am."

We continue up the hill. Our moderate pace quickly leaves her behind, struggling step by step with her load. I walk in silence the rest of the way up the hill, contemplating the visit and the last few years. How I've let my business slide. How I've traveled here to run around foolishly . . . for what? Most NGOs haven't taken me seriously enough to even return my phone calls.

Maurice reads my pensive mood and attempts to encourage me. "I've never met anyone like you before, Lisa."

I try to hide the welling tears. Maurice can see he's getting to me, so he continues, "You make me want to do something else with my life. I want to work helping other people."

It's not that I'm not touched. It's that his praise rings painfully untrue. I think back on the last five weeks: the endless hours at the hospital, the cheerleader speeches, driving up and down South Kivu. All the time, doing nothing but, what, collecting stories? Hugging women? Silly stunts. Paltry presents. Who am I against Congo? I feel ridiculous; my hurling antics at this country's problems has been like tossing teaspoons of water on a raging fire.

I AM BACK ON the terrace at Orchid, having a late-afternoon tea, when Zainab enters. I met her once, in D.C., but I'm not sure she'll recognize me. Despite all the public speaking, I'm often shy and reserved when I meet new people, especially those I greatly respect. Zainab is certainly one of those people. She glances at me, so I wave hello.

"Oh—I didn't recognize you!" she says and gives me a big hug.

Ebullient as ever, gracious to her core, she joins me for tea and a long talk, which meanders from topics like self-care—an essential ingredient to the work—to her childhood in Iraq. She explains that in Iraq they have women who attend funerals with the specific function of coaxing the grieving to cry. Zainab says she is like one of those women, only she coaxes women to tell their stories. Not only in war zones, but even after public talks in America, women often approach her and spill their life histories.

"Congo," she says, "is one of my favorite places on earth. You have the worst of humanity and the best of humanity. It's raw, but it is real."

Alice and her filmmaker friend Prathiba join us. Alice is much what I have imagined. In gray dreadlocks and loose-fitting, natural clothing, she is quiet and has a piercing gaze that makes me feel transparent. Even if I met Alice Walker poolside following a month-long relaxation retreat at a high-end spa, I would be inclined to not say much. But under the wear of Congo, I clam up and just observe. I've never spent time around this breed of women: self-possessed, comfortable in their skin, nothing put on, nothing to prove. I cannot imagine her spending a moment on anything petty. She has the aura of a visionary.

They invite me along for dinner. Alice says little through our meal. I'm quiet too, aside from a comment about my decision to not cry around Congolese women. At the end of the meal, Alice looks at me directly and, as though confirming that I am, in fact, transparent, says, "It's okay to cry with them."

CHAPTER TWENTY-EIGHT

The End of Logic

I'M NOT SURE why I told Maurice to come today. He needs a day off and I have nothing on the agenda. My time in Congo is nearing its end. I have left messages all week for the country director of an NGO who said he had planned a trip so that I could tour their facilities up north. But we were supposed to leave yesterday, so the silence has turned into a brush-off.

I feel like a fifth-year high school student, or the last lingering guest at a dinner party who's stuck in the kitchen washing dishes long after the other guests have gone home. So I am sipping my tea on the terrace at Orchid, observing the gardens and Lake Kivu in the morning light.

Maurice arrives and joins me. Perched on the edge of his chair, he hands me a scrap of paper. It's a note scribbled in French, directions of some kind and a couple of names. "Jean Paul has sent this for you," Maurice says. "The UN in Walungu has a woman who just returned from the forest."

Normally, I would not go on this kind of goose chase, especially in Congo. Especially in Walungu. But today I have nothing better to do. *What the hell, let's visit the UN and try to track her down.*

We drive through Walungu, past the church and the Women for Women compound on the edge of the town and then deeper into the town center. It is crawling with Congolese military. They are everywhere: meandering down the roads with guns casually dangled over their shabby uniforms, hanging out in front of shack restaurants, chatting with girls. Few are occupied with any meaningful task.

"This makes the Congolese very tense," Maurice comments. "So many soldiers, just . . . around."

Jean Paul's directions are vague. We cruise up and down the main drag several times, ask at the UN office, then stop at a playground nestled in the middle of a military camp, where Congolese army officers play with local children on teeter-totters and merry-go-rounds. A sign boasts this playground was constructed as a gift from Pakistani UN troops, who appear to make "hearts and minds" a priority.

We pull up to a small cement compound and Maurice runs inside with the piece of paper to get any information he can. Serge and I wait in the car, watching a Congolese army officer stumble down the road dead-drunk, yelling at himself and everyone around him. Maurice returns a few minutes later with news. The man we are looking for is away, but he will be back in a few hours. In the meantime, the UN majors manning the station would like to say hello.

They invite us into the brick compound and we meet the majors, who have been stationed here for a little over a month—one from Nigeria, one from India, and one from Uruguay. They are welcoming. Major Vikram, the major from India, is particularly friendly after I warm him up by sharing my India travel stories; I spent time there when I was in college. He offers us chai and biscuits as the men collectively answer my questions after an informal briefing. I am not allowed to film. I try to ignore the fact that one of my hosts is wearing only boxer shorts. After all, I have disrupted their Sunday morning.

They offer me a copy of the report taken on the woman we're hoping to track down. By reading the report, I get the real story. It wasn't one woman abducted, but three girls, two of them fifteen and one of them seventeen.

On Wednesday, Interahamwe came to their compounds in Kaniola and took them to the forest, but apparently the Congolese Army rescued them.

This story is a first. *Rescued? By the Congolese Army?*

Both Major Vikram and Major Kaycee, from Nigeria, disappear for a few minutes. A laminated map on the wall catches my attention. It is a map of a range of hills, with villages and hamlets on one side of the range, Kaniola included. On the other side are Interahamwe camps.

I am shocked. I've always imagined the Interahamwe as elusive bands of men roaming vast tracks of the Congo forest, evading the UN and international eye. Surely, I assumed, the reason the international community has allowed these guys to slaughter, torture, and maim civilians is because it's a complicated territory, like mountains-of-Afghanistan complicated. But this map isn't complicated at all. On one side of mountain ranges, villages. On the other, Interahamwe camps, neatly marked and color coded with flags and *X*s to note how many combatants live in each camp. No secret societies or elusive rebels here.

Major Kaycee reappears in full military fatigues—camouflage—with his UN badge on broad display. "Okay," he says. "Shall we go there?"

My chest tightens as we follow Major Vikram and Major Kaycee's UN SUV down an increasingly narrow dirt road. We chew clay-dust and hug blind curves for ten kilometers up the road to Kaniola.

Yes, *Kaniola.* The home village one of my sisters was talking about when she commented, "If it was safe to go back home, do you think we would accept to suffer in Bukavu?" The home village Generose swears she will never return to. The village where people are regularly burned alive in their houses.

Fear seeps through my body like a slow adrenaline drip. With every poverty-porn stereotype floating in my mind, I picture charred and barren hills, fresh graves lining the pathways, morbid sounds in the air, decrepit people in rags with smoke slowly rising around them, like refugees in the mist. I ask Maurice for reassurance. "Do you really think this is safe?"

I don't know why I ask. By now, I should know the answer: *Everything* is safe to the Congolese. Maurice is predictably soothing. "Oh, yes. Safe. The Interahamwe only attack here maybe twice a week."

The UN vehicle in front of us pulls over at a rusty, bullet-riddled road sign. Locals are gathered around and children lug badly beaten-up, five-gallon water jugs. The UN translator accompanying the majors asks for directions while Major Kaycee motions for me to get out.

As I emerge from my unmarked SUV, villagers stare blankly. An old man on crutches watches us suspiciously. Who can blame them? We must be quite a sight and, frankly, hard to place, with the major in combat boots and camouflage, Major Vikram in jeans, a sporty red T-shirt, sunglasses, and tennis shoes (he's dressed more for a casual day at a suburban shopping mall or football match), and me in a long skirt and flip-flops.

I'm not sure which getup will provide us more protection. Nonthreatening, feminine skirt? Major Vikram's sporty casual? Or Major Kaycee's official uniform? I love his pale blue UN cap and the UN ID tag that hangs around his neck; they're the only real protection we've got in the event we come across any evil-doers. We do not have guns.

I follow the majors down a narrow winding path, between a few compounds lined with tropical-plant fences and around a couple of blind corners, then I get my first glimpse of the valley. Some long-buried belief comes into play, lulling me into a sense of security: Bad things happen only on cold and stormy nights with howling, ominous winds. Or in dead-of-Africa-night, during the silent hours that one might expect to be filled with panic and bloodshed.

Bad things can't possibly happen during the day—or in a place—like *this*. I look over the valley and see that Kaniola is nothing like I've pictured. "It's so beautiful," I say, stunned.

Major Vikram concurs. "Too beautiful."

Yes, Major Vikram, it is *too beautiful*. These aren't the small undulating hills of Rwanda, but broad, grand hills with room to breathe. Some are solid, saturated green; others are dotted with round, thatch-roofed mud huts or shaggy igloo-shaped straw huts that might be mistaken for haystacks. I see banana patches. Tidy, sweet rows of cabbages. Sunflowers. Water flowing in gentle streams. Voices of children drifting in the breeze. Birds, who apparently failed to read the memo titled *Kaniola: Very, Very Dangerous Place*, chirp away. The Kaniola valley is mythic-pretty.

Major Kaycee points across a valley to the hills, or perhaps the mountains, just beyond. "That is the hamlet which was attacked. Maybe a twenty-minute walk."

If you were born here, you wouldn't want to leave. In fact, I don't know if I want to leave. I wonder what a little African compound on the cusp of Kaniola goes for these days. Do they have building codes? Would the village elders allow a permanent structure? Would they welcome a foreigner among them? We'd have to carry supplies in on this path to the far side of the valley, to those grass-covered hills, where I could have a compound all my own, perched on a tiny hilltop. I could grow old and someday say, "I had a farm in Africa . . ."

"You see those forested areas, those small patches?" asks Major Vikram, gesturing at the ridgeline on the far side of the valley. "The Interahamwe is that side. It's from those hills that Interahamwe come across and attack villagers."

Oh, right. Those Who Kill Together. Never mind.

Yet it is still impossible to imagine anything bad happening on this quiet, lovely Sunday afternoon in this pristine African countryside. My tension drains away, the soft breeze and sun luring me into a familiar stillness that masquerades as calm. Like the stillness of a room after the respirator has been shut off. Or the calm that descends when you're staring into the eyes of a sociopath and he doesn't *look* crazy. Or the peace I was feeling on a sunny, early autumn morning in Manhattan, after my first summer with Ted, before he rushed up the stairs to our loft, steaming coffee and toasted bagels in hand, and burst in the door to announce that the World Trade Center was on fire. I had suited up for my daily run down the West Side Highway; I planned to run to my turn-around spot, the World Trade Center. But I was feeling lazy, and Ted had gone to pick up breakfast, so I blew off the run. We scrambled to our roof with a clear view of the North Tower's gaping hole. My first thought spilled out, unfiltered: "That doesn't look like a coffee pot fire." Without commentary, without a newscaster framing the event's significance, we didn't know what was happening. An hour later, with naked eyes, I saw the North Tower fall. From two miles up the West Side Highway, it simply looked like a cloud of smoke. And then nothing.

Major Vikram and I fill the space with loud chitchat, as though we're hanging out at a local pub. We chat about *Oprah*. Debate the varieties of bananas that grow in North India. I pitch him a long-buried screenplay idea, about a man searching for his daughter, who disappeared in Major Vikram's Himalayan home state.

I talk about running. "I'm out of shape! I haven't been able to run here."

Major Vikram asks innocently, "Why?"

"Uh, I'm not sure it's safe," says the white girl going for a casual Sunday stroll next to Interahamwe territory.

"Don't worry about safety."

We both laugh. *Don't worry about safety.*

A woman passes us; she's wearing a bright green African dress, with her hair done and full makeup. I look her in the eye, *"Jambo, Habari!"*

She looks at me and nods, *"Bonjour."*

As we walk down this path into the valley, passing villagers, there is no "I've been touched by terror" evidence like I saw in Manhattan on September 11; I remember seeing a dazed bike messenger walking through Union Square, his dreadlocks caked in ash. Here, everyone looks clean and neat. We pass a tall guy, so thin, in a blazer that squares off his hollow frame. Then comes a slim older man in pressed, belted khakis, a blue oxford shirt, and lace-up dress shoes. *Wait, isn't that the uniform for the legislative aids who grab quick power lunches on Pennsylvania Avenue before heading back to a long afternoon on Capitol Hill?*

This is officially odd. What's the deal with the well-groomed people of Kaniola? Then I remember: It's Sunday. They're dressed for church.

Generose comes to mind. What is the first thing she said to her children after her home was attacked, burned to the ground, and her family assassinated in her front yard? *Thank God. I'm alive.*

A group of young women sees us and steps to the edge of the path, doing their best to avoid us. Major Kaycee calls a command to Maurice. "Papa, ask them if they know about those incidents of the ladies kidnapped."

Maurice approaches them in his mild-mannered way and speaks in a soft voice. The major shouts from behind him, "Ask any of them!"

Before Maurice can finish, the Major asks another local and calls out, "Okay! They are up there."

The girls watch suspiciously, as we continue up the path. Only months later, when I review the video, will I see that one of the girls we were looking for was among them—tense, trying to be inconspicuous, hoping her friends don't rat her out.

After hiking for a half hour we are in the middle of the valley. I am waiting for the majors outside a compound when I hear children's voices whispering behind me. I look over my shoulder to discover six wide-eyed children, all in ratty, soiled clothing. I turn my camera on them and they inexplicably flinch and step back.

I flip the viewfinder and call them back so I can show them their photo. They smile, shy but intrigued. "See what beautiful smiles you have," I say. They giggle and cover their mouths, duck behind one another, and peek out to smile at themselves in the viewfinder.

We enter the compound; a guarded older woman, around sixty, greets us. In New York or Paris, I'm sure her bone structure, cropped silver hair, and thin frame could win her a place as a catalog model. "This woman is their grandmother; we are going to her daughter's house," Major Kaycee says, then he turns to her and asks, "How far is it? Five minutes? Ten minutes? Are the girls there?"

He is measuring the investment they've made already in what they thought would be a quick walk. I'm not sure any of us thought it would be this far, especially in the direction of the hills. No one knows if the girls are home. But questions of security aside, I don't want to turn back.

I pipe up, "We'll walk. It's okay."

We get directions and set out with the troop of children, who serve as our new guides, in tow. Major Vikram pulls the UN badge from his pocket and clips it to the front of his pants, on broad display. One of our newly adopted guides, a little boy, waddles and flops in a grown-up's long-sleeve sweatshirt. Barefoot, he's stepping in time with Major Kaycee, following him the way a child clings to his daddy's leg in a crowd, moving as fast as he can, trying to stay in the thick of the manly men.

Major Vikram turns and sizes him up. The UN translator stops the boy and tells him to go home, but the child is anxious to prove himself essential by showing us the way.

As we round another bend, Major Vikram points back toward the road. "Can you see on that hilltop *something, something, something?*" It is a small collection of tents on the far side of the road, perhaps a mile from our hill, away from the forest. He adds, "That is the mobile unit, the base for opposing security. For the protection of local people."

"How long has it been there?" I ask.

"Two weeks."

"Do they patrol over here?"

"No."

I miss the cue completely. Of course they don't patrol here. They don't patrol where the attacks happen most often because it's too dangerous.

A group of young girls clustered under a big, rainbow-colored umbrella, their ages ranging from five to ten, walks toward us on the path. Some have babies on their backs and each wears a Sunday-best dress with lace trim.

They slow to a stop, trying to place the large African man in camouflage fatigues. The tallest among them takes her little sister's hand and leads them off the trail, her eyes tracking the major and Major Vikram. I recognize that look. It's the same frozen, nowhere-to-hide stare I saw on the streets of the

West Village late on the morning of September 11, when a low-flying government plane passed by. Strangers stopped cold and stared into each other's eyes, as though to ask, "Shouldn't we duck and cover?"

Major Vikram greets the girls as they pass us. They step off the trail, onto a patch of grass, poised to run. I approach them, which alerts them to my presence for the first time. They spot the camera and scatter, lugging the babies on their backs.

It finally dawns on me. *They think the camera is a gun.* I flip the viewfinder over and call them in my cheeriest, most soothing babysitter voice. "It's a camera! Do you want to see a picture of yourself?"

They approach cautiously, perhaps relieved, but too startled for quick smiles.

They relax for a moment when they see themselves on the mini-viewfinder screen. I ask them, "Did you think it was a gun?" As the Swahili word "gun" crosses Maurice's lips, their slow-growing smiles instantly drop. The children duck and run again. It's not funny or cute. There will be no warming it up now, so I wave goodbye and move on.

We hike toward the forest. Toward the Interahamwe. We wind our way up narrow paths on hillsides, and reach the top, only to recognize we have many more hills to go. I notice a hilltop church with a rusty corrugated metal roof. Banana leaves rustle in the wind. I do not notice the slow, creeping tension, or the cue from my UN escorts who ask, "Are you *sure* you want to go *there?*"

A family spots us and ducks behind bushes, watching us suspiciously. Normally, *Jambo* means "Hello," and is followed by the response *Jambo sana*, which means "Very hello." Somewhere between the road and this ridgeline, the translation has changed. As I muster up my chirpiest voice, *Jambo* now means "Relax! We're not here to kill you!"

As they pause, slowly stand up to check us out, even smile, and call back, "*Jambo sana!*" now means "Thank God!" Make that "Very thank God!"

We are much closer to the forest now. It creeps down the hills. Trees are now distinguishable in detail as we follow the last ridgeline running along this valley.

We pass a villager who stands to the side of the path with a haunting look. In an ash-gray sports jacket and pants, he stands with his arms at his side, watching, like an intern standing at attention in a concentration camp.

On a nearby path, two girls, both maybe six years old, with shaved heads and ragged little oversize frocks, see the camera and drop to the ground. One of them makes a run for it, her little body tearing down the hill for safety. Where did she learn this routine? She slows down, hides behind bananas, looks back to check on her friend. She sees the camera pointed at her. Terrified, she disappears. Her friend runs after her at top barefoot speed.

On the other side of the hill, a woman minds her fields. Hers may be the first angry face I've seen here; she is seriously annoyed that the camera is pointed at her. She puts down her hoe, stands up, and glares, as if to say, "What the hell are you looking at?"

"Is that it there? Is that where we are going?" I ask, pointing to a cluster of round mud huts with cone tops, and cabbage patches perched on top of a small hill butted right up to forest. The Forest, that is. I'm trying to sound casual as I ask Maurice again, "So, this is the spot?"

Major Vikram and Major Kaycee are equally disoriented, squabbling with each other and the translator. "No, no, no. . . ."

"Are we going this way or that way?"

"It must be up there, beyond those bushes. . . ."

We've been hiking for an hour and something has turned. Suddenly, we all know we've gone too far and are tempting fate. We're all thinking it must be just beyond the next corner. Even the idle talk with Major Vikram fades. My attempts at small talk fall flat. Major Vikram has other things on his mind, and making fun of myself for being out of shape, or my banal talk of the benefits of exercise, seems far less funny than it did an hour ago. Conversation circles around variations of "Oh my God, it's so close."

"It's no wonder they've had problems if they live that close."

"It's so near to the jungle."

"Yeah. Really near."

"You see, Lisa, if they are coming from this place. . . ."

"Anyone can come. . . ."

"It's so close."

I hear children playing. In the distance, in an open field at the top of the hill, a group of boys are playing soccer next to a wooden shack that looks like it's about to fall over. They see us and stop, stand at attention, and stare. A young man, maybe twenty, in an African-print, oxford-style shirt and baseball cap approaches and talks with the major. He is the girls' brother.

Major Vikram points to the compound, now in view. "Do you see that prominent *V* of the hills and sky? They live just there. This is the house."

The translator points back towards the main road and village. "He says all of the girls are back there at church."

"What do we do?" Major Kaycee asks me, then adds, "I think we go to see the sisters in the church. That's plenty."

It's not plenty for me.

If there is a point where numbness becomes dangerous, when lack of emotion trickles into lack of logic—a point when you leave your hand on a burning stove—then we have officially entered that terrain. I have been relying on the majors to pull the parachute string and tell me when we had crossed into the *too dangerous* zone. But the last thing any UN major wants is to be proven cowardly in front of a young woman. Who has a camera. They did not account for my tear-my-life-to-shreds impulsiveness. Nor did I. We have no business being here.

But since we've come all this way. . . .

We finally reach our destination: the very last hut in the very last hamlet before Interahamwe territory. We enter the spotless compound—it's the kind of third world clean that comes from having nothing, the lack of garbage or clutter perhaps due to the fact anything of value has long since been taken. Major Kaycee takes careful notes on his official UN pad, as Maurice translates the girls' brother's account of what happened that night.

"It was Wednesday night when the Interahamwe came from the mountains. They woke us. There were six of them; three stayed with me and my wife and three others went to the next house. They took three hens, three goats, maize flour, and my two sisters. My arm was hurt with their gun, but I escaped and ran to inform the neighbors and nearby soldiers.

"The soldiers immediately came here and fired only one bullet, but the Rastas [yet another Congolese militia] escaped. More soldiers came and we followed them into the forest, up the mountain. We tracked them to where we guessed they were keeping the women, in the Rasta camp. They were speaking in Rwandan."

This strikes me as odd. *Why were the Rasta speaking Rwandan?*

"We spotted my sisters. We commanded them to get behind us. Then we saw the other girl. Immediately there was the intervention of the Interahamwe. There was exchange of bullets."

Exchange of bullets. What a lovely understatement for "it erupted into full-on gun battle."

"After some minutes exchanging bullets, the Interahamwe ran away. The soldiers took the three women, maize flour, and goats. We ran all the way back home."

"How long were they with the militia?" I ask.

"Twelve hours."

I look around the compound, noting an empty metal feeding trough but no animals. I hear Major Kaycee ask Maurice, "How did you know they were Rasta, not Interahamwe?"

I circle back around. "Yeah, that's a good question."

"Because they were speaking in Rwandan and they are taller than Congolese," Maurice translates.

In unison, both majors and I say, "They were Interahamwe."

Maurice retreats; he's been caught. Purposely mistranslating? Major Kaycee invites his translator to step in. Maurice looks me in the eye, knowing he's been called out for his blatant editorializing. It's the first moment in five and half weeks I've been angry with him. The brother continues, "Even the soldiers we were with said it was FDLR, not Rasta."

I wander around the compound and enter the simple straw hut; inside, a fire pit is lined with logs. Straw is strewn around for comfort.

Outside again, a sweet-faced child stands in front of me, smiling with warm eyes, leaning against the fence, wearing flaming red. The hills are just beyond her. So here it is, the mythical "forest." A two-minute walk away.

I scan the trees, wondering if I could throw a stone or spit a cherry that far. Who might be staring back at me? Does my pale skin stand out, bright like a traffic light, against the lush, green landscape? If they see me here, what might it cost this family? Does the Interahamwe operate using the simple equations that rule life in the Bukavu slums: *Muzungu* = Money = Attack?

I rejoin the others, trying to encourage the brother. "Tell him he is a hero!"

The brother is still, with his arms folded, casting his eyes to the ground. He nods, allowing a slight smile of acknowledgement to leak out. He bites his lip with embarrassment.

After the long trek back to the road accompanied by the girls' brother, we load into our respective SUVs and drive up the road to park outside what in Africa qualifies as a mega-church. The one institution left standing, it is maybe three stories high and marks the center of Kaniola. We wait a long time for the brother to haul his sisters out of the service. Finally, as church is letting out, the brother runs back out to the car. The girls are embarrassed and don't want to attract attention to themselves. It hadn't occurred to me they would not want to be seen, in front of the whole village, being picked up after church by vehicles boldly marked UN. This would, effectively, mark them as "Raped Women."

We pull up a hundred yards down the road. A few minutes pass and the brother, two girls, and a man in a shiny green sports jacket slip into our unmarked car and encourage Serge to gun it before their friends notice.

While we drive, I'm introduced to Chantal, fifteen; Nadine, seventeen; and Christophe, their quiet-mannered father. Both girls are plump, with a healthy glow, but with the skeptical aura true to teenagers the world over. They are not remotely anxious to impress; instead they watch me, the white lady, with the detached reserve one would expect of American kids with Converse tennis shoes and nose rings who smoke clove cigarettes at the local café. A girl may live in the worst place on earth, but she can still be cool, after all.

As we stop and settle into a private field off the main road, dark clouds roll in and thunder crashes in the distance. *(That's more like it.)*

Chantal picks at the grass as we talk. Christophe gives his permission for the girls to talk to me on camera. "We know you will film, and whatever you film will maybe pass on television, and this will help end the situation," he says.

The situation.

The girl's story is identical to their brother's. "They used belts to tie our hands, like cows. After they got our neighbor, Rahema, they looted whatever they found in house goods—hens, maize flour—and took us with them."

Chantal, still picking at the grass, looks down as she tells the story. "After we climbed up the mountain they realized we had forgotten our clothes, so we went back. We got all our clothes and climbed the mountain again. We didn't know our brother had gone for help."

I don't have a clue why Interahamwe would care if the girls had forgotten their clothes, but it was critical because it allowed the army enough time to catch up with them on the seven-hour hike through the forest towards the militia's camp. They did not know they were being tracked.

"We stopped to rest, the soldiers slaughtered a hen, and they sent us to get water so they could prepare food."

The father stops us to say, "Excuse me. Here is their friend."

The third girl joins us. Rahema is also fifteen and a bit more shy than the others. We continue, as Chantal holds a bandana over her mouth. "Rahema was carrying the maize flour, so she stayed behind when we went to get water. That's when we heard the guns. We saw the Congolese soldiers. They ordered us to get back. The militia guarding us ran away. We hid behind them while they shot towards the guys who had Rahema. The militia released her and ran into the forest. We recovered Rahema and all the things robbed from the village. That's when we saw our brother with the soldiers."

"How do you feel about staying in your village now, after this has happened?" I ask.

"We would like to move, but we don't have family in another place. We are frightened."

Christophe interrupts. He is quiet and direct, if not desperate. "I would like to add something. The militia knows everybody, everywhere. So even if we move from Kaniola to another place, we are sure we will find militia in that place. So we prefer to stay at home."

The father looks broken by his inability to protect his girls.

"Is the militia interested in these three girls in particular? Or do they just take anyone?" I ask.

"They are always interested in women and animals."

"Did they hurt you?" The girls shake their heads no.

"I have one more question. But I'm wondering if all the men can go for a minute."

The men leave, but the brother and father stay. I have to ask them again to give us a minute alone. Chantal tries to leave with them. I take it she knows the next question. I ask her to stay. She sits back down and faces away from me.

"Did they . . . Maurice, you know what my question is. Can you think of a delicate way to put it?"

Maurice nods, and asks them.

"They did not rape us," one of the girls says. "The problem was time. We were running. But on the way, they kept telling us once in the camp, we will be their wives."

"How did you feel about that?" I ask.

"I was afraid, but really, what could I do?" Nadine responds.

"Is there anything you would like to tell people in America?"

"Help us, so we can put an end to the situation. Help us to help fight militias, so we can live in peace."

"And you, Chantal?"

She is so done with this conversation. "I don't have anything to add. Maybe my parents know what to say."

I realize Rahema, who joined us late, has said nothing. I turn to her and ask, "Is there anything you would like to tell me about what happened that day?"

"After they separated me from the other girls, the militia began to touch me . . . wherever," she says without affect. "Immediately, Congolese soldiers appeared and they ran away."

After the interview, I stand above the road, watching the three girls casually walk away together, like teenage girls anywhere. They are laughing, talking, maybe gossiping. Major Vikram leans over to me and says ominously, "They are safe . . . for now."

We all know. We all feel it. But he says it anyway, "Now the Interahamwe know where they live. They will definitely be back."

Christophe stays behind, standing with arms crossed next to the UN majors, ready to talk man-business. He addresses Major Kaycee, asking, "What's next? What will you *do*?"

The sinking feeling is palpable. Now that he's had their ear, Christophe thinks the UN is going to actually help. Major Vikram and Kaycee squirm with the awkwardness; it's like each is being asked, after a casual hookup with a woman, "So will you call me?" Collecting the report was the pinnacle of action, the big event. Followed by the brutal truth. What's next? *Get real. Nothing's next.*

I dig around in my purse for paper and find an already-scrawled-on envelope. I rip it in half and scribble a note in bold block letters, as though emphatic handwriting and exclamation points could tip the scales.

Please enroll these girls. I will pay. If you have questions, contact Hortense or Christine in Bukavu. Thank you!!!

LISA SHANNON

FOUNDER, RUN FOR CONGO WOMEN

Christophe nods, despite his confusion, as Maurice tries to explain Women for Women. I picture the girls carefully following my instructions, walking eight miles into Walungu's town center.

They cannot be enrolled, but I won't learn this until tomorrow, when I visit the Women for Women office to implore Jules, the head of sponsorship, to help.

"But Lisa, the time of the Walungu enrollment has passed."

"You don't understand. The Interahamwe are coming back for them."

"Anyway, they are too young."

"But *I'll pay.*"

Jules will smile at the painfully awkward position I'm putting him in. "It is against the regulations."

"Forget the regulations! We have to get them out of there!"

He will stare at me, unwilling to budge. After five and a half weeks of taxing Women for Women staff, there will be no more *muzungu* credits left in the bank. I will have no rank left to pull.

If force of will would work, I would grab Jules, shake him as though he's the gatekeeper to saving Congo, and make him understand the urgency. If screaming, or throwing a diva fit, or banging on the doors of the powers that be would change the situation, I would do all of it shamelessly. But I know the rules here, and none of it would work.

There's only one tactic left. I will beg.

"Please. Please do this. Jules. *Please.*"

He will simply hold up his hands.

I am standing at the hard edge of the "one person can make a difference" story I've been telling myself, with my arms draped at my sides, watching the girls disappear towards the hills. They are still innocent. They follow the long, winding path back to the compound that sits at the far edge of civilization, where they will *burn like a field of poppies at the edge of a rainforest.*

CHAPTER TWENTY-NINE

These Fragments

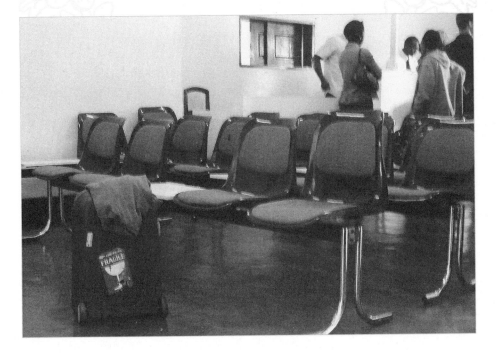

*I*IN THE TINY Rwandan hilltop airport, which overlooks Lake Kivu and Congo's hills beyond, I file past security. Zainab, Alice, and Prathiba pull up and emerge from their car. They will be on my flight to Kigali, the only flight this airport will host today.

Passports stamped.

Fees paid.

Luggage checked.

I wave my final goodbye to Serge and Maurice and proceed to the pale cement waiting room while Zainab and Prathiba navigate their way through the bureaucracy. Alice has already cleared her paperwork and stands alone by the wall, wearing a do-not-disturb look. Instinct tells me to leave her alone—but come on. It's Alice Walker, fresh out of Congo. I can't resist. I set my bags down and approach her. With desperate curiosity I ask, "What were your impressions?"

She looks at me, seemingly shocked at my question. "I could not begin . . . It will take months."

Embarrassed, I slink across the waiting room and find an empty wall. I stand under the TV and face the waiting room, its tattered couches and plastic seats hosting twenty or so bored-looking travelers. I'm already feeling raw and shaky; I'm wired on caffeine and sugar from a lunch of Coke and french fries at the airport snack bar, where Maurice, Serge, and I moped, dreading our imminent goodbye. I asked Serge, who claimed to speak no English, "What will you do when I'm gone?"

Serge grumbled, "Some f——ing job."

We burst into laughter that ended with the quiet heartbreak you feel when you look into the eyes of someone dear, unsure if you will ever see that person again. Maurice shrugged and said, "We are like orphans."

Adrenaline woke me at four this morning. With the finish line in view, something was rumbling inside me. Ted called around 4:30 AM to let me know the house sold following a bidding war. Our move-out date is set for three weeks from now.

We drove to Panzi after breakfast to say a last goodbye to Generose. Bonjour's mom approached me in the parking lot and, with a big hug, told me Bonjour is okay. *"Aksanti sana."* Thank you so much.

Later, in the light-filled office with a view of the lake, a Women for Women staff member and I talked about memorials. She said, "We are not like Rwanda. It is not possible here in Congo to leave the dead on display. We bury our dead."

I know of the genocide memorials she was referring to, though I'd had no time to visit. "I imagine this is why some journalists say Congo doesn't photograph well," I said "They're thinking, Where are the bodies?"

"Exactly," she says. "If you come across a body, you must bury it, even if you don't know the person. Otherwise, we believe they will haunt you."

The conversation went no further; I understood the point. I thought of the foot-square box, the three mini-urns, and the Build-a-Bear that hold my father's ashes.

Now, standing against the wall in the airport, I scan the couches, noticing the blank stares fixed on the TV above me, the mix of stoic aid workers and African businessmen. I'm hoping the embarrassment doesn't show in my face. No such luck. Alice reads my expression and approaches to ask, "What were *your* impressions?"

The question slaps me like an alarm bell sounding during a deep night's sleep. I scramble for words, but I'm at a loss. My defenses seem to have crept away, abandoning their posts somewhere between my last breakfast on Orchid's terrace and Generose's final call to Maurice's cell phone, which came as we chugged up the smooth, Rwandan road above Lake Kivu. Generose called to announce that she had "fainted from grief" after we said goodbye.

What are my impressions?

"You see how difficult that is?" Alice asks, rhetorically.

I don't have impressions. No well-formed ideas, no neat prescriptions. Only fragments, unedited and unfiltered. In my embarrassment, the raw and shaky feeling is giving way to something nameless, something that's roaming into the territory of pain.

As Zainab finishes up her paperwork across the waiting room, she flashes me a knowing look and winks. Prathiba approaches to usher Alice away, like a security guard who is making up for slackened duty. "Perhaps we should move outside into the sunshine."

Alice asks me, "Are you taking a day in Kigali?"

I can't speak. I shake my head.

"You fly straight back? Oh, that will be hard on your rear." As they move to the sunny corridor, Alice says, "It's okay to cry about it."

I face the room of travelers with their eyes glued to the TV above my head; it's as though I'm on stage. I can't stop it. I burst. As everything goes blurry with tears, I shield my face, my wet hands spread open to cover my eyes. My shoulders are shaking, my belly heaving. I am doing my best to be silent. The packed waiting room pretends they don't see my full-on melt down. I shrink down the wall.

I huddle on the floor of the waiting room in unending sobs.

CHAPTER THIRTY

In-Between

I'M ON STAGE in front of a public meeting hall, alone. I scan the sparse audience. Blank or pained expressions stare back at me as some remove their hands from their mouths or ears. I've just told Generose's story. An African woman towards the back of the room gets up and dashes towards the bathroom, followed by her American companion.

I look down at my outline, written in block letters on yellow legal paper. I'm not even halfway through. I stray from my notes, "This is really long . . . and dark. . . ."

They still stare at me blankly. The African lady's friend discreetly grabs their things from the pew and the two exit quietly through the back door. I dump my outline and make a mad dash for the finish line, quoting every hopeful anecdote I can come up with.

As the stragglers find their way to the door, one of my mom's friends stops me. She has booked me for a talk at her church, so she emails often, anxious to hammer out the details. Now she lays down the law. "That was way too dark for my church."

Though I try to reassure her it's no problem to edit a talk to be church-appropriate, she follows up by demanding an advanced copy of my speech to preapprove.

AND THAT'S HOW it will be this year; every speaking engagement will be a prenegotiated tightrope walk between taste and truth. A more strategic mind might break it down carefully, analyzing the lines and the limits. Instead, I retreat to my easier-to-digest, pre-Congo talking points, which are laced with only occasional illustrations from my trip and result in an unavoidably flat delivery.

The hard truth is that I made no plans beyond Congo. After years of cashing in every karmic credit I had for this work, it is time to face reality: tanking stock-photo sales reports and, in front of me, the years it will take to untangle my business and financial bonds with Ted.

We have only a few weeks to endure together before we turn over the house to the new owner and execute complicated plans to avoid each other until Ted finds a place in New York and I move into my new house here in Portland. In the interest of civility, we go out to breakfast. Ted and I slip into a booth at a hipster dive, each sipping cups of tea while waiting for brunch to arrive. He stirs the milk in his Earl Grey, his head dropped. A tear hits the table. His lips shake as he struggles to form words. "I've been thinking; I wasn't there for you when you needed me. I'm sorry."

I watch him. He seems like someone running after a bus, pounding on its side after it has pulled into traffic. It is the beginning of Ted's months-long campaign to get back together, which I meet with patient sympathy and a clear view of the impossibility of two lives now on radically different trajectories.

Eventually, Ted gets it. At the coaching of his bachelor buddies in New York, Ted invests fifteen minutes posting his profile on a dating website. It turns out to be an instant remedy for unrequited love. He responds to one of the first four applicants, a woman who works in design for a corporate chain store. They carve out a love nest in Brooklyn and plan to marry.

Months after our return, Kelly and I have lost touch. She doesn't organize another run. I invite her to come down and speak at the Portland Run for Congo Women finish-line celebration, but she can't make it. My heart sinks as I read her scant, post-Congo blog entries. In a tailspin of doubt, she has turned in on herself; she's searching for that perfect soul-place she questioned in me as we stood beneath the Capitol building two years ago. She laments her inability to cleanse the blood out of the oppression-drenched American soil on which she's built her suburban dream, along with her fruitless attempts to scrub her way out of her white skin. . . .

And then, for ages, nothing. No posts.

She has processed herself into oblivion.

Oh, love. I hardly ever drink. But I want to take her out for a Bloody Mary brunch. We could get fabulously drunk and I might say the right thing to talk her down. But I can't stand to listen to my own platitudes or truisms anymore. Even buckets of pepper and tomato juice and vodka at noon won't help me produce any answers for myself, much less for her.

I TRAIN FOR the 30-mile run in only six weeks, a feat made possible because of my new secret weapon: iced coffee. I pound it back at strategic points along the trail and manage my third 30-mile run without incident. At the finish line, I collapse on the park lawn and don't talk much. I watch my mom run around like mad, coordinating. She could just as easily peel away from the crowd and whimper on the sidelines, "I can't do it!" as she could camp at the T-shirt table, offering Japanese acupressure tips to injured runners, or telling volunteers about the summer she wandered the Northern California woods, feeling the power of the earth surge through her as she entered the river naked.

No, she isn't perfect. The decidedly unglamorous details of organizing these fundraising runs have been a Herculean effort for that right-brained lady. But then, I don't think the thought of perfection has ever crossed her mind, much less slowed her down. She's been too busy throwing her wild-hearted energy into getting sound permits, making photocopies, and coordinating porta-potties. She's worked her butt off for Congolese women. Just as she's been doing for years.

Despite all the fits and rages and screams of "I want out," she's still here.

I'm sure she does it because she wants to support me, but if that were all, the mother-daughter tension would have sent her packing years ago. She is still here simply because, in a strikingly personal way, she loves Congolese women and believes herself connected to them. Looking at my mom across the park lawn in my post-run daze, I burst into a smile, which is tempered only by my embarrassment over how long it's taken me to get how wonderful she is.

Actually, my two-person staff—Mom and me—has become the bottleneck. It's time for Run for Congo Women to grow beyond our limited capacity. Women for Women is ready to take it over so they can help it grow with fully funded staff that operates from checklists based on a proper development strategy and will never miss an email. They will handle the logistics, while I continue my role as spokesperson and founder on the volunteer basis with which we have built up the project.

The network interest in my footage is lukewarm. I never make a documentary. I knew while sitting on the little airplane next to Alice and Zainab that I wasn't walking away from Congo with a film. I turn over the footage to Women for Women, who hand it off to an editor to make a web video of me and my trip. A male movie-trailer voice booms, "While watching an episode of *Oprah*, Lisa Shannon learned that four million people. . . ." I find it unbearable. When I see it, I want to climb under the table and stay there.

The blank space in my life grows cavernous in the absence of fourteen-hour workdays, even though I'm interrupted by the occasional conference call or speaking engagement.

I KEEP D ON HAND the way one keeps good wine in the cellar. I bury myself in him the way one reflexively covers an exposed nerve. Both of us are reeling from the shell shock of lives in collapse. The connection is forged without plans, professions, or sentimentality.

In the summer, we escape to a cabin on a remote bay in the northern wilderness. "It doesn't get better than this," D says. The insistent invitation of his stare is like a knock at the door when you'd rather pretend no one is home. He lists the food, the wine, the trees, the light, the reflections on the water, as though I would miss it without his itemized list. As though I can't feel the wine on my tongue or the breeze on my skin. As though I can't see his face. As though I won't remember.

I retreat to my three-by-five notecards inside the glass cabin, scribbling down thoughts, moments, scenes from Congo, shifting them around the table. I don't have a film, but I wonder if I might have a book—if only I can find the narrative through-line.

In deep winter, we stand on opposite sides of a snow-covered bridge. We are silent as I watch the water flow past the last open patches of the stream crusted over in ice. He calls this meditating. We've walked for an hour in the snow, past farms and forest. I'm not sure if we've been talking; it felt like silence. And silence feels perfect. It's early December. I would rather not speak. I didn't want to come here, afraid soft and sweet would scrape at the edges of my raw state. Instead it feels like a refuge.

In early spring, we are in D's townhouse bathroom. It is the most inviting room in his house, not because of the floor-to-ceiling marble, steam shower, or spa tub. It's the light. In it, I can breathe.

We slip into opposite ends of the bath. Again with the insistent stare, he asks, "How have you been?"

Our eyes meet for a second. I could spill everything: I'm lost. Reeling. Empty.

"Good," I say.

I shut my eyes.

We have plans to see each other before and after my trip out East. But for reasons too convoluted to recount, in a rapid-fire text message exchange, we end it. I'm on a subway in New York, with two valid e-ticket itineraries still sitting in my in-box, but I know which plane I'll step on tomorrow, all the same. I won't see him again and as I sit here, it seems fitting. As the dirty metal cars rock back and forth, faces shutter past like out-of-sync movie frames. I think of the unspoken undercurrent between us since we met at Orchid, the energy we've spent pretending things are casual, of how I have ignored the fact that when he looks in my eyes, I sense something rare. I write him a message, something like "life is too short to be so guarded." I erase it when I realize the message is more like a note to self. The moment has come and gone.

WHILE DIGGING AROUND in the basement, I purge stack upon stack of plastic crates filled with stock photo props. They're now destined for the local women's shelter—the plastic flowers, white slipcovers, colorful dresses for little girls' summer days with fake families. Mixed in among the props and Christmas ornaments, I notice water-damaged, mildewed boxes labeled LISA: CHILDHOOD. I remember a smaller, carved wooden box that is buried in one of these boxes. I picked it up in India, to keep important letters, photos, and keepsakes in. And in that box—it's astounding I have forgotten it all these years—is a handwritten note from my father, the only one he wrote to me in my life, presented on the verge of my departure to India, when I was sixteen. My mom had corralled her New Age friends for a going-away "blessing ceremony" for me. This note was Dad's effort to participate privately, without over-the-top ritual displays. I pull out the plain piece of paper with perforated edges; it was torn from an eighties dot matrix printer, folded in quarters, and labeled in barely legible man-handwriting:

A Blessing for Lisa
7-28-91
Writing a blessing or a deep wish somehow implies doubt, which I
don't feel. So I prefer to affirm the blessings, talents & characteristics

that you already have clearly demonstrated, that I believe will serve
you well in India and the rest of your life.
1. Courage: As a child and later you often seemed fearless in pursuing
your objectives, whether in a game or telling a prejudiced stranger off.
This tenacity has been linked with a strong sense of inner direction.
You seem never to doubt your objective and then be willing to act.
2. Your inner directedness seems to be leading you to areas of meaning,
purpose, and high values. You seem always to be concerned with more
than just yourself, indicating a maturity far beyond your years.

Thus I know you will do well in the tasks you set for yourself and I
am proud to be your father.

> *Love,*
> *Dad*

As if Dad's trying to temper me with another parting message, I later find a small collection of mini digital video tapes that have been scattered and lost in a junk drawer. I interviewed my dad on video in his final weeks. When I asked about his work and finding meaning through helping others, he responded, "I don't think you can be focused on, 'Oh, gee, I want to make a difference.' It has to be spontaneous. If it's not . . . there's some kind of egotistical thing going on. That's a red flag. You hope you impact people on the deepest level you are capable of at the time. Sometimes you hit it, sometimes you don't. You're trying."

I WAKE IN MY empty attic-bedroom, three stories up, with windows overlooking the top branches of the two ancient walnut trees that guard my empty Craftsman-style house. Like the rest of the place, my bedroom is void of furnishings, except for some clothes on a rolling rack and the crisp white sheets and comforter that engulf me on a mattress on the floor. I get up, wander downstairs, get a cup of tea, and check my email. There is a message from Eric with the subject line "Seventeen Knifed to Death in Kaniola."

"I am forwarding you an article about 17 persons who were killed by knives in Kaniola. Do you remember there?"

Yes, Eric, I remember there.

What part of Kaniola? Oh, God. Was it the area I hiked to? Was it people I've met?

I burst into tears and cry half the day, scanning the footage, searching my memory, swimming in images of the children who ducked when I pointed the camera at them. The waddling little boy. The grandmother. The boys playing soccer on the hilltop. The three still-innocent girls. Their brother, our guide. The father. Oh God, the father. Is it Christophe? It must be.

I remember—today is Memorial Day.

I've spent too many days scribbling down notes—shreds of paper that get lost in stacks and "to sort" boxes—with pleading faces in my head, telling me I promised to continue until the coming of Jesus. As time goes on, I'm all too aware I am slowly becoming another one of those *muzungu* bullshitters who said they care, who said they'd be back, who said they'd do something. Maybe the problem isn't me straightening out the story. Maybe it isn't complete. I have unfinished business.

CHAPTER THIRTY-ONE

Missing

UNDER THE WEIGHT of fluorescent lights and jet lag, I watch the unclaimed plastic suitcases make their final rounds on the baggage belt. I've combed the pile of bags set to the side, waiting to be claimed, and scoured nearby belts to see if my bag could have maybe, possibly, been put on the wrong cart.

It's late night in Nairobi, 15 months since I was last in Africa, and time to face facts. The bag is still in England, lost with tens of thousands of others in the abyss of Heathrow's new Terminal 5 chaos. All the carefully selected presents, my clothes, videotapes, malaria pills, tampons . . . I'm going to Congo with no stuff.

I get in line behind the other British Airways passengers who share my fate, comforting myself by taking stock of what I do have. The essentials: my camera bag, my white three-ring binder, a catalog of photos, printed from video, of every person I passed in Kaniola on the Last Walk.

At least having no stuff breaks the ice as I cross the Congo border, pulling the passport-stamp guy into my little drama. "I have no bags for you to search."

"You didn't get your bag?"

"No."

He looks at me, deadpan. "I'll loan you a pair of my trousers."

See that? The spirit of giving.

Ah, Congo, the familiar air of a war-ravaged land. It feels like home. I already dipped my toes into the familiar paranoia back at home, when I hit a major snag in my travel preparations. Maurice and Serge are now being quoted US$300 per day for SUV rentals. Even on a ten-day trip, that adds up fast. As with all my Run for Congo Women work, including my prior Congo visit, this jaunt through Africa is strictly self-funded. After all, I am a never-published, would-be author working on spec.

I put out the word, emailing all my contacts if they know how I can find a more reasonably priced vehicle (around US$100 a day). Less than a week before departure, I got one hit from a friend.

MAMA LISA,

I RECEIVED A CALL FROM RENÉ THIS MORNING. HE SAID HE HAS A JEEP FOR RENT.

HE WILL BE DRIVING IT HIMSELF.

NICE DAY!

I SPENT TWO DAYS swimming in thoughts of *El Presidente* hovering behind me, overseeing every interview, every roadside stop, and wondering if he knows I was responsible for getting him fired. (After our drive, I approached his boss at an international NGO, who was unaware of his affiliations. He was fired immediately and since then has struggled to find work—even calling me for a job reference at a ridiculous hour after he was forced to abandon "political affiliations incompatible with humanitarian work.")

I offhandedly mentioned René's offer to drive me in an email to D when I was encouraging him to buy Eric an SUV. (If the inflated rental rates are tough on me, they must be killing Eric's little nonprofit with his hour-and-a-half commute!)

D didn't respond much; he just cautioned me. "Be careful."

But, funny thing, I got an email from Eric about an hour later. He had just gotten off the phone with D and just happens to have a neighbor who will rent me an SUV at US$90 a day.

D plays dumb when I mention the coincidence.

Later Eric will tell me about the call, how D urged him to take care of me, since I don't always maintain the strictest safety standards for myself. (It's true, a lot of experienced Congo travelers think I am nuts. I prefer to think of myself as having a high threshold for risk.)

Oh, and D agreed to buy Eric that SUV.

ORCHID IS A WHOLE different scene this time around. The Last Belgian is away and the place is crawling with middle-management types, mostly mining subcontractors clearing the way for a massive goldmine that is only a short helicopter ride from town.

Over breakfast, some managers strike up a conversation with me and ask about the purpose of my visit. I see no reason to sugarcoat the matter. I mention the Kaniola massacre matter-of-factly, as I would tell any friend inquiring about my plans for the week. They fidget with their napkins for a moment and quietly rise. Someone murmurs, "Well."

They walk away without further niceties, but one of them remains. So I start with the basic traveler's intro. "What brings you here?"

"Environmental work."

"I have a lot of friends who have environmental projects here. What kind?"

"Mining."

In remarkably unfiltered fashion, he explains he's been hired by a mining company with offices in the hotel to do an environmental impact assessment. The company wants to claim that all the pollution and other damage to rivers near a new gold-mining project they're starting in Eastern Congo already existed—and was done by local artisanal miners—prior to mine and hydroelectric construction. "So no one can pin it on us," he says.

In another lifetime, I might have found this intriguing, even scandalous. But foreign mining interests are no secret in Congo. Why pretend it's shocking? Why be shy? He's not. Like all good corporate spin-machines, he has resolved the ethical issues, hovering above the conflict like the helicopter that flies in and out every day, cruising across the Congolese landscape just high enough to avoid being bothered by the little things, like people.

"Americans did this in their own West," he reminds me. "Is it fair to say in Congo, they shouldn't do what the West did?"

I can't help myself. "Who's 'they?' The Congolese people? Last time I checked, they aren't responsible for most of the mining or timber harvesting here and they don't seem to benefit. And it's brought the war."

"I suppose that's true," he says. "But is it different than all of history? We used to all have colonies, only now, we label it *bad*."

I can't disagree: War profiteering. Genocide. Global warming. All generally thought of as "bad." "We do," I agree.

The conversation makes me tired, too tired to feel hostile or even annoyed. Beneath the thick Afrikaans accent, here is a man clinging to a dying ideology. The grasping mindset, the moral compromise that won't even get him big bucks, just a stab at a life's work that involves travel to exotic corners of Africa. That may be enough for a neocolonialist. I look at him and feel sad.

I ask, "But isn't it a question about who we are? Choosing the role we will play in this world?"

He chews this over for a moment. "I suppose it is."

As he gets up to leave, as though offering me some kind of truce, he hands me his card. I realize he thinks we've been flirting when he says, "If you ever need a place to stay when you're in South Africa. . . ."

I WANT TO GET the return visit to Kaniola out of the way immediately, if nothing else to combat my shaky nerves. At Major Vikram and Kaycee's former station in Walungu, I am greeted by Major Alejandro, a warm, slim South

American who is new to this post. I describe the attack and what I'm after: a return trip to Kaniola and any information about the massacre.

"I know nothing about this," Major Alejandro says, "as I have only been here four days. But there is one man left from that time. He's in Bukavu today. Come back tomorrow, he will be here. It will be his last day."

In the meantime, I am directed to the Pakistani Battalion in Walungu to secure permission for a Kaniola visit, which now requires clearance.

I end up on a sunny hilltop, on a patio lined with roses and yellow cosmos that overlooks the vast valleys beyond Walungu, with a handful of Pakistani military commanders. Shared cups of juice served in glass and gold goblets aren't enough to bridge the massive cultural divide, especially when it comes to their questions about my scant credentials. "You've written a book before?"

"No."

"Who is publishing this book?"

"I don't know yet." I cut to the chase. "I don't need guides. I can go on my own. . . ."

"I'm sorry Madame. You'll need written permission from HQ in Bukavu."

BACK IN BUKAVU, I am poised for another "we couldn't have less in common" meeting as I am led into a grand office at UN headquarters. Instead, Colonel Khan is gracious, carrying himself with restraint and formality. He's genuinely trying to be helpful. I sip my requisite apple juice while he scans his desktop files for any information about the day of the massacre.

As he scrolls through his reports, I see file names and pictures in the lefthand margin of his screen. I zero in on the thumbnail photos scrawling by: severed heads and limbs, stacks of bodies. Part of me strains to see them, hoping to catch a clue about the massacre. The other half is relieved I can't make out the details from across the desk, grateful my mind has been spared the gory imprint.

He grants us permission to return to Kaniola and arranges for a security-escort several days from now. Colonel Khan emphasizes, "If there is anything you see there that warrants our attention, anything our people can make improvements on, I hope you will do me the favor of reporting back to me."

He cannot, however, release the reports.

THE DELAY WHILE WAITING for the security-escort is perfect.

So, about singing "Kumbaya" with the people. Snarky swipes aside, there's something that has bothered me all year. In my pursuit of Congo horror stories, there were a lot of questions I didn't ask. Like who was lost. I didn't even ask their names.

THERESE STEPS OUT of a cement building that's covered in peeling paint, on a private compound in the village. It's a Sunday, so few others are around. There is no grand reception, just a long hug with my first Congolese sister. She's wearing the same yellow Sunday-best dress she did nearly a year and half ago. I present her with one of the only gifts that made it in my carry on bag: a green scarf in raw silk. Therese wraps it on her head. It happens to be the perfect complement to her favorite dress. Another translator is filling in, a staff lady who speaks fluent Mashi, Therese's regional dialect. "Therese would like to know about your tribe, your clan."

We talk for hours. I tell her all about my Catholic clan in Arkansas, my Protestant clan from Oklahoma, my immediate family, and my tribe of friends.

I ask about her family.

"I was singer in the church choir, and a greeter at church. My husband was prayer-group treasurer. We would come to the parish here to give reports on the groups. It was a two-and-a-half-hour walk, so it was a chance to be together. We fell in love."

I ask about the time her husband was taken to cook for the Interahamwe.

"Some people told me he died, but I was not convinced. I felt he was still alive. I waited and waited until he came back. I had served the evening meal to my mother- and father-in-law when I heard a voice like my husband's, greeting his parents. His father was astonished. He said, 'Your voice is like Pascal's voice. Who are you, man?'

"He said, 'I am your son, Pascal.'

"I couldn't imagine he had come back. I thought he was dead.

"He walked in. I hugged him. The children, who were already sleeping, got up. The youngest asked me, 'Is he really my father?'

"I said, 'Yes, he is your father.'

"We expressed our joy in dancing and singing.

"Before my husband went to the bush, he was not kind. He was lazy; he didn't want to work. I was taking care of my husband and my children. But since he's come back, he helps me feed the children. His mind has changed. He's kind. When I go farming for other people, my husband goes as well. In the evening, I bring what I got, he brings what he earned, and we feed our children. I'm more happy now than before."

"Can you tell me more about your little girl who died?" I ask.

"She was five years old. Children always bring happiness to parents. Each child has their own manner of acting. When I see what the two children are doing, helping me with housework, I always think about my first child. I imagine if she was still alive.

"She was kind; she loved her grandparents so much. She had the habit of bringing plates when I served food. She always served her grandparents first. She liked to serve others, to wash dishes after dinner."

I interject, "We would call her a 'little helper.'"

Therese says, "Nsemeru. Her name means 'I love you.'"

WANDOLYN IS WAITING with her husband in a private room at the Women for Women Walungu center. Once we are settled, she blurts out, "I don't want to talk about the *event* anymore."

I smile and reassure her, "I just wanted to see you."

After I left, Wandolyn spent nine months in a psychiatric ward, while the nuns cared for Nshobole. When Wandolyn was finally well enough to return home, the nuns had fallen in love with the little girl and wanted to keep her. "Of course I want the child with me, but she receives better care with the nuns. She eats better than my other children! And they will send her to school. We visit her once a month."

I packed photos of the two of them together, but they were lost with my bag. Instead, I pull out my laptop and scroll through photos of their family, images of Wandolyn with Nshobole strapped to her back, panoramic views of Congo beyond them. Excited, Wandolyn and her husband point and smile, nostalgic for the time their daughter lived with their family.

Generose bursts into tears when she sees me. *"Karibu.* Welcome." She wears a beautiful sky-blue African dress. On her crutches, she leads me to her new, little wooden house, with its corrugated metal roof and bright blue trim. She stops at the front door, next to a tall tropical plant sprouting bold red flowers. She picks both blooms and presents them to me. "I grew the flowers for you, so someday, when you came back, I could give them to you."

We tour the compound with her children in tow. Her youngest is over-the-moon enthusiastic, jumping and silly, exchanging funny faces with me. When we step inside, I'm tense. The house is not what we had agreed upon. It's smaller than we discussed and the floors are not cement. They are bumpy with stones. I ask Maurice and Hortense pointed questions about what happened. Generose interrupts, "It is not their fault, Lisa. Prices went up after you left. But I bought the stones and filled the walls myself for around two hundred and forty dollars. I used the money I've raised from my business."

She leads us around to the backyard, bursting with pride at her cassava liquor distillery. "I sell only the best," she boasts, explaining the distillation process. I'm not sure how I feel about keeping the local men liquored up, but her pride is contagious. "I wanted to have some for you to taste, but I sell out after only one day. I can make two batches per month, for a profit of seventy dollars per month."

Considering the fact that most families here live on US$20 per month,

I'm impressed. She's making enough to send her kids to school, buy plenty of food, grow veggies in the back, and bit by bit improve her house. A woman joins us and shakes my hand. Generose nods, raising her eyebrows as she introduces her. "She is among the ones who help."

An employee? This little house is her new empire!

Inside, we pull the curtains closed and wait for the neighbors and children to disperse, so we can talk privately. It's dusk and we talk by candlelight. I ask about her son.

"He was a child I loved so much," she tells me. "The fact that he is the only one who refused to eat a part of me marked my heart."

"What was your son like?" I ask.

"He was nine years old, in third grade. He loved to play soccer and to go fishing on his grandparents' compound. He loved to create cars with banana leaves or to make paper airplanes. He liked to provoke others. He took a toad and put it in his friend's bag. So we were called to the school to justify his behavior. The first thing he used to ask when he came home was, 'Where is the food?' If there was no food, he would get angry with everyone in the house, 'Why is the food not ready?' Or 'Why don't you put salt on the fish? Is the problem poverty, or what?' Or 'You prepare vegetables every day. I don't want vegetables. When I visit my aunt, she makes meat. Why don't you prepare meat?'"

Maurice and I laugh and I say, "Quite a fiery little man."

But Generose looks blankly at the wall.

"Do you remember the last thing you said to your child?"

"What I remember is the last speech he gave to the killer."

"What did he say?" I ask.

"To his father's killer, he said, 'I do not accept to eat a part of my mother.'

"They said, 'Then we are going to kill you.'

"He said, 'If you kill me, kill me. But I will not eat a part of my mother.'"

Generose spaces out, slowly rocking back and forth, while Maurice translates, "They said, 'Then you better pray, because you are going to die.'

"He said, 'You're asking me to pray to God? Why? I do not love you. I am angry with you. How can I pray to God when I have such a bad heart against you?'"

We are quiet for a moment. Then I ask her, "What did the soldiers say?"

"They said nothing. They shot him. I heard the sound of many bullets, but what I saw was the one that entered here." She points to the middle of her forehead.

"What was his name?"

"Lucien."

"And your husband?"

"Claude."

"How did you meet your husband?" I ask.

"My husband was ill, and he came to the hospital where I was a nurse. In treating him, the love began between us. I loved him first because he was handsome. Second, because he gave me advice. After the treatment, he left the hospital, but after two days, he came back to visit me. In one week, he came back with his father to bring a hen as a sign of thanks. After that, he began the habit of visiting. He did this for two years. After two years, he decided to come see my parents.

"There was a great ceremony. My husband's family brought my parents two cows and six goats. We went to the priest so he could bless us. Afterward, we organized a big party."

"What was he like as a person, a man, a husband?" I ask.

"The type of husband I dreamed of since I was a child. Someone very tall, who's not a drunk and doesn't smoke. When I met him, he had all these qualities, and I said, 'This is the man.'

"As a husband, he was responsible. As the father of my children, he was responsible up to the end of his life. He had a habit. When I was very tired he would say, 'Today, it is not your chore. I will prepare food for the whole family.' He prepared eggs and rice. That was his dish. This created a problem with his family. They said, 'How can a man prepare food for his wife? This must be a problem of witchcraft.'

"But there was no witchcraft. Only love.

"We say when you love one another very much, you don't have a long life. Sometimes I have candidates, men who come and would like me to be with them, but when I remember the love my husband had for me and I know those men have their own wives, I say, 'No. You can't give me love as given by my husband. You only want to joke with me. No. No.'"

"I have one last question," I tell her. It has been on my mind for a year. "My father didn't die in a violent way. He had cancer. But when I think of him, the first thing that comes to mind is the way he would slowly run his finger around the edge of his coffee cup while we would talk for hours. I miss that." His habit used to annoy me when he was alive. But when I think of it now, I remember it like the slow hum of a Tibetan singing prayer bowl. "What do you miss about your husband?"

She doesn't hesitate. "When I was pregnant, very heavy with a baby, my husband would wash my body. It was very intimate."

CHAPTER THIRTY-TWO

Salt

WHY? THAT'S THE burning question I've had for years.

I have a unique opportunity to talk with one of the very few people who might have the answer. I'm sitting down with a former Interahamwe rebel who is staying at the child soldier rehabilitation center. André walks into the empty boys' dorm, which is lined with wooden bunk beds and barred windows. I'm surprised. He is a chubby-cheeked seventeen-year-old in jeans and a T-shirt—and he's Congolese. He carries himself with the mild, respectful manner common to boys who have been through serious military training.

In 2002, André was at school when the Interahamwe showed up to "recruit." They forcibly took every boy in the fourth, fifth, and sixth grades. He was eleven years old.

André lived as a member of the Interahamwe for six years. "Life in the forest was very, very hard," he tells me. "It was not possible to wash with soap. We had to eat food without salt. It was impossible to eat food prepared in pans, to have clothes. We had hair everywhere on our bodies. We ate tree roots. We passed many years without seeing anyone in society."

I ask, "If Interahamwe rebels could have normal lives once they leave the militia, how many would simply walk away?"

"If you leave, you are killed. If there was really a possibility, if they had authorization to go home, maybe eighty out of a hundred would accept. Easily."

For a boy who never finished fifth grade, he is as close to the mark as any Washington policy wonk. Those I have spoken to estimate would-be Interahamwe deserters at around 70 percent.

"The other twenty—why would they stay?" I ask.

"The twenty are afraid of judgment. They recognize they have killed a lot of people in Rwanda. One person may have killed more than a hundred persons in Rwanda, so they say, 'Instead of going back to my country, I prefer to shoot myself and die here in the forest.'"

The Interahamwe are responsible for the most sadistic violence in Eastern Congo. But perhaps worse, this force of six to eight thousand provides the excuse for other militias to exist—and terrorize—in the name of protecting civilians from the Interahamwe. The combined presence of these militias has cost 5.4 million mostly innocent civilian lives. But how many die-hard Rwandan *genocidaires* lead the militia, while effectively holding their fellow FDLR combatants hostage? I'm not often shocked, but I'm skin-burning astonished when I learn *fewer than one hundred* set the agenda, and in turn, fuel instability throughout Eastern Congo and by extension central Africa.

Fifteen years into this mess and the international community still has no plan to deal with the Interahamwe.

But there's still something I don't get. I ask André, "Why kill the villagers? Why torture them? One woman I know, they cut off her leg and fed it to her children. They cut out villagers' eyes or nose. Why? What's the logic?"

André bites his lip. "What you heard about, it is true. This is only to show the hard conditions in which the Interahamwe live. Even a child of ten years old—or less—was raped. I saw with my own eyes victims of cutting—breasts, nose, mouth. It is only to show the Interahamwe are no longer persons like us. They are like animals."

"It's because Interahamwe are bitter for being stuck in the forest?" I ask. "It's like revenge on humanity?"

"That's it. A kind of revenge. How can some people spend a good life when others spend a bad life in the forest?"

"How many people do you think you've killed?" I ask him.

"When we talk in terms of killing, I was under orders. We were sent to ask for money. To ask for salt. Because salt was precious. Whenever you do not have salt and you do not give us money, I have orders to kill you. And really, I killed."

Because salt was precious.

CHAPTER THIRTY-THREE

The Hidden Face

ALEJANDRO GREETS US anxiously. He has been calling around, trying to track down the only UN guy who was stationed here in Kaniola at the time of the massacre. But it's turned out there is no such person; none of the foreign UN officials stationed in Walungu at that time is still in Congo. So Alejandro has taken the initiative of asking local UN staffers if they know anything about it. Frankly, I'm not sure it's worth the effort. I'm only looking for a few details that weren't included in the report, plus the names of anyone affected.

Alejandro has run into another roadblock. "Everyone is acting very strange. Even the cleaning lady, when I ask her, is like this." He imitates her by hemming and hawing, avoiding our eyes. No one will talk.

"Of course, I want to help you," he says. "But now I want to know why everyone is acting this way!"

Alejandro calls for another UN staff member, Joseph. He is a short local man, reserved and precise, who speaks better English than almost any Congolese person I've met. He worked closely with Major Vikram and Major Kaycee. I chat him up about Major Vikram, mentioning the emails we exchanged about that day. Joseph is evasive. "I think I remember something like that in 2005."

"No, this was in May."

"I don't know. Talk with others maybe."

"If Major Kaycee and Major Vikram went to the site of that attack, you would have gone with them," I say. "Right?"

"I would go with them, of course."

"Surely if you were there, if you saw seventeen dead bodies, you would remember, wouldn't you?"

"Maybe," he answers. "I don't remember when exactly. Maybe if you look at the daily security reports. . . ."

When did this turn into an interrogation scene? I didn't come here looking for intrigue. I just want to know if the people I met that day are okay. "I don't understand why this is so secret. It was an international news story. So what's the big deal? I just want a few more details about what happened."

"Do you have clearance?" Joseph asks.

"Of course," I tell him. "The Pakistani Battalion is taking us to Kaniola."

Alejandro jumps in. "I have told you, you are free to talk with them."

Joseph sticks to his guns. "Do you have *written* permission?"

"No," I fess up.

Alejandro pushes him. "You are free! Help these people help your country!"

Joseph is growing frustrated. "Look at the report. I think you will find . . . especially in that spot—"

Alejandro cuts him off. "Yes, but as we say in my country, these are cold words. You are a living, breathing person! You were there!"

Poised to burst, Joseph spits out, "I have plenty to say."

He reins himself in, retreating to a more officious tone. "Read the report and you can ask me questions."

The UN doesn't turn over the report. It's classified.

WE GO TO Women for Women's Walungu center, where a few participants from Kaniola agree to talk with us. "The family with seventeen people killed are my neighbors," says a young woman with a red dress and cornrows. "The

Interahamwe came, started cutting people, killing them and burning houses. We spent the night here in Walungu. In the morning we went back to Kaniola. There were government soldiers there already. We felt safe and remained. They were burning dead bodies."

"You saw that?"

"Yes."

"When was the last attack in Kaniola?"

Another woman offers, "February, when they took my two nieces."

They're all in agreement. It's been three months since the last attack. And that's actually an improvement, compared to the twice-weekly attacks that were happening before.

"It's the government's Commander X who masters security in Kaniola," someone says. "Whenever he's there, nobody dares attack because he is strong. When he goes to Bukavu to visit his family, attacks happen."

I present my white binder, as though I'm conducting a one-woman war tribunal and each blurry, pixilated eight-by-ten video print will immortalize its subject. They crowd around the white notebook, flipping page by page, looking at their friends and neighbors. It might be a silly exercise. Watching them scan the pages, I realize that I have no idea what I want to *do* with my notebook full of fuzzy video printouts. I just need to know.

"Do you know that little boy?"

They shake their heads.

"I know four of the children," another woman says. "The militia killed their grandfather."

"What about these little girls?" I ask.

"I recognize that one," another woman answers. "They got into her compound, killed her father, and burned people in the house next door. Burned them alive. About a year ago."

They point to a photo of a man on the roadside, waiting next to the children with the plastic water tubs. "He disappeared. It's as if he was killed. His sister went a year ago to the bushes for sex slavery."

"This one died," a woman says, pointing at another man. "The Interahamwe killed him nine months ago."

The women gather in closer. They are pointing at someone, discussing her among themselves. It's the first woman I passed on my Sunday walk in Kaniola; she was on her way to church. She wore a beautiful dress and had pretty hair and makeup.

"Do you know her?" I ask.

"After a week of marriage, she was taken in the bushes. It was less than six months ago."

As the women watch, I scrawl notes across the bottom of the photograph, like my video log has somehow preserved time. As if I could go back and stop her on that trail. Warn her. Give her money to take her groom and move far away.

"Has she come back? Has she been seen since?"

"They killed her."

I gasp. I only said *jambo*. I didn't know her. But I feel sick, the same way you might feel upon learning that someone at work just died, someone you used to joke with around the water cooler.

"Any of these?" I show them a clear photo of the three girls with Christophe.

"She's there, the girl in the blue scarf."

"They are still in the village?" I say.

"The one in green is a schoolteacher." She's talking about the girls' father, Christophe.

"But is he okay?" I say, pressing them

Pointing to Nadine, someone says, "This one was taken to the forest, and she has never come back. She escaped the first time. When she thought it was quiet, she came back. They took her that time."

I mumble, "I met her once."

They start to back off, straightening their dresses, gathering their things. They've grown tired of the exercise.

"These children, they're okay?" I say, anxiously trying to rope the women back in.

"Some children were taken to the forest. The parents were charged a fine."

"These children?" I say.

"None of these."

A staff member interrupts the meeting. One of the original four Walungu sisters is waiting for me outside; she's reporting that her brother-in-law was killed last night. When she enters, I recognize her and remember her name: Isabelle. I give her a big hug. The other women linger, arms folded. They've all heard the story. He was their neighbor.

"He died or he was killed?" I ask.

"They shot him," Isabelle answers.

"Who's 'they'?"

"Local government soldiers."

"*Why?*" I ask.

"We don't know why."

"To punish him?" I say. "To steal from him?"

"They waited for him on his way back home."

"So they knew him?" I ask. "Is that common? The Congolese Army just . . . assassinating people?"

They all nod emphatically, all too aware of the truth. *"Ndiyo."* Yes.

"Who else have they killed?"

One of the women calls out, "Three cases in two months of government soldiers killing someone."

Everyone ticks their tongues, a Congolese gesture of agreement and disapproval. I'm trying to get my bearings. Looting and rape are standard fare for the Congolese Army. But killing civilians? This is the first I've heard of it.

"We don't know why?" I persist. "They must have a *reason.*"

"It's a matter of conflict between people. When people are in trouble, they bribe soldiers to avenge them. They are hired to kill."

I AM SITTING on the terrace back at Orchid when a group of Pakistani UN officers wanders out onto the terrace. One lingers by my table, waiting for an invitation to practice his English. I notice that the patch on his uniform reads PAK ARMY.

The officers look beyond the gardens to Lake Kivu. The man near me says, "Very beautiful country."

I'm bored and happy enough to engage. "Yes, so beautiful."

"But the people . . . not good. Very black." Coaxing me to join his anti-African club, he adds, "Don't you agree?"

I slowly turn my neck and look at him, dead cold. "The people here are wonderful. Huge hearts."

His buddies inch away.

"Work hard . . ." he says.

I can hear a "but" coming, so I shoot him down before he can start. "Yes, they work so hard."

"Okay." His colleague seems aware of the breach and is eager to usher him onward.

MAURICE, SERGE, AND I park on the side of Walungu's main drag and wait in the car. A credible anonymous tipster with UN connections has heard about our inquiry into the massacre. He was verifiably present with my UN major escorts at the massacre site. He approached asking us to meet him at a rendez-vous point. He stayed up late last night copying the files.

A handful of Congolese military men lurk on the opposite side of the road and seem to find me the most interesting attraction. One of them is especially keen to stare and I'm inclined to stare back. His face is shrouded with an army-green ski-cap. Creepy. I'm desperate to take his photo, but photographing the military is not legal and his is not a friendly stare. I pretend I'm watching some women who are struggling up the muddy road in the rain, their loads covered in dirty plastic, while I hold my camera sideways and try to capture a shot of Ski-Mask Guy. But all I manage to grab are a series of photos of raindrops on the car window. He's blurry and out of focus in the background. It's too bad, it would have made a great visual metaphor. I mentally title the photo I didn't get: The Hidden Face of the Congolese Army.

"Okay," Maurice says, motioning. Enough time has passed. We weave our way through Walungu's back pathways to a private home where our source has been waiting for us. We slip inside; the floor is damp and the faint sound of running water comes from somewhere within the dark hut, which is lit only by the sunlight coming through the doorway. We teeter on wooden benches opposite each other. He produces a small stack of papers and hands them over: carefully copied daily reports from Kaniola, as well as incidents of recent assassinations by the Congolese Army. He says, "You will need to copy it."

"We can't just keep this?"

"Not in my handwriting."

I would be amused were it not for the weight of what he's inching towards telling me. I see the list of names labeled *Chihamba*. Eighteen persons killed. Twenty-five tied up and taken to the forest. Three goats looted.

I dive in with my questioning. "You were there that day."

He is calm and direct. "Yes."

"What happened?"

"They cut out the eyes, nose, and mouths of all those people killed."

"So it was the Interahamwe."

"It was almost obvious it was meant to look like the Interahamwe."

That's a pregnant way to put it. What a stunning thing to say.

"What do you mean, 'almost obvious,'" I ask him. "Meant to *look like* the Interahamwe?"

"The disfiguring was like an imitation of Interahamwe signature attacks," he says.

"How can you tell the difference between the Interahamwe and an imitation?" I ask.

"The Interahamwe does not kill eighteen people for three goats and cell phone. Understand?"

No. I don't understand at all. "Why would someone imitate the Interahamwe?"

He's quiet for a moment, squirming. "There are tensions. Sabotage actions. Different brigades behave like rivals."

"You're saying it was a Congolese perpetrator? *The Congolese Army?*"

"I am confident."

I look at the notes on other attacks which read: "*Comment = probably to create illusion*" and "*Global context of the incident: troop units shifting in and out.*"

He continues. "Brigade Y was handing over the area to Brigade X, under Commander X. There were subsequent confrontations between the rival units, under the command of a certain Commander Y. Once Brigade Y was transferred away, the disturbances ended."

Is he telling me this just to be dramatic? My gut tells me no.

Even in this anything-goes place, I am astounded.

The Congolese Army mutilating and murdering civilians, staging their actions to make it look like the Interahamwe was to blame, for the benefit of rivalry?

His story is not so far-fetched. Months from now, the *New York Times* will report high-level collaboration between Interahamwe leadership and top-ranking Congolese military officials. Satellite phone records will show lengthy, frequent conversations between the two. As it turns out, collaboration between the Interahamwe and Congolese government is common knowledge.

"The people were promised an investigation would be carried out," he tells us now, in the dark hut. "But the locals wait and wait. There was no investigation."

CHAPTER THIRTY-FOUR

Furaha

FROM BEHIND MY sunglasses, I watch the sunlight reflect on my eyelashes, forming little rainbows. I'm sitting in a patch of sunshine while the cleaning guy mops the otherwise empty Orchid terrace with citronella. Old-world French accordion music drifts in as I sip my tea. For a moment, the moldy corners disappear and the patio borders on elegance. I shut my eyes. *Why are we all here?*

Henry Morton Stanley—the real one—comes to mind. The mining guys, the aid workers, me . . . aren't we all trying to live one of those "create-your-own-adventure" books we read as children? Pick option A, B, or C: do you want to help rape victims or child soldiers, rake in the cash as a mining guy, or take down a warlord?

A European mining guy sits down in the next cluster of chairs to sop up a cigarette and a juice. He's looks like a frat boy lost in Thailand, wearing floppy shorts, prayer beads around his wrist, and well-worn flip-flops. As he smokes, he watches me as if he's watching a traffic accident or street fight from a distance; he's cool and detached. He's staying in the room next to mine. I wonder if he heard me crying last night.

An hour or so later I'm still on the terrace, though I've shifted to the table in the corner. French-lady aid-workers smoke and laugh loudly, as if to draw attention to themselves, while keeping an eye out for anyone worth talking to. A collection of blasé Scandinavian businessmen in jackets, pleated khakis, and blue striped or checkered oxford shirts sip wine. I'm not sure any of us belong here, sucking the marrow out of Congo. I keep my eyes down and watch the tiny flies flailing around on my dinner plate. It's a bad day in Congo. The kind that leaves me haunted by futility and failure, and swimming in images of pixilated, freeze-framed faces labeled "abducted" and "murdered."

I want to vent, to scream. But then there's that nagging question: Vent to whom? Despite the fact that it has been months since we've shared a bed, and that we've never been in the territory of "I love you," D comes to mind. I text him:

Here with your mining buddies on the terrace at Orchid.
Found out four people I met last year were killed.

Back in my room, it's late. I'm bent over the mildew-ringed bathtub, washing my only outfit, jeans and a T-shirt that have grown thick with road dust and sweat. I wring the clothes out and prop them on the chair, knowing they'll likely be more wet than damp by morning, but perhaps dry by noon.

I climb inside my cocoon, pull down the mosquito net, tuck it under the mattress. I lie down, carefully positioning myself in the middle of the bed so as not to touch the net. I'm still aching. I stare at the dimly glowing light bulb. I run my fingers across the sheets. They always feel damp here. I study the little rips and mended tears in the net, and I start to cry.

My BlackBerry rings.

D.

I could pick up. I could cry into the phone. I could tell him everything. A piece of me would rather not. In fact, all of me would rather not. I won't.

But I pick up anyway.

"Did I wake you?"

"No," I say quietly, my voice shaking.

"How are you?"

I let out a long sigh, crying.

"That's what I thought. That's why I called."

I spill it. All of it. The massacre. The Congolese Army. The assassinations. And my deepest doubts. "What am I doing here? They live in hell and I give them peanuts. . . ."

I can't talk anymore. I just cry.

D says, "Someone has to do it. Someone has to be a witness."

I cry for a long time. Then D tells me about his beautiful new office. His view of the trees. He brings up the cabin we stayed in on the bay. He reminds me of the wonderful time we had; it's as if he is coaxing me back to life with his itemized list of little joys. Cradling the phone, curled under my mosquito net, we talk longer than anyone should from America to Congo.

I WAKE UP EARLY, my stomach acidic and nervous. We are scheduled to go to Kaniola today. When I went before, I was too numb and off-guard to be scared. Not so this time. I know what's coming and I'm petrified.

I WANT TO BARK at one of my Pakistani Army UN escorts, "Stand down, soldier!" He is pointing his gun squarely at a seven-year-old boy. The little guy's only infraction was to move a few steps closer to me after we exchanged *jambos*.

We are in Kaniola at the trailhead of what Major Vikram referred to as The Last Walk, a point marked by the rusty, bullet-ridden sign on the side of the road that matches my video-print photos. Never mind my camera being mistaken for a gun. We have real guns this time, and a crew of five armed and jumpy men committed to securing my perimeter. They've only been stationed here in Congo for a few days and this is their first visit to Kaniola. They've heard the stories. But they don't quite grasp the security threats on hand; they're drawing on military exercises that don't apply here. There are no child suicide-bombers in Kaniola. The Interahamwe don't hide in thatched roofs waiting to pounce. They announce themselves and kill openly here, so there is no point in harassing children who just want to say hi. I'm not going to let the ambiguity of who's in charge get in my way. I'm the only one who has been here before. I smile at my security guy and kindly request, "Don't point the gun at children, please."

He eases off the boy. But as we set out on our walk through the stunning, now-familiar valley, their tense, by-the-letter approach continues. One stays in front, another in back, both with guns poised for action. In theory, having guns should make us safer, but in a place like this, I'm not sure if guns protect or provoke. They do not endear us to the locals. We approach a group of young men, ranging in age from late teens to early twenties. Though they gather and tolerate my trigger-happy guards, who are stalking the periphery of the crowd, my questions about security land flat.

"There is nothing wrong. Everything is okay."

I can see it in Maurice's discomfort. They are unwilling to talk.

Around the next bend, I spot a familiar old woman: the grandmother. She's heading towards her compound. I call out, *"Jambo, Mama!"*

She sizes up the group, unimpressed with the lurking armed security. As Maurice approaches, she turns and walks away. I follow her and say, "Mama, I wish you would talk to me."

"I'm too hungry to talk!" she calls behind her. Maurice and I follow with the guards running to stay in position in front and behind.

"But I met you last year," I say. "Do you recognize me?"

She ignores us, continuing on. I chase her. "I've been worried about you all year. I've traveled all the way from America to make sure you and your family are okay."

She slows down and turns around to size me up.

"Here is your photo. Do you remember?"

She looks at the fuzzy photo of herself, baffled. "I can't think of anything but hunger."

She caves and agrees to talk for a few minutes. One of the guards searches the compound for any lurking evil-doers on the roofs or in the hedges and huts. The grandmother perches on a little wooden bench and laughs. "Can you give me clothes, so I can be beautiful?"

She wears a tattered gray sweater and has calloused, cracked bare feet. "You already are beautiful. I wish I had clothes to give you," I tell her.

"It is difficult for a woman like me," she says. "I am alone. I've already lost my husband and relatives. I live only with my grandchildren. I don't have a hen, a goat, nothing for myself. Not even clothes."

She introduces us to one of the five puffy-cheeked kids who have been watching from a distance; it's her granddaughter, who's maybe five years old. Both the girl's parents died four years ago, when she was still an infant. She curls in towards her grandmother, who keeps a hand on the child's arm.

"If you have nothing, no money to feed yourself, why did you take in this little girl?"

"She had nowhere else to go."

On the way out, I slip her ten dollars.

We trek along the last ridgeline on the far outskirts of the village. The clusters of huts and cabbage patches are unchanged from last year. But then we approach the soccer field. It's become a small Congolese Army camp. Temporary straw shelters, something like tents, with ditches dug in front of them, dot the field that is otherwise overgrown with grass. The hilltop is windy, which adds a haunting feeling to this outpost at the edge of civilization.

A plainclothes Congolese soldier sees us and calls out, *"Commandant! Commandant!"*

A clean-shaven young man, with the fresh face of a virgin soldier, emerges from one of the huts. He's wearing a tracksuit jacket and fashion jeans. Embarrassed to be caught out of uniform, he disappears and greets us again in full, crisp uniform, complete with creases and a green beret. He gives a formal salute for the benefit of the UN major. He straps on his gun, trying to impress the UN, desperate to prove himself. He has just been transferred from the west; this is his fourth day in Eastern Congo. His first assignment is this last ridgeline in Kaniola. Their unit is split, with five soldiers at this camp and four on a neighboring hillside. He's heard the stories. He points to the hills, the forest. "This place is attacked; they come from over there."

The UN commander cuts him short. "But there has been no such incident since last May."

"That's what they said," I comment, thinking of the edited information we may have gotten, given our guns. "Have you had any attacks since you've been here?"

"The day before yesterday, I saw four flashlights during the night, right there, coming down the mountain from the forest. I fired three shots," he says, pointing to a spot on the opposite hill. "Then I saw the flashlights climb back up the mountain."

Three shots and they ran way? *Wow. That's how it's supposed to work.*

He talks discreetly, confiding in the major. "Our commander left us up here with no supplies. No food. We sent someone the day before yesterday to ask for something, and again yesterday, but nothing yet. We hope our commander will send something soon."

Apparently he's not yet initiated to the ethics of Eastern Congo. I ask him, "What have you been doing in the meantime?"

"The villagers share with us."

So it begins.

We continue on our walk with local guides, who say they will take us to see one of the girls in her new home, which is a few compounds away from the one we visited last year. We wait twenty minutes or so, then a familiar young woman enters the compound, which is filled with baby goats and calves. It's Nadine! She's bewildered to find me waiting for her. An oversize sweatshirt reading "Charge Spicy Sporty" hangs over her swollen belly. She is not maimed or mutilated or slaughtered or taken to the forest. She's married! Pregnant! It's the height of good fortune for an eighteen-year old girl in these parts. I embrace her, squealing, *"Jambo!* Look at you! You've had a good year!" Her young husband stands close to her. We've been waiting with him, indulging his English. He wraps his arm around her and with a broad smile pronounces in English, "My woman!"

His possessiveness would be annoying were it not for the obvious pride. He has scored the woman of his dreams, the envy of the hamlet. She seems amused, like she's tolerating her husband's enthusiasm. He adores her.

I pull out my white notebook and show her a photo from our interview last year; she can't contain her smile. I ask, "Are they all okay?"

"They are all okay."

I ask about the massacre.

"This is Mashirata; the massacre happened at Chihamba," she says, pointing out the next hill.

On the way home, I'll think about Chihamba, questioning whether I should feel any better that seventeen people were murdered there, not here. But after a year of worrying, I'll decide to enjoy the moment.

Another girl enters the compound. Rahema! She looks years older. She's put on weight and wears her hair cropped short and sophisticated, without a headscarf. I hug her and size her up. I'm just so thrilled, I cry, "How have you been! You are okay!?!"

She looks at me like I'm completely crazy, but I don't care! She smiles, half amused, the way you smile at that barely tolerable long-lost auntie who squeezes your cheeks and talks about how much you've grown since the last time she saw you. "I am okay," she says. "I am healthy. There is no problem."

"You have no idea how happy I am to see that."

SISTERS CROWD AROUND the gate of the Walungu Women for Women compound, waiting for us. I'm surprised, and I shoot Hortense a disapproving look. We were only supposed to meet with the women from Kaniola I talked with last year. I shake my head and say, *"Secret* visit. No receptions."

But as the car slows and I emerge, I wave, smile, and give a short stump speech.

As I slip inside a spare meeting room, it quickly fills with more than twenty women. "What's going on? I don't have time to meet with a huge group."

The truth is that the prospect of a group meeting is painful because I feel terrible for not being able to give each woman the attention she deserves.

Hortense is mildly defiant. "You said, 'sisters from Kaniola,'" she says. "These are all your new sisters from Kaniola."

Twenty-one brand new sisters from Kaniola. I look at each of their sponsorship booklets. Each one reads: HOME VILLAGE: KANIOLA. SPONSOR: RUN FOR CONGO WOMEN.

"I am so happy to be here to meet all of you," I say, scanning the room as they smile slightly, intrigued. "But I am sorry because although I packed gifts of scarves and earrings and postcards, the airline lost my bags. I feel bad showing up empty-handed."

From the back of the room, one of the women says quietly, "We need you first. Things come second."

Indeed. I need you first too.

Things come second.

I've been thinking about what André said. He may have been on to something. Whether it is cell phones or sailboats or salt, isn't this—the war, the atrocities, the world's response, and even my own journey—all really about what we deem precious? However silly or grandiose or blind, my efforts for Congo have ultimately boiled down to the simple act of pushing the reset button on my life and putting human beings before stuff. As I look around the room, it's humbling to realize that *people first* was never even a question for these Congolese women.

I ask the group, "How many of you have taken in orphans?"

Seventeen out of twenty-one raise their hands. Eighty percent. Even in this group of women who live in Kaniola.

Those Who Kill Together may come knocking. They may chase these women from their homes, burn their families alive, take them to the forest, rape them, rob them of everything, leave them with no means to support themselves. But then these women see a child who has no one and they take that child in.

As I describe Run for Congo Women, they squint and lean in to hear clearly; a few lift their eyebrows. Several mumble quietly to themselves, "Please, may you continue this work."

We go around the room. "We were living in Kaniola. We left after my husband and my child were killed, burnt in the house. . . ."

I don't need to collect more horror stories. I already have enough to fill volumes, and most I will never share. As each woman talks, I look into her eyes. How do I spin each sweet face that hangs in desperation? How do I turn her into a talking point? I can't. And I don't want to anymore. I picture their long walk home to Kaniola. I picture myself on a plane. I don't want them to go home tonight. I don't want to let them go.

A woman speaks. Her tall, slender frame and pronounced cheekbones give her a majestic beauty. She wears a dress printed with religious scenes from the Last Supper. While she speaks, she instinctively places her hand on her heart. I hear the word Interahamwe.

As Hortense translates, the lady dwells on her memory. She wipes her eyes with the sleeve of her tattered jacket. "At 8:00 PM, we saw the flashlights. We went to hide in the bushes as usual. Women went to the stream, men to the cassava fields. We only heard the men screaming, but we couldn't do otherwise. They killed two of them. I held my baby in the stream; he was about to cry, so I took grasses. . . ."

She turns her neck, pressing hard against the cement wall, crying. I get up, abandoning Hortense's translation, which trails off behind me as I walk across the room.

"I heard the cry of the men. It wasn't easy for us. . . ."

I put my hands on her shoulders. She looks at me. Sisters mumble behind me. I can't hear the translation. I'm not listening anymore. The specifics don't matter.

I look in her despondent, deep-set eyes and say, "I'm so sorry." She doesn't know what I'm saying. She doesn't need to know.

I don't know how to stop the atrocities. I don't know how to make people care.

But looking in my sister's eyes, we seem to have carved out something between us that none of the madness can touch.

Invisible threads.

I take her hand and lead her across the room, making a place for her next to me, resting my hand on her back for the remainder of the meeting.

I discreetly dig in my purse and count to make sure I have enough. I do. I distribute one crisp five-dollar bill to each of them. I'm so embarrassed. Five dollars is nothing. Peanuts.

Yet, you would think I've just handed each one a US$10,000 check. They leap to their feet, erupting in a Congo-style *fete d'amore*, like the hundreds of women I've met before have done.

I take a photo of each woman, as though this will help me lock her away somewhere safe.

I choke back tears. I don't know what they're singing, but it reminds me of the only Swahili song I know, the one sung to me in endless repetitions at the meeting with the Panzi group and again on the peninsula, when Hortense leaned over to me and said, "Do you hear that? They are singing your name. The song goes: *Hey, Lisa, stay with us! You are a child of Congo now.*"

I put down the camera as my sisters grab me by both hands. They pull me into the celebration. With tears in the corners of my eyes, I dance with them. Women doubled over in pain just a few moments ago are now beaming. Each one embraces me, pressing her forehead to mine.

I whisper to one of them, "*Furaha.*"

She whispers back, "*Furaha sana.*"

Joy. So much joy.

EPILOGUE

BY THE END of 2008, we still haven't raised a million dollars. But we have sponsored more than a thousand Congolese sisters. These women are collectively raising more than five thousand children.

And, little thanks to me:

Journalists flocked to Congo to document the unrest, giving the conflict unprecedented media coverage.

Lisa F. Jackson's film *The Greatest Silence* won the Special Jury Prize at the Sundance Film Festival. The film aired on HBO and was screened around the world.

Eve Ensler announced that the 2009 V-Day campaign will benefit women in Congo.

Celebrities like Ben Affleck, Ashley Judd, Mia Farrow, Emile Hirsch, and Robin Wright spoke out about or traveled to Congo.

Senator Barack Obama, an original sponsor of the 2006 Congo bill, was elected President of the United States.

Even Kelly shook the white-girl angst and started work on her own Congo initiative.

More than 1,700 people participated in Run for Congo Women.

I spent the year in a one-woman, full-time Write for Congo Women.

The United States Holocaust Memorial Museum hosted the first national-al grassroots conference for Congo.

The Enough Project launched the Raise Hope for Congo Campaign.

And that, my friends, is a movement.

MEMORIAL

YOU ARE MISSED

Claude

Lucien

Nsemeru, "I Love You"

Mama Annie

Mama Annie's Husband

The Kaniola Bride

The Kaniola Groom

The Kaniola Wedding Party

The Beerseller Munisha

The Beerseller's Wife

Alain, aspiring conservationist

The Six Park Guards

The Pygmy Husband

The Cowherd of Kaniola

The Pastor of Kaniola

Shuza, "Answer"

Venciana's Baby of One Day

André's Three Classmates

The Villager with Money

Ten Villagers Who Had No Salt

The Lady on the Path

The Man at the Bus Stop

Most of Furaha's Family

Maribola, beloved child of Fitina

Makambe, beloved child of Fitina

Liza, beloved child of Fitina

Ruben, beloved child of Fitina

Nape, beloved child of Fitina

Five Unnamed Children of Fitina

Therese's Uncle

Therese and Pascal's Eight Neighbors

"One of Us in the Canoe"

The Man at the Front Gate

Two Young Men on Lookout

The Thirteen-Year-Old Girl

The Twins and Their Baby Sibling

Three Children Who Ran Away

Some Babies of Baraka

Fifteen-Year-Old Grandson in Kaniola

Yvonne's Daughter, mother of five

Yvonne's Infant Granddaughter

Venciana's Grandfather

Venciana's Cousin, father of five

Venciana's Other Cousin,
    father of seven

Wandolyn's Little Girl

Suzanna's Father

Suzanna's Younger Sister

Suzanna's Aunt

Suzanna's Three Nieces

Nabito's Husband

Nabito's Brother

Nabito's Nephew

Nabito's Uncle

Nabito's Neighbors

The Couple Who Lived Next to Noella

Noella's Other Neighbors

Hortense's Younger Sister

Hortense's Husband

Alisa's Husband

Alisa's Older Brother

Lisa's Sister

Lisa's Brother-in-Law

Esperance's Husband

Esperance's Firstborn Child

Faida's Baby Grandchild

Jannette's Husband

Sophia's Husband

Wandolyn's Brother

Anna's Husband

Victorine's Husband

Sabina's Mother

Sabina's Aunt

Kenisla's Husband

Christine's Two Girls

Rahema's Mother

Marianna's Father

Cecile's Husband

Baraka's Sister's Husband

Josephine's Five-Month-Old
    Baby Girl

A Baby of Two Months

Walengamine's Son

Faila's Daughter

Zaina's Little Boy

Mesha's Little Boy

Mesha's Little Girl

Asende's Three Boys

Asende's Little Girl

Veronique's Little Boy

Veronique's Three Little Girls

Byamonea's Four Daughters

Byamonea's Son

Maria's Two Sons

Fatuma's Little Boy

Mwashite's Little Girl

Mwashite's Little Boy

Tchala's Son

Mawazo's Daughter

Mawazo's Son

Kiza's Three Little Boys

Anna's Two Sons

Elisa's Little Girl

Elisa's Little Boy

Josephine's Daughter

Joyce's Daughter

Joyce's Son

Mariam's Two Daughters

Mwajuma's Daughter

Mwajuma's Son

Nyota's Little Boy

Pauline's Two Little Girls

Rebecca Furaha's Little Girl

Esperance's Son

Esperance's Daughter

Charlotte's Two Boys

Charlotte's Two Girls

Deodatte's Little Girl

Deodatte's Little Boy

Benita's Daughter

Theresia's Two Daughters

Anastasia's Son

Anastasia's Daughter

Esperance's Son

Esperance's Daughter

Charlotte's Little Girl

Ernestine's Daughter

Jeannine's Little Girl

Josephine's Three Sons

Annonciate's Three Little Boys

Annonciate's Little Girl

Nyota's Two Daughters

Nyota's Son

Franciose's Girl Child

Beatrice's Two Young Children

Antonia's Husband

Furaha's Husband

Appoline's Husband

Mapendo's Husband

Immacule's Little Girl

A Girl Child

A Woman of Kaniola

Some Children of Appoline

A Villager of Uvira

Mpondo M'Lusisi

Florida M'Murhebwa

M'Birego, wife of Christophe

Mr. Mutijima Mudekereza

M'Mastaki Mapendo,
    citizen of Nalubuze

Chance Chirhuza,
    citizen of Nalubuze

Olivier Mandiko Muhusi,
    citizen of Nalubuze

Espoir Chirungu,
    citizen of Nalubuze

M'Rugamba Chirungu,
    citizen of Nalubuze

M'Saveri, citizen of Nalubuze

Mukengere Chirungu,
    citizen of Nalubuze

Merci Muranga, citizen of Nalubuze

Bihama Kaborongo,
    citizen of Nalubuze

Maria M'Kahumba,
    citizen of Nalubuze

Ngomora Buhendwa,
    citizen of Nalubuze

Olivier Bukengo Laurent,
    citizen of Nalubuze

Sylvie M'Chihebeyi,
    citizen of Nalubuze

Mapendo M'Gerenge,
    citizen of Nalubuze

Jospeh Kirhero Ntabala,
    citizen of Nalubuze

Nzungu Chigokere,
    citizen of Chihamba

Mbiribindi Mudekereza,
    citizen of Chihamba

Nine of Eric's Neighbors

Citizens of the President's Village

Asende's 500 Neighbors
    in the Forest

702 Citizens of Makobola

5.4 Million Unknown
    Children of Congo

KEY TERMS

Banyamulenge: A Tutsi-Congolese ethnic group (not a militia).

CNDP: National Congress for the Defense of People (in French, *Congrès National pour la Défense du Peuple*), a Tutsi-Congolese militia lead by General Laurent Nkunda.

FARDC: The Armed Forces of the Democratic Republic of the Congo, or the Congolese Army (in French, *Forces Armées de la République Démocratique du Congo*).

FDD: Forces for the Defense of Democracy (in French, *Forces pour la Défense de la Démocratie*), a Burundian militia.

IDP: Internally Displaced Person. Someone who has been forced to leave his or her home. Similar to the term "refugee," but IDPs have not crossed any international borders.

Interahamwe or FDLR: Democratic Liberation Forces of Rwanda (in French, *Forces Démocratiques de Libération du Rwanda*). A Rwandan Hutu militia linked to the 1994 Rwandan Genocide. Also known as the Interahamwe, "those who kill together."

Kabila, Joseph: President of the Democratic Republic of the Congo since January 2001. Son of Laurent Kabila.

Kabila, Laurent: President of the Democratic Republic of the Congo from 1997 until January 2001, when he was assassinated.

Kagame, Paul: President of Rwanda since 2000.

LRA: The Lord's Resistance Army. Ugandan rebel group based in far north-eastern Congo.

Mai Mai: A Congolese militia, or "local defense force," known for its members' use of traditional African medicine. Translates to "Water Water" in Swahili.

Mobutu Sese Seko: Dictatorial president of Congo (then known as Zaire) from 1967 to 1997.

MONUC: United Nations Organization Mission in the Democratic Republic of the Congo (in French, *Mission de l'Organisation des Nations Unies*). United Nations peacekeeping force in Congo.

NGO: Nongovernmental Organization. Nonprofit organization that is not affiliated with any government or political party. Many advance humanitarian causes.

Nkunda, Laurent: Tutsi Congolese general who was head of the CNDP until 2009, when he was captured and arrested by Rwandan troops.

Rasta: A militia comprised of former Interahamwe and Congolese.

RCD: Rally for Congolese Democracy. Rwanda-backed militia that sparked the 1998 "RCD War," and later morphed into a political party.

UN: United Nations

UNHCR: United Nations High Commission on Refugees.

ACKNOWLEDGMENTS

HOW DO I BEGIN? Thousands of people have been the lifeblood of this story. My deep appreciation goes out to everyone who has played a part, large or small. These acknowledgments just start to scratch the surface.

Very special thanks to my parents. To my mom, Ann Shannon, an unsung hero for women in the Congo. Run for Congo Women would not have happened without your undying support, unconditional love, dogged work, and lifelong lessons in compassion. And to my father, Stewart Shannon, who never failed to see the beauty underlying even the most terrifying places in the human spirit. Though you died before I could even pick Congo out on a map, you have nonetheless been my silent guide though all of it. What a rare treasure to have had a man of your depth and compassion as my father.

I extend my deep gratitude to Zainab Salbi for founding an organization with such heart and vision, for providing endless encouragement, for being my personal hero, and especially for being among the first in the world to serve Congolese women and to bring their stories to the world's attention. Deep gratitude also to Oprah Winfrey, Lisa Ling, and Liz Brody for telling the stories no one else would touch, and to Nancy Haught, Michelle Hamilton,

Jerome McDonnell, and Megan McMorris for their critically important early press coverage of Run for Congo Women.

Thank you to Alice Walker, for wise words at exactly the right moments, and to Lisa Jackson for being a mentor, a friend, and one of the first grassroots voices for Congo.

Thank you to every Run for Congo Women organizer past and present, including Geni Donnelly, Jen Parsons, Amy Hing, Gisela Ferrer, Monica Ianelli, Marya Garskof, Tracy Ronzio, Tracey Dennis, Lynda Hermsmeyer, Mary Jo Burkhart, Robin Potawsky, Ranny McKay, Stephanie Bond, Shannon Sansoterra, Susan and Laurie Rumker (I can't wait to see the woman you become!), Becca Loring, Jesse Cox, Kristine Lebow, Ariel Sherman-Cox, Francisca Thelin, Zan Tibbs, Christina Pagetti, Tonya Sargent, Sara Ryan, Holly Gerloff, Monica Hunsberger, Lynda Sacamano, Carrie Kehoe, Nita Evele, and Carrie Crawford. Thanks to Jerry and Kristianyi Jones and Emily Deschanel for their critical early and continued support.

Thank you to my beloved family and friends, especially Lana Veenker, Tammy and Amit (Kai, Lia & Neha) Singh, Julie Shannon-Miller, Aria Shannon, Adriana and Julian Voss-Andreae, Shelley Jacobsen, Rick Jacobsen, Phil Atlakson, Garry Wade, Aileen Adams, Rae and Hack Fuller, Deidre McDermitt, Felicity Fenton, Sam Shannon, Dirk Simon, Kristin Leppert, Almine Barton, Tobias Hitsch, Lisa Maeckel, Shannon Meehan, Ashley Muhlherr and Tim. And, of course, to D, for being a refuge.

Thank you to the entire Women for Women International staff (past and present), especially Ricki Weisberg, Patty Pina, Trish Tobin, Alison Wheeler, Erica Tavares, Karen Sherman, and Jennifer Morabito.

My thanks go out to Dr. Richard Brennan of the IRC, Adam Hochschild, Eve Ensler and V-Day, John Prendergast and everyone at The Enough Project and Raise Hope for Congo Campaign, The United States Holocaust Memorial Museum, The Chicago Congo Coalition, Congo Global Action, and Friends of Congo (who were working on Congo ages before I came along).

Thanks to Christine Karumba and the entire Women for Women Congo staff. To Maurice, Serge, Jean Paul, Hortense, and Moses, because I was never really alone in Congo. To Murhabazi Namegabe and BVES, the Panzi Hospital and Dr. Roger, and Eric.

Thank you to my publisher and editor, Krista Lyons, who read the proposal and declared, "Seal Press needs to publish this book." To my agent, Jill Marsal, for believing in the project and invaluable manuscript feedback, as well as to the Sandra Djikstra Literary Agency, especially Sandra Djikstra and Elise Capron.

Thanks to my writing mentors: Cynthia Whitcomb, Betty Sargent, and Maureen Barron. And special thanks to Blake Snyder, who spent many hours helping me find the elusive through-line, even if it meant looking petty or self-aggrandizing or just plain bad in the interest of an honest story. He passed away before reading this book, and thank you. You're missed, Blake! To Yusef Komunyakaa, for writing a poem that would still haunt me eighteen years after reading it. To Wesleyan University Press, for permission to reprint it in this book. And to everyone who read and gave me feedback on the book proposal and manuscript.

My thanks go to everyone in Congo who shared their stories with me. To everyone who donated to Generose's house. To everyone who has ever donated, run, hosted a house party, volunteered, or in any way supported Run for Congo Women.

And to my beloved Congolese sisters.

BIBLIOGRAPHY

Associated Foreign Press. "17 Villagers Knifed To Death in Congo." May 27, 2007, as forwarded via email from "Eric."

Blumenauer, Rep. Earl. Statement prior to passing of the "Democratic Republic of the Congo Relief, Security, and Democracy Protection Act of 2006." The Congressional Record, 152, no. 133 (December 6, 2006).

Brody, Liz. "I Am Starting To Throw Away My Worries One by One." O, The Oprah Magazine, December 2006.

CNN. "Logging Decimates African Rainforest." CNN, April 16, 2007.

Enough Project, The. "Congo Quick Facts." www.enoughproject.org, 2009.

————. "Key Terms." www.enoughproject.org, 2009.

————. "Roots of the Crisis." www.enoughproject.org, 2009.

Enough Project Team, The, with the Grassroots Reconciliation Group. "A Comprehensive Approach To Congo's Conflict Minerals." Stragic paper, The Enough Project, April 24, 2009.

Freeley, Rebecca, and Colin Thomas-Jensen. "Past Due: Remove the FDLR from Eastern Congo." Strategy paper, The Enough Project, June 3, 2008.

Gettleman, Jeffrey. "Congo's Army Clashing with Militias." New York Times, October 25, 2007.

Greenpeace International. "Conning the Congo." Investigative report, Greenpeace International, July 2008.

Hamilton, Michelle. "2006 Heroes of Running." Runners World, December 2006.

Harkins, George W. "Letter to the American People," dated December 1931.

Sequoyah Research Center, American Native Press Archives. www.anpa
.ualr.edu.

Haught, Nancy. "Hearing the Cries, and Running to Help." *The Oregonian*, August
26, 2005.

Hochschild, Adam. *King Leopold's Ghost: A Story of Greed, Terror, and Heroism in
Colonial Africa*. New York: Mariner Books, 1999.

Human Rights Watch. "DR Congo: Militia Leader Guilty in Landmark Trial." March
10, 2009. www.hrw.org.

International Crisis Group. "Mortality in the Democratic Republic of the Congo: An
Ongoing Crisis." Special report, released January 2008. www.theirc.org.

———. "Congo: Ex-Rebels in Army Are Accused of Now Looting, Raping, and Killing," The Associated Press, *New York Times*, May 19, 2009.

———. "Congo Violence Reaches Endangered Mountain Gorillas." *New York Times*,
November 18, 2008.

———. "In Congo, a Little Fighting Brings a Lot of Fear." *New York Times*, November 3, 2008.

———. "Mai Mai Fighters Third Piece in Congo's Violent Puzzle." *New York Times*,
November 21, 2008.

———. "Rape Epidemic Raises Trauma of Congo War." *New York Times*, October
7, 2007.

———. "Rape Victims' Words Help Jolt Congo into Change." *New York Times*,
October 18, 2008.

———. "Rwanda Stirs Deadly Brew of Troubles in Congo." *New York Times,* December 4, 2008.

Keane, Fergal. *Season of Blood: A Rwandan Journey*. London: Viking, 1995.

Kigali Memorial Centre. "Francine Murengezi Ingabire." www.kigalimemorialcentre.
org.

Komunyakaa, Yusef. "You and I Are Disappearing," in *Dien Cai Dau*. Middletown,
CT: Wesleyan University Press, 1988.

Koppel, Ted. "Heart of Darkness." *ABC News Nightline,* DVD release date September
18, 2006. Originally aired 2002.

Kristof, Nicholas. "Crisis in the Congo." *New York Times*, October 29, 2008.

Lacey, Marc. "War Is Still a Way of Life for Congo Rebels." *New York Times*, November 21, 2002.

McMorris, Megan. "The Accidental Activist." *Fitness Magazine*, March 2007.

Munch, Edvard. "When we stood close. . . ." in *Munch In His Own Words*. Edited by
Poul Erik Tojner. New York: Prestel, 2003.

O, The Oprah Magazine, "Postcards from the Edge." February 2005.

Omaar, Rakiya. "The Leadership of Rwandan Armed Groups Abroad with a Focus on the FDLR and RUD/URUNANA." The Rwanda Demobilization and Reintegration Commission, December 2008.

Polgreen, Lydia. "Congo's Death Rate Unchanged Since War Ended." *New York Times,* January 23, 2008.

———. "Congo's Riches Looted by Renegade Troops." *New York Times,* November 16, 2008.

———. "Fighting in Congo Rekindles Ethnic Hatreds." *New York Times,* January 10, 2008.

———. "A Massacre in Congo, Despite Nearby Support." *New York Times,* December 11, 2008.

———. "Militias in Congo Tied to Government and Rwanda." *New York Times,* December 13, 2008.

———. "Resolving Crisis in Congo Hinges on Foreign Forces." *New York Times,* December 19, 2007.

———. "Rwanda's Shadow, From Darfur to Congo." *New York Times,* July 23, 2006.

———. "War's Chaos Steals Congo's Young by the Millions." *New York Times,* July 30, 2006.

Powell, Alvin, with Michael Van Rooyen and Jocelyn Kelly. "Rape of the Congo: Making Sense of Sexual Violence in Central Africa." *Harvard Public Health Review,* Spring 2009.

Ruxin, Josh. "Calm in Kigali, Horror in Congo." *New York Times,* October 20, 2008.

———. "A Solvable Problem." *New York Times,* October 24, 2007.

———. "Peace in Congo?" *New York Times,* February 9, 2009.

Timberg, Craig. "For Congo's Mothers, Unceasing Loss." *Washington Post,* February 12, 2005.

Vidal, John. "Sold Down the River." *The Guardian,* September 22, 2007.

———. "World Bank Accused of Razing Congo Forests." *The Guardian,* October 4, 2007.

Winfrey, Oprah. "Ricky Martin Travels To Meet Tsunami Orphans." *The Oprah Winfrey Show,* January 24, 2005.

ABOUT THE AUTHOR

LISA J. SHANNON is founder of Run for Congo Women, which began with her lone thirty-mile trail run and quickly blossomed into a global, volunteer-driven grassroots effort to raise funds and awareness for women in the Democratic Republic of Congo. She previously owned a photography production company, where she served as art director and producer. Shannon lives in Portland, Oregon.

INDEX

Run for Congo Women events, 50–52, 57, 272–273, 317

Runner's World, 56–57

running events, 42–45, 47–48, 50–52

Rwanda: background information, 64–65; military conflicts, 18, 65, 92, 111–116

S

Salbi, Zainab, 37, 70–72, 238, 239, 244–245, 266, 268

salt, 294

Samson, Trevor, 38–39

Save the Children, 190

Second Annual Portland Run for Congo Women, 51

Serge, 84, 93–95, 242, 266–267, 301

sexual violence: gang rape, 98–104, 143–144, 164–166; Mai Mai, 90–91, 212–213

Sifa, 121–124

sister visits, 126–130, 132–138, 140–146, 148–154, 164–167, 172–175, 239–244, 312–315

South Kivu Province, 18–19, 116–117

speaking engagements, 270–271

speech to rape victims, 100–103

sponsorship program, 43–45, 77–78, 127–130, 132–136

stock photography, 29

Sumana, 56

T

tantalum; *See* coltan mining

tax collection operations, 115–117

Ted: birthday trip, 40; breakup of relationship, 57–58, 271; business partnership, 28–29, 35, 83; family visits, 36; flashlights, 181; long distance call, 197, 267

Therese, 132–138, 285–286

Thomas, Kelly: Baraka trip, 156, 159–160, 170–172, 178–183, 189–191; Congo visit, 69–70, 81–82; grassroots activism, 52–54; Panzi Hospital visit, 98–102; post-Congo activities, 272, 316; sister visits, 136

Trail of Tears, 123–124

traumatic fistula, 98–99, 103–104

tropical forests, 110

Tutsis, 65, 217

Twa, 65

U

Uganda, 18

UNICEF, 78

United Nations High Commission on Refugees (UNHCR): Kaniola visit, 249–264, 308–311; military conflicts, 65; Pakistani Army, 301; presence in Congo, 190; refugee camps, 111, 163

United Nations peacekeeping forces, 19, 65

V

Vikram, Major, 249–253, 255–258, 263, 296–297

Voss, Susan, 132

W

Walker, Alice, 238, 239, 245, 266, 268

Walungu, Congo, 140–146, 220–225, 248–251, 286–287, 297–301

Wandolyn, 140–146, 286–287

War Child, 190

Washington D. C. visit, 54–57

"When We Stood Close" (Munch), 7

Wildwood Trail run, 42–45, 47–48

Winfrey, Oprah, 14, 28, 36–37

witchcraft, 158, 216–217

Women for Women; *See also* Christine: Baraka, 164; country directors, 52; enrollment process, 223–225, 263–264; headquarters visit, 56; Run for Congo Women events, 273; sister visits, 126–130, 132–138, 140–146, 148–154, 164–167, 172–175, 239–244, 312–315; sponsorship program, 43–45, 77–78, 127–130, 132–136; Walungu visit, 286–287, 297–301

worst wedding day, 57–61

Wyden, Ron, 55

Y

"You and I Are Disappearing" (Komunyakaa), 231–232

Z

Zaire, 18, 111–116

Zanzibar visit, 228–235

Zimbabwe, 18

FIND YOUR
OWN FURAHA

WHAT YOU CAN DO FOR CONGO RIGHT NOW

BEFORE YOU PUT this book down, check your email, make dinner plans, or remember there was one more thing you meant to do . . .

1. Sponsor your own Congolese sister. (3 minutes, $27 per month, www.womenforwomen.org)
2. Run (or walk or bike or swim or whatever) for Congo Women. Ask 12 friends to join you on a short run, each of you pitch in $30 and—ta-da!—you have enough to sponsor and change a woman's life. Or dedicate a solo run to women in the Congo. Or register for a Run for Congo Women near you. (1 hour–6 months, starting at $30, www.runforcongowomen.org)
3. Join the Raise Hope for Congo Campaign. (1 minute, www.raisehopeforcongo.org)
4. Share this book with friends. Start a book club. (1 hour to organize, 2 to discuss)
5. Purchase a copy of Lisa F. Jackson's film *The Greatest Silence: Rape in the Congo*. Host a screening in your home, then ask your guests to sponsor a

woman in Congo. (2 minutes to order the film, plus 2 half-days to plan and host the gathering, $29.95, www.wmm.com)

6. Protect Congo's forests. Offset your carbon footprint through Eric's North American partners Zerofootprint. (1 minute to calculate your footprint, 2 minutes to pay online to offset that footprint, www.zerofootprint.net)

7. Urge President Barack Obama and Secretary of State Hillary Clinton to craft and implement an intelligent, comprehensive, diplomatic strategy to permanently deal with the Interahamwe, a.k.a. the FDLR. (2 minutes, www.whitehouse.gov/contact)

8. Friend me on Facebook. I post the latest news from Congo daily. (2 minutes)

9. Visit my website, which contains links to all of groups and organizations mentioned above. (1 minute, http://athousandsisters.com)

10. Dream up something new, like I did.